Cooperation among Nations

A volume in the series

Cornell Studies in Political Economy

EDITED BY PETER J. KATZENSTEIN

A full list of titles in the series appears at the end of the book

Cooperation among Nations

EUROPE, AMERICA, AND NON-TARIFF BARRIERS TO TRADE

JOSEPH M. GRIECO

CORNELL UNIVERSITY PRESS

Ithaca and London

First published 1990 by Cornell University Press.

International Standard Book Number 0–8014–2414–3 (cloth)
International Standard Book Number 0–8014–9699–3 (paper)
Library of Congress Catalog Card Number 89-46166
Printed in the United States of America
Librarians: Library of Congress cataloging information
appears on the last page of the book.

♾ The paper used in this publication meets the minimum requirements of the American National Standard for Permanence of Paper for Printed Library Materials Z39.48—1984.

In memory of my father,
Mauro Grieco, 1910–1986

Contents

Tables   viii

Acknowledgments   xi

1. Anarchy and Cooperation among Nations   1
2. Realism, Neoliberal Institutionalism, and the Problem of International Cooperation   27
3. The Tokyo Round Regime on Non-tariff Barriers to Trade   51
4. Rule Compliance and Dispute Settlement in the Tokyo Round NTB Regime, 1980–1987   69
5. Rule Construction in the Tokyo Round NTB Regime, 1980–1987   103
6. The Tokyo Round NTB Regime and Neoliberal Institutionalism   135
7. The Tokyo Round NTB Regime and Realist International Theory   168
8. Realism and Cooperation among Nations   216

Appendixes
1. Operative Rule Construction, Technical Committee on Customs Valuation, 1981–1987   235
2. Operative Rule Construction, Committee on Technical Barriers to Trade, 1980–1987   238
3. Highlights of November 1986 Package of GPR Code Improvements   241

Index   243

Tables

2.1   Major propositions in liberal institutionalism, neoliberal institutionalism, and realism   32

2.2   An Amended Prisoner's Dilemma game   43

2.3   Neoliberal and realist views on states and international cooperation   49

4.1   Valuation methods of signatories to the Code on Customs Valuation   72

4.2   Notifications of measures under the Code on Technical Barriers to Trade, 1980–86   77

4.3   Compliance with comment periods recommended by the Committee on Technical Barriers to Trade, 1980–86   78

4.4   Rule-compliance and dispute-settlement experiences associated with the Tokyo Round NTB codes, 1980–87   100

5.1   Rule-construction activities associated with the Tokyo Round NTB codes, 1980–87   132

6.1   Effectiveness of rule compliance and dispute settlement in the Tokyo Round NTB codes, 1980–87   137

6.2   Effectiveness of rule construction in the Tokyo Round NTB codes, 1980–87   138

6.3   Impact of U.S.-EC interactions on NTB code rule compliance and dispute settlement, 1980–87   139

6.4   Impact of U.S.-EC interactions on NTB code rule construction, 1980–87   140

6.5   U.S.-EC discord and setbacks in NTB code rule compliance and dispute settlement, 1980–87   141

6.6   U.S.-EC discord and setbacks in NTB code rule construction, 1980–87   142

6.7   Compliance with comment periods recommended by
       the Committee on Technical Barriers to Trade,
       advanced countries, 1980–86   145
6.8   Major-signatory contracts awarded under the Code on
       Government Procurement, 1983   147
6.9   Contracts awarded under single-tendering procedures
       of the Code on Government Procurement, 1983   148
6.10   Notification of subsidies to the Committee on Subsidies
       and Countervailing Measures, advanced-country
       signatories, 1984   149
6.11   Frequency of meetings of NTB code committees,
       1980–87   154
6.12   Number of signatories associated with NTB codes,
       1980–87   156
6.13   Composition of committees for NTB codes, 1987   157
6.14   EC balance of initiated anti-dumping actions, 1980–86   161
6.15   EC balance of initiated countervailing measures,
       1980–86   162
6.16   Notifications made to the Committee on Technical
       Barriers to Trade, showing EC absolute gains, 1980–86   163
6.17   EC balance of Article-10 enquiries under the
       Committee on Technical Barriers to Trade, 1983–84   164
6.18   EC balance of contracts covered by the Code on
       Government Procurement, 1983   166
7.1   Anti-dumping actions initiated among all signatories to
       the Code on Anti-Dumping Practices, 1980–86   173
7.2   Anti-dumping actions initiated among major signatories
       to the Code on Anti-Dumping Practices, 1980–86   174
7.3   Countervailing measures initiated among all signatories
       to the Code on Subsidies and Countervailing Measures,
       1981–86   176
7.4   Countervailing measures initiated among major
       signatories to the Code on Subsidies and Countervailing
       Measures, 1981–86   177
7.5   Significance of subsidies: major signatories to the Code
       on Subsidies and Countervailing Measures, 1970–82   178
7.6   Estimated economic effects of liberalized agricultural
       markets, advanced countries   180
7.7   Technical notifications to the Committee on Technical
       Barriers to Trade, by signatory, 1980–86   190
7.8   Value-added tax rates in the European Community,
       1988   197

7.9   Significance of public enterprises, major signatories to
       the Code on Government Procurement, 1970s   199
7.10   Foreign participation in major GPR code-signatory
       government-procurement markets, 1983   201

Acknowledgments

In writing this book, I benefited enormously from the criticisms and support of many individuals and institutions. My first and greatest debt is to John Mearsheimer. When my arguments were in their least developed and most vulnerable form, he generously and unfailingly gave me vital intellectual guidance and encouragement. He pushed me to strengthen my arguments and to pursue them to their logical conclusion. And, perhaps most important, when the research was not going so well, he reassured me that the project had value and that I ought to persevere and complete it. For his support and friendship I will always be grateful.

I also offer special thanks to Louise Hodgden. She read every chapter many times and offered extremely important criticisms and suggestions on how I might clarify my theoretical ideas and empirical analysis. I am also especially grateful to Claudio Cioffi-Revilla and George Tsebelis for their guidance in thinking about how one might specify a realist-informed utility function for defensively positional states.

I thank my friends and colleagues who read the entire manuscript and offered many recommendations on how to improve it: Hayward Alker, Robert Bates, Ole Holsti, Peter Katzenstein, Robert Keohane, Friedrich Kratochwil, Peter Lange, Roy Licklider, Jack Snyder, Daniel Verdier, and Gilbert Winham. I also benefited greatly from comments on chapters of the book or papers related to it provided by Stephan Haggard, Robert Jervis, William Keech, Stephen Krasner, David Lake, Timothy McKeown, Joseph Nye, John Ruggie, Glenn Snyder, Stephen Van Evera, Stephen Walt, and Kenneth Waltz. I also thank Victoria Haire and Roger Haydon for their editorial guidance.

In collecting data for the project, I received assistance from government officials and international civil servants in Bonn, Brussels, Geneva, London, Paris, and Washington; to all of them I am deeply grateful. William Bernhard, Joy Langston, and David Strom served as excellent research assistants for the study, and Elizabeth Franklin, Kimberly Holder, and Angela Whitson provided secretarial support of the highest quality.

Portions of Chapters 1, 2, and 8 first appeared as "Anarchy and the Limits of Cooperation: A Realistic Critique of the Newest Liberal Institutionalism" in *International Organization* 42:3 (Summer 1988), 485–507, © 1988 by the World Peace Foundation and the Massachusetts Institute of Technology. Adapted by permission of the MIT Press. Parts of Chapters 2 and 8 earlier appeared as "Realist Theory and the Problem of International Cooperation: Analysis with an Amended Prisoner's Dilemma Model," first published in *The Journal of Politics* 50:3 (August 1988), 600–624, adapted by permission of the University of Texas Press.

For their generous financial support of this project, I thank the German Marshall Fund of the United States; the Center for International Affairs at Harvard University, where I served during 1985–86 as a Paul-Henri Spaak Fellow in U.S.-European Relations; the Duke University Research Council; and the International Affairs Program of the Ford Foundation in a grant to Duke University's Center for International Political Economy.

JOSEPH M. GRIECO

Durham, North Carolina

Cooperation among Nations

CHAPTER ONE

Anarchy and Cooperation
among Nations

International cooperation is a subject of manifest importance for anyone concerned about the prospects for world peace and order. Most students of international relations recognize that international anarchy makes cooperation among nations difficult to achieve even when they have common interests. There is considerable disagreement, however, as to how and why international anarchy constrains the willingness of states to work together. Two theories—modern realism and the newest liberal institutionalism—dominate the contemporary debate on that crucial question.[1]

My goal is to examine these two competing theories and to determine which one best explains the problem of international cooperation. This endeavor involves two steps. First, I examine each theory to

1. Major realist works include: E. H. Carr, *The Twenty Years' Crisis, 1919–1939: An Introduction to the Study of International Relations* (New York: Harper Torchbooks, 1964); Hans J. Morgenthau, *Politics among Nations: The Struggle for Power and Peace*, 5th ed. (New York: Knopf, 1973); Raymond Aron, *Peace and War: A Theory of International Relations*, trans. Richard Howard and Annette Baker Fox (Garden City, N.Y.: Doubleday, 1973); Kenneth N. Waltz, *Man, the State, and War: A Theoretical Analysis* (New York: Columbia University Press, 1959); Waltz, *Theory of International Politics* (Reading, Mass.: Addison-Wesley, 1979); Robert Gilpin, *U.S. Power and the Multinational Corporation: The Political Economy of Foreign Direct Investment* (New York: Basic, 1975); and Gilpin, *War and Change in World Politics* (Cambridge: Cambridge University Press, 1981). Major neoliberal institutionalist works include Robert O. Keohane, *After Hegemony: Cooperation and Discord in the World Political Economy* (Princeton: Princeton University Press, 1984); Robert Axelrod, *The Evolution of Cooperation* (New York: Basic, 1984); Axelrod and Keohane, "Achieving Cooperation under Anarchy: Strategies and Institutions," *World Politics* 38 (October 1985), 226–54; Arthur Stein, "Coordination and Collaboration: Regimes in an Anarchic World," in Stephen D. Krasner, ed., *International Regimes* (Ithaca: Cornell University Press, 1983), 115–40; and Charles Lipson, "International Cooperation in Economic and Security Affairs," *World Politics* 37 (October 1984), 1–23.

determine which provides the stronger analytical argument regarding the impact of anarchy on states as they evaluate opportunities to cooperate. Second, I test the two theories by applying them to an important arena of action in the modern international political economy—the Tokyo Round regime for the reduction of non-tariff barriers to trade.

Both realism and neoliberal institutionalism contribute to our understanding of world affairs. However, the principal conclusion of this book is that realism is the more powerful theory of international cooperation. Both theories are built on the assumptions that states are the key actors in world affairs and that they are powerfully influenced by their anarchical political context. Yet neoliberalism mis-specifies the effects of anarchy on the character and goals of states. This defective analysis of anarchy and states leads neoliberalism to paint a more roseate picture of the prospects for cooperation than is actually warranted. Realism, in contrast, is based on a better understanding of the effects of anarchy on states, and thus it offers a more compelling logical analysis of interstate collaboration.

This conclusion is verified, the study suggests, through an empirical test of the two theories in circumstances that favored neoliberalism. Neoliberals concede that their theory has had little explanatory power so far in security affairs or what is sometimes called the "high politics" of the international system. Realism, they acknowledge, is typically the appropriate theory for the analysis of the political-military goals and actions of states. Neoliberals would maintain, however, that there is much more to the international system than military interactions, that there is a growing network of trade, monetary, capital, and technology flows among states constituting an international political economy. Neoliberals argue that realism provides an inadequate understanding of "low politics" outcomes in the international political economy, and especially of the successes and failures of cooperative efforts among states in this increasingly important domain of international action. The international political economy, neoliberals assert, is where their theory has a decisive advantage over realism.

Given that neoliberals concede the dominance of realism in the political-military realm, the question that arises is whether neoliberal institutionalism is, in fact, superior to realism in explaining outcomes in the international political economy. This book addresses that question by focusing on the efforts during the 1980s of the leading industrial states to cooperate to regulate non-tariff barriers to trade (NTBs). By the early 1970s the world's major trading nations had rendered tariffs almost obsolete as an instrument of protection in their relations with one another. At the same time, however, NTBs were becoming so pervasive that there were increasing fears that they constituted a "new protectionism" threatening the world trading system.[2] The industrialized states made a concerted effort to deal with NTBs in the 1973–79 Tokyo Round of multilateral trade negotiations and constructed a new regime consisting of six codes of conduct. Neoliberal claims notwithstanding, the successes and failures that followed as the code partners—especially the United States and the European Community (EC)—tried to implement and build on the rules articulated by the Tokyo Round agreements are best explained by realism, not neoliberalism. If this case can be made, there would be weaker grounds for the neoliberal claim that realist theory is suited only for the analysis of political-military matters. In fact realism would be shown to be superior to neoliberalism in the latter's supposed domain of choice, that is, the international political economy.

REALISM AND NEOLIBERAL INSTITUTIONALISM

Realist political theory has dominated the study of international relations at least since World War II.[3] Realism has three basic assumptions. First, states are the major actors in world affairs.[4] Second, the international environment severely penalizes states if they fail to protect their interests or if they pursue objectives beyond their means; hence they are "sensitive to costs" and behave as unitary-rational

2. The concept of a "new protectionism" is discussed in Melvyn B. Krauss, *The New Protectionism: The Welfare State and International Trade* (New York: New York University Press, 1978); and Bela Balassa, "The 'New Protectionism' and the International Economy," *Journal of World Trade Law* 12 (1978), 409–36. For the arguments that lead to acceptance of neoprotectionism, see Wolfgang Hager, "Protectionism and Autonomy: How to Preserve Free Trade in Western Europe," *International Affairs* 58 (Summer 1982), 413–28. For an analysis of the recent movement toward neoprotectionism in Western Europe, see Miles Kahler, "European Protectionism in Theory and Practice," *World Politics* 37 (July 1985), 475–502.

3. This book does not draw a sharp distinction between "realism" and "neorealism," because on crucial issues—the meaning of international anarchy, its effects on states, and the problem of cooperation—such modern realists as Waltz and Gilpin are very much in accord with such classical realists as Carr, Aron, and Morgenthau. For an alternative view, see Richard Ashley, "The Poverty of Neorealism," in Robert O. Keohane, ed., *Neorealism and Its Critics* (New York: Columbia University Press, 1986), 255–300. Kenneth Waltz highlights the differences between classical and modern realism in "The Origins of War in Neorealist Theory," in Robert I. Rotberg and Theodore K. Rabb, eds., *The Origin and Prevention of Major Wars* (Cambridge: Cambridge University Press, 1988), 39–52.

4. Morgenthau, *Politics among Nations*, 10; see also Waltz, *Theory of International Politics*, 95.

3

agents.[5] Third, international anarchy is the principal force condition-ing the external preferences and actions of states.[6] On the basis of these assumptions, realists have developed two major propositions concerning international cooperation. First, realists argue that states are preoccupied with their security and power; by consequence, states are predisposed toward conflict and competition, and they often fail to cooperate even when they have common interests.[7] Second, realists claim that international institutions can mitigate the inhibitory effects of anarchy on the willingness of states to cooperate only marginally.[8]

The major challenger to realism has been liberal institutionalism. Before the current period, it appeared in three successive presenta-tions: functionalist integration theory in the 1940s and early 1950s, neofunctionalist regional integration theory in the 1950s and 1960s, and interdependence theory in the 1970s.[9] Liberal institutionalists sought to refute the realist understanding of world politics.[10] First,

5. Waltz, "Reflections on *Theory of International Politics*: A Response to My Critics," in Keohane, ed., *Neorealism*, 331.

6. Waltz, *Man, State, and War*, 224–38; Waltz, *Theory of International Politics*, 79–128; Aron, *Peace and War*, 6–10; and Stanley Hoffmann, *The State of War: Essays in the Theory and Practice of International Politics* (New York: Praeger, 1965), 27, 54–87, 129.

7. Aron, *Peace and War*, 5; Robert Gilpin, "The Richness of the Tradition of Political Realism," in Keohane, ed., *Neorealism*, 304.

8. Waltz, *Theory of International Politics*, 115–16; see also Morgenthau, *Politics among Nations*, 512; and Stanley Hoffmann, "International Organization and the Internation-al System," in Leland M. Goodrich and David A. Kay, eds., *International Organization: Politics and Process* (Madison: University of Wisconsin Press, 1973), 50.

9. For functionalist international theory, see David Mitrany, *A Working Peace System* (Chicago: Quadrangle, 1966); see also Ernst B. Haas, *Beyond the Nation-State: Functional-ism and International Organization* (Stanford: Stanford University Press, 1964). On neo-functionalism, see Haas, *The Uniting of Europe: Political, Social, and Economic Forces, 1950–1957* (Stanford: Stanford University Press, 1958); Haas, "Technology, Pluralism, and the New Europe," in Joseph S. Nye, Jr., ed., *International Regionalism* (Boston: Little, Brown, 1968), 149–76; and Joseph S. Nye, Jr., "Comparing Common Markets: A Revised Neo-Functional Model," in Leon N. Lindberg and Stuart A. Scheingold, eds., *Regional Integration: Theory and Research* (Cambridge: Harvard University Press, 1971), 192–231. On interdependence theory, see Richard C. Cooper, "Economic Interdepen-dence and Foreign Policy in the Seventies," *World Politics* 24 (January 1972), 158–81; Edward S. Morse, "The Transformation of Foreign Policies: Modernization, Interde-pendence, and Externalization," *World Politics* 22 (April 1970), 371–92; and Robert O. Keohane and Nye, *Power and Interdependence: World Politics in Transition* (Boston: Little, Brown, 1977).

10. Liberal institutionalist theories may be distinguished from three other variants of liberal theory. One of these, trade liberalism, articulated by Richard Cobden and John Bright, finds that international commerce facilitates greater interstate cooperation: for Cobden, see Arnold Wolfers and Laurence W. Martin, eds., *The Anglo-American Tradi-tion in Foreign Affairs* (New Haven: Yale University Press, 1956), 192–205; with respect to both Cobden and Bright, see also Waltz, *Man, State, and War*, 98–99, 103–7. A second variant, democratic structural liberalism, posited by Immanuel Kant and Woodrow Wilson, finds that democracies based on national self-determination are conducive to

they rejected realism's assumption about the centrality of states.[11] For functionalists, key new actors in world politics were specialized international agencies and their technical experts; for neofunctionalists, they were labor unions, political parties, trade associations, and supranational bureaucracies; and for the interdependence school, they were multinational corporations and transnational and transgovernmental coalitions.[12] Second, institutionalists attacked the realist view that states are unitary or rational agents.[13] Authority was already decentralized within modern states, functionalists argued, and it was undergoing a comparable process internationally.[14] Similarly, modern states, according to interdependence theorists, were increasingly characterized by "multiple channels of access," which, in turn, progressively weakened the grip on foreign policy previously held by central decision makers.[15]

---

greater international cooperation. For Wilson, see *Anglo-American Tradition*, 263–79; for Kant and Wilson, see Waltz, *Man, State, and War*, 101–3, 109–11, 117–19, and Michael W. Doyle, "Liberalism and World Politics," *American Political Science Review* 80 (December 1986), 1151–69. Finally, a liberal transactions approach suggests that private international interactions promote international integration; see Karl Deutsch et al., *Political Community and the North Atlantic Area* (Princeton: Princeton University Press, 1957); and Bruce Russett, *Community and Contention: Britain and America in the Twentieth Century* (Cambridge: MIT Press, 1963). In a recent essay, Nye refers to the first two variants as commercial and democratic liberalism, respectively, and suggests that the third might be termed sociological liberalism. See Joseph S. Nye, Jr., "Neorealism and Neoliberalism," *World Politics* 40 (January 1988), 246.

11. World systems analysis also challenges the realist focus on states, suggesting that states are themselves resultants of the development of a single world capitalist economy. See Immanuel Wallerstein, "The Rise and Future Demise of the World Capitalist System: Concepts for Comparative Analysis," in Wallerstein, *The Capitalist World System* (Cambridge: Cambridge University Press, 1979), 1–36; and Wallerstein, *The Modern World System*, vol. 1 (New York: Academic, 1974).

12. See Mitrany, *Working Peace System*, 17, 85–87, 133–34; Haas, *Beyond the Nation-State*, 32–40; Haas, *Uniting of Europe*, 16–31, 113–239, 283–340; Nye, "Comparing Common Markets," 195–206; and Robert O. Keohane and Joseph S. Nye, Jr., "Introduction," and "Conclusion," in Keohane and Nye, eds., *Transnational Relations and World Politics* (Cambridge: Harvard University Press, 1972), ix–xxix, 371–98.

13. A substantial body of literature that is not based on liberalism nevertheless shares the latter's skepticism about the unity and rationality of states. It finds that subsystemic forces, such as organizational and bureaucratic politics, small group dynamics, crisis decision making, and individual psychology, all undermine state coherence and rationality. See Graham T. Allison, *Essence of Decision: Explaining the Cuban Missile Crisis* (Boston: Little, Brown, 1971); Irving J. Janis, *Groupthink*, 2d ed. (Boston: Houghton Mifflin, 1980); Ole R. Holsti, *Crisis Escalation War* (Montreal: McGill University Press, 1970); John D. Steinbruner, *The Cybernetic Theory of Decision* (Princeton: Princeton University Press, 1974); Alexander L. George and Juliette L. George, *Woodrow Wilson and Colonel House: A Personality Study* (New York: Dover, 1964); and Robert Jervis, *Perception and Misperception in International Politics* (Princeton: Princeton University Press, 1976).

14. Mitrany, *Working Peace System*, 54–55, 63, 69–73, 88, 134–38.

15. See Mitrany, *Working Peace System*, 20, 32–38; Haas, "The New Europe," 152,

Liberal institutionalists also argued that states were becoming less concerned about power and security. Internationally, nuclear weapons and mobilized national populations were rendering war prohibitively expensive.[16] Moreover, increases in economic contacts between nations were causing states to be increasingly dependent on one another for the attainment of such national goals as faster economic growth, full employment, and price stability.[17] Domestically, industrialization had created the present "social century": the advanced democracies (and, more slowly, the socialist and developing countries) were becoming welfare states oriented less toward power and prestige and more toward economic growth and social security.[18] Thus liberals rejected the realist proposition that states are fundamentally disinclined to cooperate, finding instead that states increasingly view one another not as enemies but as partners needed to secure greater comfort and well-being for their home publics.[19]

Finally, liberal institutionalists rejected realism's pessimistic assessment of international institutions. For functionalist theory, specialized agencies such as the International Labor Organization (ILO) could promote cooperation because they performed valuable tasks without frontally challenging state sovereignty.[20] Neofunctionalist theory presented a similar argument; Ernst Haas suggested that supranational bodies like the EC were "the appropriate regional counterpart to the national state which no longer feels capable of realizing welfare aims within its own narrow borders."[21] Interdependence theory reached the same conclusion; Robert Keohane and Joseph Nye claimed that "in a world of multiple issues imperfectly linked, in which coalitions are formed transnationally and transgovernmentally, the potential

---

155–56; Keohane and Nye, "Introduction," xxv, and "Conclusion," 375–78; Morse, "Transformation," 387–89; Cooper, "Interdependence," 177, 179; and Keohane and Nye, *Power and Interdependence*, 33–35, 226–29.

16. Mitrany, *Working Peace System*, 13; Morse, "Transformation," 380–81; Keohane and Nye, *Power and Interdependence*, 27–29, 228.

17. Mitrany, *Working Peace System*, 131–37; Haas, "The New Europe," 161–62; Cooper, "Interdependence," 161–68, 173–74; Keohane and Nye, *Power and Interdependence*, 26, 228.

18. See Mitrany, *Working Peace System*, 41–42, 95–96, 136–37, 144–45; Haas, "The New Europe," 155–58; Morse, "Transformation," 383–85; and Keohane and Nye, *Power and Interdependence*, 227.

19. See Haas, "The New Europe," 158, 160–62, 166–67. See also Mitrany, *Working Peace System*, 92–93; Morse, "Transformation," 383–85; and Cooper, "Interdependence," 164–67, 170–72, 179.

20. Mitrany, *Working Peace System*, 133–37, 198–211; see also Haas, *Beyond the Nation-State*.

21. Haas, "The New Europe," 159.

role of international institutions in political bargaining is greatly increased."[22]

Postwar events, and especially those of the 1970s, appeared to support realism and to invalidate liberal institutionalism. States remained autonomous in setting foreign policy goals; they retained the loyalty of government officials active in "transgovernmental networks"; and they demonstrated that they could readily manage the terms of their relationships with such seemingly powerful transnational actors as high-technology multinational corporations.[23] Industrialized states varied in their economic performance during the 1970s in the face of similar challenges (oil shortages, recession, and inflation), and scholars linked these differences in performance to continuing divergences, and not growing convergence, in their domestic political-economic structures.[24] In the 1970s and early 1980s the use of force still was a pervasive feature of world politics, as demonstrated by increases in East-West tensions and the continuation of the Soviet-American arms competition; direct and indirect military intervention and counterintervention by the superpowers in Africa, Central America, and Southwest Asia; and the Yom Kippur and Iran-Iraq wars.[25] Specialized international institutions such as the ILO and the United Nations Educational, Scientific, and Cultural Organization (UNESCO) appeared to be unable to reshape state interests; instead,

22. Keohane and Nye, *Power and Interdependence*, 35; see also 36, 232–34, 240–42.

23. See Stephen D. Krasner, *Defending the National Interest: Raw Materials Investments and U.S. Foreign Policy* (Princeton: Princeton University Press, 1978); Robert W. Russell, "Transgovernmental Interaction in the International Monetary System, 1960–1972," *International Organization* 27 (Autumn 1973), 431–64; and Joseph M. Grieco, *Between Dependency and Autonomy: India's Experience with the International Computer Industry* (Berkeley: University of California Press, 1984).

24. See Peter J. Katzenstein, ed., *Between Power and Plenty: Foreign Economic Policies of Advanced Industrial States* (Madison: University of Wisconsin Press, 1978); Katzenstein, *Corporatism and Change: Austria, Switzerland, and the Politics of Industry* (Ithaca: Cornell University Press, 1984); Katzenstein, *Small States in World Markets: Industrial Policy in Europe* (Ithaca: Cornell University Press, 1985); John Zysman, *Political Strategies for Industrial Order: State, Market, and Industry in France* (Berkeley: University of California Press, 1977); Zysman, *Governments, Markets, and Growth: Financial Systems and the Politics of Industrial Change* (Ithaca: Cornell University Press, 1983); and Peter Gourevitch, *Politics in Hard Times: Comparative Responses to International Economic Crises* (Ithaca: Cornell University Press, 1986), 181–217.

25. On the continuing utility of force in the nuclear age, see Alexander L. George and Richard Smoke, *Deterrence in American Foreign Policy: Theory and Practice* (New York: Columbia University Press, 1974); Barry M. Blechman and Stephen S. Kaplan, *Force without War: U.S. Armed Forces as a Political Instrument* (Washington, D.C.: Brookings Institution, 1978); Kaplan, *Diplomacy of Power: Soviet Armed Forces as a Political Instrument* (Washington, D.C.: Brookings Institution, 1981); John J. Mearsheimer, *Conventional Deterrence* (Ithaca: Cornell University Press, 1983); and Richard Betts, *Nuclear Blackmail and Nuclear Balance* (Washington, D.C.: Brookings Institution, 1987).

they were often embroiled in and paralyzed by East-West and North-South disputes.[26] Finally, nascent supranationalism in Western Europe increasingly appeared to be little more than old-fashioned intergovernmental bargaining, and the advanced democracies frequently experienced serious trade and monetary conflicts and sharp discord over economic relations with the Soviet Union.[27]

Yet international cooperation did not collapse during the 1970s as it had during the 1930s.[28] In finance, private banks and governments in developed countries worked with the International Monetary Fund (IMF) to contain the international debt crisis.[29] In trade, the advanced states completed the Tokyo Round negotiations under the General Agreement on Tariffs and Trade (GATT).[30] In energy, the advanced states failed to coordinate responses to the oil crises of 1973–74 and 1979, but cooperated effectively—through the International Energy Agency (IEA)—following the outbreak of the Iran-Iraq war in

26. On East-West disputes in the ILO, see Walter Galenson, *The International Labor Organization: An American View* (Madison: University of Wisconsin Press, 1981). North-South struggles within UNESCO are described in "Symposium: Focus on UNESCO," *Comparative Education Review* 30 (February 1986), 108–56. More general analysis of North-South conflicts within international institutions is provided by Stephen D. Krasner, *Structural Conflict: The Third World against Global Liberalism* (Berkeley: University of California Press, 1985).

27. On the problem of European integration, see Donald J. Puchala, "Domestic Politics and Regional Harmonization in the European Communities," *World Politics* 27 (July 1975), 496–520; and Paul Taylor, *The Limits of European Integration* (New York: Columbia University Press, 1983). On trade conflicts during the 1970s, see John H. Jackson, "The Crumbling Institutions of the Liberal Trade System," *Journal of World Trade Law* 12 (March-April 1978), 93–106; Bela Balassa and Carol Balassa, "Industrial Protection in the Developed Countries," *World Economy* 7 (June 1984), 179–86; and Kahler, "European Protectionism." On monetary disputes, see Susan Strange, *International Monetary Relations of the Western World, 1959–1971*, vol. 2 of Andrew Shonfield, ed., *International Economic Relations of the Western World, 1959–1971* (Oxford: Oxford University Press for the Royal Institute of International Affairs, 1976), 320–53; and Benjamin J. Cohen, "Europe's Money, America's Problem," *Foreign Policy*, no. 35 (Summer 1979), 31–47. On disputes over economic ties with the Soviet Union, see Stephen Woolcock, *Western Policies on East-West Trade*, Chatham House Papers, no. 15 (London: Routledge & Kegan Paul for the Royal Institute of International Affairs, 1982); and Bruce W. Jentleson, *Pipeline Politics: The Complex Political Economy of East-West Energy Trade* (Ithaca: Cornell University Press, 1986).

28. Stephen D. Krasner, "Preface," in Krasner, ed., *International Regimes*, viii.

29. See Charles Lipson, "Bankers' Dilemmas: Private Cooperation in Rescheduling Sovereign Debts," *World Politics* 38 (October 1985), 200–225; and Miles Kahler, ed., *The Politics of International Debt* (Ithaca: Cornell University Press, 1986).

30. See Gilbert Winham, *International Trade and the Tokyo Round Negotiation* (Princeton: Princeton University Press, 1986); see also Charles Lipson, "The Transformation of Trade: The Sources and Effects of Regime Change," in Krasner, ed., *International Regimes*, 233–72; and Jock A. Finlayson and Mark W. Zacher, "The GATT and the Regulation of Trade Barriers: Regime Dynamics and Functions," in Krasner, ed., *International Regimes*, 273–314.

1980.[31] Finally, in high technology, the European states initiated and pursued during the 1970s a host of joint projects in high technology such as Airbus Industrie, the ARIANE rocket program, and the ESPRIT information technology effort.[32] Governments had not transformed their foreign policies, and world politics were not in transition, but states achieved cooperation through international institutions even in the harsh 1970s.

These developments set the stage for a formidable new liberal challenge to realism in the 1980s. Breaking away from earlier liberal formulations, the newest liberal institutionalists assert that they accept the realist views that states are the main actors in world politics and that international anarchy profoundly inhibits the willingness of states to cooperate. In particular, the new liberals claim that they recognize that states—as "rationally egoistic" agents interested only in themselves—find it hard to work together in the face of anarchy because cheating is both feasible and profitable.[33] However, neoliberal institutionalists argue that international regimes—or, more generally, international institutions—can reduce the attractiveness of cheating and thus are able to promote cooperation. This is because regimes and institutions facilitate the pursuit by states of a strategy (that of reciprocity) that reduces the attractiveness of cheating and the uncertainties states otherwise may have about the faithfulness of partners. Thus neoliberal institutionalists argue that realists are excessively pessimistic about international institutions and interstate collaboration, for the former can help rationally egoistic states to achieve the latter.

By highlighting the compliance problem in interstate arrangements, neoliberals have helped us understand the problem of international cooperation. Much more problematic, however, is their claim that they can undercut realism even while using the latter's own basic premises and propositions. The next chapter demonstrates that neo-

31. See Robert J. Lieber, *The Oil Decade: Conflict and Cooperation in the West* (New York: Praeger, 1983); Daniel Badger and Robert Belgrave, *Oil Supply and Price: What Went Right in 1980?* (Paris: Atlantic Institute for International Affairs, 1982); and Keohane, *After Hegemony*, 217–40.

32. See Bruce L. R. Smith, "A New Technology Gap in Europe?" *SAIS Review* 6 (Winter–Spring 1986), 219–36; and Walter A. McDougall, "Space-Age Europe: Gaullism, Euro-Gaullism, and the American Dilemma," *Technology and Culture* 26 (April 1985), 179–203.

33. Thomas Schelling has observed that the notion of mixed motives "refers not, of course, to an individual's lack of clarity about his own preferences but rather to the ambivalence of his relations to the other player—the mixture of mutual dependence and conflict, or partnership and competition." See Schelling, *The Strategy of Conflict* (New York: Oxford University Press, 1963), 89.

liberal theory is in fact not truly grounded in realist theory and that, compared to realism, neoliberalism offers a partial and ultimately defective analysis of the implications for states of their anarchical political context. It shows that realist theory correctly rejects the neoliberal contention that anarchy causes states to be rational egoists; instead, realism finds with greater logical rigor than is evidenced in neoliberalism that states in anarchy must be in greater or lesser measure what I shall call "defensive positionalists." Realists recognize that states worry that partners may cheat them. However—and more significant from the realist viewpoint—states are fundamentally concerned about their physical survival and their political independence. Survival and independence both result from and depend upon a state's own efforts and thus its relative capabilities. As a result, states want to know what the impact will be of virtually any relationship on their relative defensive capabilities: hence the realist insight that states in anarchy are generally defensive positionalists. Defensive state positionalism, in turn, generates a relative-gains problem for cooperation: a state will decline to join, will leave, or will sharply limit its commitment to a cooperative arrangement if it believes that gaps in otherwise mutually positive gains favor partners.

In sum, neoliberals claim that states in anarchy are rational egoists; realists assert in contrast that states are defensive positionalists. Neoliberals argue that states find cooperation in mixed-interest situations difficult to achieve primarily because of fears of cheating, and they suggest that management of the cheating problem opens the way to successful joint action. Realists argue that states are inhibited about cooperation in such situations because of fears about cheating and, in addition, and in greater or lesser measure, because of fears about relative achievements of gains. From a realist viewpoint, if the problem either of cheating or of relative gains arises but is not resolved, cooperation is likely to fail.

Realism and neoliberalism thus compete on two important dimensions. First, they compete for our acceptance as the more appropriate basis for the study of the problem of international cooperation: neoliberalism would lead us to focus on compliance problems; realism would lead us to investigate both compliance and distributional issues. Second, the two approaches compete for our attention in devising mechanisms to promote mutually beneficial forms of interstate collaboration: neoliberalism would lead us to stress strategies and institutions that reduce cheating; realism would emphasize the cheating problem and, independent of that, the need to address the relative-gains concerns of disadvantaged members in such an endeavor. Thus, for both theoretical and practical reasons, it is useful and necessary to explore and estimate the comparative veracity of realism and neo-liberal institutionalism.

A TEST OF REALISM AND NEOLIBERALISM

This book attempts to demonstrate that realism is logically superior to neoliberal institutionalism. It also seeks to determine whether realism or neoliberal institutionalism provides greater insight into the actual behavior and interactions of states. To test neoliberal and realist claims about anarchy and states, this study follows the advice of Kenneth Waltz and begins by identifying the two approaches respective "expectations about outcomes associated with anarchic realms."[34] This is necessary because, as John Ruggie notes, "ordering principles [such as anarchy] constitute the 'deep structure' of a system, shaping its fundamental social quality. They are not visible directly, only through their hypothesized effects."[35] Thus the first task in assessing the comparative empirical strength of neoliberalism and realism—and one of the tasks undertaken in the next chapter—is to derive competing hypotheses that are generated by the two approaches and that are the result of their divergent understandings of states and anarchy. Empirical investigations can then determine whether observed state behavior supports realist or neoliberal expectations.[36]

In selecting an international issue-area to serve as a testing ground for neoliberalism and realism, I could have tried to prejudice the outcome of the study in favor of the latter by focusing on military interactions of political adversaries, for the latter are extremely likely to be worried about the effects on their relative capabilities of any

34. See Waltz, *Theory of International Politics*, 102.

35. See John Gerard Ruggie, "Continuity and Transformation in the World Polity: Toward a Neorealist Synthesis," in Keohane, ed., *Neorealism*, 135.

36. Employing this method of competitive theory testing, Barry Posen has demonstrated that the military doctrines developed by France, Britain, and Germany during the interwar period more closely match expectations derived from a systemic-oriented, balance-of-power theory than from approaches that focus on organizational politics. See Posen, *The Sources of Military Doctrine: Britain, France, and Germany between the World Wars* (Ithaca: Cornell University Press, 1985). Similarly, Stephen Walt has recently shown that a major realist hypothesis—that states prefer to balance power rather than to "bandwagon"—accounts for more instances of state alliance behavior than hypotheses derived from competing theories stressing such factors as ideology or domestic structures. See Walt, *The Origin of Alliances* (Ithaca: Cornell University Press, 1987), chaps. 2, 7; also see Walt, "Testing Theories of Alliance Formation: The Case of Southwest Asia," *International Organization* 42 (Spring 1988), 275–316.

security-oriented interaction, whether it be cooperative or otherwise. That is not the path taken here. Instead, I seek to demonstrate that realism is superior to neoliberalism in explaining important political-economic events, namely, U.S.-EC relations in the Tokyo Round regime on NTBs, and their impact on the effectiveness of that regime during the 1980s. For a variety of reasons articulated by the neoliberals themselves, this case selection gives neoliberalism significant initial advantages over realism in a competitive test.

First, neoliberals claim that states typically find it easier to cooperate in economic than in security matters. Charles Lipson, for example, suggests that "our analysis has emphasized the possibilities for strategic cooperation that foster the development of rules, norms, and political institutions in the world economy, and the more impoverished possibilities in security affairs."[37] More generally, Keohane suggests that neoliberalism "insists on the significance of international regimes, and the importance of the continued exploration of the conditions under which they emerge and persist," and he observes that "judging from the literature in international relations journals, this battle has been won in the area of international political economy: studies of particular international economic regimes have proliferated."[38]

Involving economics as opposed to security matters, analysis of the NTB regime should favor neoliberalism over realism. In addition, according to neoliberal arguments, the fact that the particular economic issue-area covered by the NTB regime involves cooperative efforts to reduce trade barriers ought to give neoliberalism a further edge over realism. For example, Robert Axelrod suggests that "a good example of the fundamental problem of cooperation is the case where two industrial nations have erected trade barriers to each other's exports. . . . the problem is that each country has an incentive to retain trade barriers, leading to a worse outcome than would have been possible had both countries cooperated with each other."[39] Axelrod goes on to observe that a model is needed to understand mixed-interest situations so well represented by efforts to reduce trade barri-

37. Lipson, "International Cooperation," 18.
38. Robert O. Keohane, "Neoliberal Institutionalism: A Perspective on World Politics," Introduction to *International Institutions and State Power: Essays in International Relations Theory* (Boulder, Colo.: Westview Press, 1988), 14. It should be noted that Keohane suggests that it would be very useful if neoliberals applied their approach to political-military affairs: see Keohane, *After Hegemony*, 7, and "Neoliberal Institutionalism," 35, 38–40.
39. Axelrod, *Evolution of Cooperation*, 7.

ers; he argues that the Prisoner's Dilemma is precisely that model, and he then proceeds to develop a theory of how the Prisoner's Dilemma can be resolved so that cooperation in such circumstances can evolve.[40]

Most of the members of the NTB codes are advanced democratic states that are already on very good political terms, and indeed are in many cases military allies, and this too should favor neoliberalism over realism. This is because, as Keohane suggests when justifying his focus on relations among the advanced democracies, it is those relationships "where common interests are greatest and where the benefits of cooperation may be easiest to realize."[41] Neoliberal theory also finds that cooperation among the advanced democracies is easier to achieve because particular collaborative ventures are typically "nested" in a network of other economic and political joint arrangements.[42] The NTB codes, firmly embedded as they are in the GATT trade regime, certainly meet this test.

The final reason that selection of the NTB regime ought to bias a competitive test of neoliberalism and realism in favor of the former is the fact that neoliberals have already suggested that the NTB codes are an important example of the validity of their ideas. For example, having noted that the danger of cheating is lower in economic than in security relations, Lipson observes that "timely monitoring is important but rarely vital since most economic actions are reasonably transparent. A few, such as nontariff barriers or short-term Mexican debt, may be opaque, but most are matters of public record." NTBs are thus difficult for states to regulate collectively. However, Lipson observes in a footnote that "making nontariff barriers more visible to foreign producers was a major accomplishment of the Tokyo Round of trade negotiations."[43] Similarly, Keohane notes that preservation of a liberal trade order requires "institutional innovations that will respond to the international bargaining realities and domestic political pressures of our day." Finding that the ideas of one author "leads us to begin thinking along those lines," Keohane concludes that "so do the Tokyo Round codes, which permit tit-for-tat strategies to promote

40. Ibid. A similar use of trade relations as an important illustration of Prisoner's Dilemma-type situations is presented in Stein, "Coordination and Collaboration," 124.
41. Keohane, *After Hegemony*, 7. It should be noted that Keohane invites the "careful extension" of his arguments to North-South and East-West relations.
42. On the "nesting" of regimes, see Keohane, *After Hegemony*, 90–91; and Vinod K. Aggarwal, *Liberal Protectionism: The International Politics of Organized Textile Trade* (Berkeley: University of California Press, 1985).
43. See Lipson, "International Cooperation," 17 and footnote 50 on 17.

liberalization and fairness while retaining an open, multilateral structure of rules to which all participants in GATT may adhere."[44]

The NTB codes involve circumstances that appear to be highly
favorable to successful application of neoliberal institutionalism. The
very same circumstances are extremely unfavorable to realist theory.
With its emphasis on the problem of state survival and state independence, realism would appear to be more suited to the "high politics"
of geo-strategic military issues and would seem to be surely unsuited
for discussions of the more mundane "low politics" of international
trade. In addition, realist theory is typically the form of analysis that is
brought to bear on relations between adversaries, and, except for
analyses of military alliances, realism is not usually applied to relations
among states that are on friendly terms. Thus, if realist expectations
as to the operation of the relative-gains problem are ever going to be
disproved, one would have expected it to be in cases involving trade
(or other economic) relations among the advanced democratic states.
At the same time, if realism's expectations are corroborated by the
NTB code experience, the factors it finds significant must be truly
potent, for they would have induced their expected outcomes in precisely those circumstances that should have vitiated their impact.

If realist theory helps us understand the differences in the level of
European-American cooperation in the Tokyo Round NTB codes
during the 1980s, and therefore the variation in the effectiveness
achieved by the agreements, then it will have done so in precisely
those circumstances in which the opposite should have occurred. Similarly, if neoliberalism has difficulties in accounting for U.S.-EC code
interactions and thus differences in code effectiveness, its shortcom-
ings as an analytical approach will have been highlighted in circumstances likely to have validated the theory. Hence the NTB code experience may approach the status of a crucial experiment.[45] Such an
experiment in principle generates findings that simultaneously constitute strong disconfirming evidence for one theory (that is, refuta-
tion in circumstances highly biased in the theory's favor) and strong
confirming evidence for another, competing theory (that is, failure to

44. See Robert O. Keohane, "Comment on Multilateral and Bilateral Negotiating
Approaches for the Conduct of U.S. Trade Policies," in Robert M. Stern, ed., *U.S. Trade
Policies in a Changing World Economy* (Cambridge: MIT Press, 1987), 407. The paper on
which Keohane commented had been prepared by John H. Jackson.

45. On the concept of a crucial experiment, see Arthur Stinchcombe, *Constructing
Social Theories* (New York: Harcourt Brace, 1968), 20–28. Also see Harry Eckstein,
"Case Study and Theory in Political Science," in Fred I. Greenstein and Nelson W.
Polsby, eds., *Strategies of Inquiry*, vol. 7 of *Handbook of Political Science* (Reading, Mass.:
Addison-Wesley, 1975), 118-20.

refute or even affirmation of the theory in circumstances least favorable to it). To a great degree, the NTB code experience may satisfy both these conditions, for it places neoliberal institutionalism at risk in precisely those circumstances most favorable to it while possibly lending support to realism in the most hostile of environments.

Of course, to test the two theories, it is necessary first to specify what it is about the Tokyo Round NTB code experience that requires explanation. As already noted, the major trading states made a comprehensive effort to address the problem of non-tariff barriers during the Tokyo Round of 1973–79.[46] This seventh trade round produced a regime consisting of six international codes and an associated network of committees of signatories. The codes articulated rules in regard to six types of NTBs: customs-valuation methods, import-licensing procedures, technical barriers, anti-dumping practices, government procurement, and subsidies and countervailing measures. In turn, the code committees were to serve as institutionalized forums through which members could verify one another's compliance, raise complaints and resolve disputes, and facilitate and sponsor negotiations to interpret or extend code rules.

Initial expectations about the new NTB regime were high. Robert Baldwin, for example, suggested that the NTB codes were "the most important part of the agreements reached" during the Tokyo Round and that the "scope and detail of the new nontariff codes represent a brilliant accomplishment."[47] Similarly, John Jackson suggested in 1983 that the Tokyo Round had been an "extraordinary trade negotiation" because "for the first time important attention was given to nontariff barriers as well as to tariffs."[48] The GATT secretariat itself suggested that the code negotiations "constituted one of the major features that distinguished the Tokyo Round from earlier rounds,"

46. The negotiation of the codes during the 1970s is fully analyzed elsewhere: see Winham, *Tokyo Round*; Leslie Alan Glick, *Multilateral Trade Negotiations: World Trade after the Tokyo Round* (Totowa, N.J.: Rowman & Allanheld, 1984); and Victoria Curzon Price, *Industrial Policies in the European Community* (London: St. Martins, 1981), 1–16.

47. Robert E. Baldwin, *The Multilateral Trade Negotiations: Toward Greater Liberalization?* Special Analysis no. 79–2 (Washington, D.C.: American Enterprise Institute, 1979), 1, 2. It should be noted that Baldwin warned that "if the liberal-trade goal is to be implemented and the Multilateral Trade Negotiations are to go down in history as a forward rather than backward step in expanding world trade on a rational basis and in promoting international political stability, it is necessary that private groups and the government make every effort to see that the codes are enforced." See Baldwin, *Multilateral Trade Negotiations*, 8.

48. John H. Jackson, "GATT Machinery and the Tokyo Round Negotiations," in William R. Cline, ed., *Trade Policy in the 1980s* (Washington, D.C.: Institute for International Economics, 1983), 165.

and observed that, in light of the growing threat of non-tariff barriers to international trade, "the core of the Tokyo Round results consists of the agreements, or codes, aimed at reducing, and bringing under more effective international discipline, these non-tariff barriers."[49]

The U.S. Executive also initially viewed the NTB codes in a very hopeful light. In April 1979, for example, U.S. Special Trade Representative Robert Strauss reported to Congress that the codes were the "key achievement of the Tokyo Round," and in another context Strauss noted that, despite their limitations, "the agreements are an historic achievement."[50] The Commission of the European Communities, which had been responsible for EC negotiations during the Tokyo Round, also presented an optimistic assessment of the NTB codes. It reported that the tariff reductions achieved in the Tokyo Round had been large but that "the major significance of the negotiations . . . lies in agreement on a series of codes and other legal texts—such as on customs valuation, subsidies and countervailing duties, government purchasing, standards, and import licensing."[51] The commission reported further that "taken together with the machinery of enforcement of each code in terms of committees of signatories," the NTB codes represented "a considerable updating and strengthening of the GATT." With the new codes, the commission suggested, "the way has thereby been cleared for allowing the GATT to continue to play a major role in reducing uncertainty for traders and promoting trade flows."[52]

The preceding statements need to be discounted in some measure as political rhetoric; however, even if such an allowance is made, they suggest that U.S. and European officials, as well as outside academic observers, believed at the close of the Tokyo Round that the NTB codes marked a potentially important achievement. But by the mid-1980s it became clear that the NTB regime had fallen short of the goals set for it during the previous decade. For example, Michael Aho and Jonathan Aronson argued in 1985 that although the NTB regime had "suggested that GATT might become a more responsive, adap-

49. GATT, *Activities in 1979 and Completion of the Tokyo Round Multilateral Trade Negotiations (1973–1979)* (Geneva, 1980), 20–21.

50. See "Statement of Ambassador Robert S. Strauss," in U.S., House, Committee on Ways and Means, Subcommittee on Trade, *Multilateral Trade Negotiations* (Washington, D.C., 1979), 484; and Robert S. Strauss, "Foreword," in *Symposium on the Multilateral Trade Agreements*, special issue of *Law and Policy in International Business* 11, no. 4 (1979), 1258–59.

51. Commission of the European Communities, "Tokyo Round: Substantial and Balanced Results," *Bulletin of the European Communities* 12, no. 10 (1979), 7.

52. Ibid., 8.

tive trade policy organization," actual experience suggested that "it has not worked out that way, in part because of the limited number of countries which have subscribed to the codes and in part because some of the rules were left deliberately fuzzy where countries could not agree on which practices should be ended."[53] Aho and Aronson went on to recall that many had hoped that the code committees "would serve as continuing negotiating fora" and that therefore "some commentators even suggested that there would be no need for another formal round." But, they argued, "the committees have not worked out very well," and "now that the trading system is gradually deteriorating, the arguments for a round are again being advanced."[54] Similarly, William Diebold observed in 1987 that governments reluctantly agreed to a new trade round because their piecemeal approach after the Tokyo Round had "not produced very good results." According to Diebold, one cause for the poor performance of the GATT after 1979 was that "the codes . . . proved to be weak, not by accident but because governments were not willing to make them stronger or use them more effectively."[55]

Dissatisfaction with the Tokyo Round codes was also expressed in the 1985 report of the "GATT Wisemen." Established in November 1983 by the GATT director-general, and reflecting international concerns that the extremely severe recession of 1981–82 had seriously harmed the international trade system, this group of seven eminent persons representing developed- and developing-country viewpoints warned that "the trading rules set under the General Agreement on Tariffs and Trade are increasingly ignored or evaded."[56] The Wisemen offered fifteen proposals for ameliorative action, including the initiation of a new trade round.[57] In addition, the Wisemen proposed that "the GATT 'codes' governing non-tariff distortions of trade should be improved and vigorously applied to make trade more open and fair." The Wisemen explained that the Tokyo Round NTB codes "represent an important step"; however, they stressed they had nev-

---

53. C. Michael Aho and Jonathan David Aronson, *Trade Talks: America Better Listen!* (New York: Council on Foreign Relations, 1985), 19.

54. Ibid., 135.

55. William Diebold, "Political Implications of US-EC Economic Conflicts (III): American Trade Policy and Western Europe," *Government and Opposition* 22 (Summer 1987), 283; also see 297.

56. GATT, *Trade Policies for a Better Future: Proposals for Action* (Geneva, 1985), 5. The members of the group were Senator Bill Bradley (U.S.), Pehr G. Gyllenhammar (Sweden), Guy Ladreit de Lacharriere (France), Fritz Leutwiler (chair, Switzerland), Indraprasad G. Patel (India), Mario Henrique Simonsen (Brazil), and Sumitro Djojohadikusomo (Indonesia).

57. Proposal no. 13, in ibid., 10, 47.

ertheless found that some of the provisions in the codes were "inadequate and should be corrected."[58]

Thus, by the mid-1980s, within the international trade policy community there was discontent with the Tokyo Round NTB regime. Yet this disenchantment resulted in large measure from highly visible failures that were sustained not by all but instead by some of the codes. As demonstrated in Chapters 3, 4, and 5, some of the NTB codes went much farther than others during the 1980s in meeting their goals and contributing to international discipline over non-tariff barriers. In general, the codes and committees of signatories responsible for customs-valuation methods and import-licensing procedures attained a substantial level of effectiveness, as did the rules on countervailing measures contained in the agreement on subsidies and countervailing measures; the subsidies portion of the latter accord was markedly ineffective; and the codes on anti-dumping practices, technical barriers to trade, and government procurement achieved mixed levels of effectiveness.

This variance in code effectiveness, in turn, was largely (but not exclusively) driven by the level of U.S.-EC cooperation and discord regarding the particular code in question. The discussion in Chapters 4 and especially 5 shows how the Nordic countries—Sweden, Norway, and Finland—played an important role in developing and proposing compromises when disputes arose or when negotiations on rules were undertaken in several of the NTB code committees during the 1980s, and Japan was often the target of criticisms by fellow code signatories during that period. However, those chapters also demonstrate that the United States and the EC were the major actors in the code committees and were usually the main protagonists in code-related disputes.[59] During the 1980s cooperation between these two GATT partners was high with respect to the rules on countervailing measures

58. Ibid., 41.

59. This finding is in keeping with Robert Baldwin's recent observation that "a minimum requirement for a viable trading system is the active support of both the United States and the member countries of the European Community. . . . Other major trading groups have generally been willing to accept the leadership of the United States and the EC in initiating multilateral negotiations aimed at reducing protection and modifying the rules of the General Agreement on Tariffs and Trade." See Robert E. Baldwin, "An Introduction to the Issues and Analyses," in Baldwin, Carl B. Hamilton, and Andre Sapir, *Issues in US-EC Trade Relations* (Chicago: University of Chicago Press for the National Bureau of Economic Research, 1988), 1. Furthermore, the fact that most of the disputes concerned with the NTB codes during the 1980s involved the United States and the EC is in keeping with the long-term evolution of GATT politics: see Robert H. Hudec, "Legal Issues in US-EC Trade Policy: GATT Litigation, 1960–1985," in Baldwin, Hamilton, and Sapir, eds., *US-EC Trade Relations*, 17–64.

and the agreements on customs valuation and import licensing; it was low in regard to subsidies; and it was of an intermediate character in their interactions involving government procurement and technical barriers. European-American cooperation was rather high in the anti-dumping code; the setbacks of that agreement, the discussion below demonstrates, were due in part to U.S.-EC consensus regarding a code-related issue.

Given its critical role in determining the effectiveness attained by the Tokyo Round NTB regime, and because it allows for a testing of the relative veracity of the two most important systemic theories of the problem of international cooperation, this study seeks to account for the variation in European-American cooperation across the NTB accords during the 1980s. Neoliberal theory would argue that if EC support varied across the codes, this should have been due to variation in the levels of cheating (either by the EC or its partners) in the codes. Neoliberal theory would also argue that the severity of cheating problems would vary in response to four specific conditions: the number of partners, the presence of advanced-country participants, the degree to which interactions among partners were iterated, and the size of the gains from each code. If EC support varied across the codes, neoliberalism would expect to find correlated variance across the agreements in these four conditions *from the EC's viewpoint.*

This book concludes that, in fact, neither U.S.-EC cooperation nor the success of the NTBs codes covaried with the presence or absence of the particular factors thought by neoliberal theory to restrain state cheating. In addition, EC cheating or EC fears of cheating do not appear to have figured more prominently in the less successful codes than in the more successful codes or in the codes where there was less rather than more U.S.-EC cooperation. Therefore neoliberal institutional theory does not appear to be effective in accounting for the study's empirical findings that there was in fact very great variance in EC support for, and thus success of, the NTB codes during the 1980s.

Realist theory, in seeking to explain the variance in EC policy toward the codes, would expect that the EC supported each agreement during the 1980s in rough proportion to its belief that relative achievements of resulting gains did not favor others. Chapter 7 demonstrates that the EC had good reason to be satisfied with its absolute and relative gains from the codes that were characterized by greater cooperation between the EC and the United States, and that achieved greater effectiveness—the customs code and the rules on countervailing measures in the subsidies agreement. European-American conflicts over the subsidies portion of the latter code resulted from a

combination of EC concerns about relative gains and from EC perceptions that it was in a zero-sum situation in which U.S. gains would
come at the expense of the EC.

Most significant, the EC and its member-countries, because of their
perception of sharp differences between the United States and Europe regarding domestic institutional structures and policy trends,
harbored grave doubts about the capacity of the EC countries to benefit to the same degree as the United States from the codes on technical
barriers and government procurement. As a result of these relative-
gains concerns, and because the EC believed that the issue-areas covered by the two accords were of vital importance to its future as a
strong, independent actor in the world economy, it followed a minimalist interpretation of the codes, bringing it into frequent conflicts
with the United States and the latter's maximalist interpretation of
and attitude toward them. Indeed, there were even instances in which
the EC gave up opportunities to achieve absolute gains for its member-
countries rather than accept bargaining outcomes with the United
States regarding the two codes in which both would benefit but the
United States would benefit more than the EC. The resulting disagreements between the United States and the EC limited the effectiveness achieved by the two accords during the 1980s. Finally, setbacks in the anti-dumping code that were not driven by U.S.-EC
disagreements were nevertheless also the result of relative-gains problems perceived by Canada, Australia, and Argentina.

In sum, the empirical section of the book seeks to show that realism
and its specification of a relative-gains problem for cooperation are
able to shed light on important elements of the NTB code experience—elements that would go unexplained if neoliberalism were the
only available analysis of the dynamics of interstate collaboration. If
this case can be made, realism will have demonstrated a greater capacity than neoliberalism to explain behavior in precisely that international domain which would appear to be most resistant to the former
and most amenable to the latter. If realism can do that, then it will also
have shown that it remains the best theory available to explain the
interests and behavior of states, not only in security matters, but in the
international political economy as well.

SYSTEMIC-LEVEL ANALYSIS OF STATES
AND INTERNATIONAL COOPERATION

The political system composed of states lacks centralized authority:
it is anarchic. For states this means that "formally, each is the equal of

all the others. None is entitled to command; none is required to obey."[60] In these circumstances, any and all security, wealth, or prestige attained by states is the result solely of their own efforts, for, in an environment in which no other agency is responsible for their fate, each state must act on the basis of national self-help. International anarchy, then, is the underlying political-structural condition whose impact on the willingness of states to undertake cooperation this study seeks to explore and understand.

This book is concerned with the calculations and actions of states; yet the empirical focus is on interactions between the United States and the European Community. I do not imply that the EC is some new trans-state community. Instead, the assumption underlying the discussion—an assumption based on the key scholarly works on EC policy making—is that the arguments presented by the EC Commission in the context of the GATT, as in other international forums, are based on and driven by the interests and preferences of the individual EC member-states and especially the EC's core countries, Britain, Germany, and France.[61] Thus references in the study to EC policy are a

60. See Waltz, *Theory of International Politics*, 88; also see Waltz, "Response to My Critics," 323. Waltz notes that the definition of a political structure also includes the level of differentiation and specialization of the units in the system, and the distribution of power among these units: see Waltz, *Theory of International Politics*, 88–101. For Waltz, changes of international structure involve changes in its ordering principle and especially the distribution of power, and he excludes as a definition of systems change the issue of differentiation and specialization of units. This, in turn, has been criticized by Ruggie in his "Continuity and Transformation in the World Polity," 141–52; and for Waltz's rejoinder, see Waltz, "Response to My Critics," 323–30. The present book finds that because anarchy leads states to seek to constrain their level of international specialization and differentiation, this element of structure importantly affects state preferences and behavior. This effect of structure is also noted in Waltz's discussion of systemic constraints on the willingness of states to become dependent on others in the context of a cooperative endeavor: see *Theory of International Politics*, 106–7.

61. As Joan Pearce and John Sutton recently suggested, while other EC members are often able to tip the balance in policy discussions, they often follow the lead of Britain, France, or Germany, and, at least to the present, "as the three largest countries in the Community they carry the most political and economic weight." See Pearce and Sutton with Roy Batchelor, *Protection and Industrial Policy in Europe* (London: Routledge & Kegan Paul, 1986), 57. For analyses of EC policy making that stress the importance of France and Germany, see, for the early period of the Community, F. Roy Willis, *France, Germany, and the New Europe, 1945–1963* (Stanford: Stanford University Press, 1965); and, for more recent developments, Haig Simonian, *The Privileged Partnership: Franco-German Relations in the European Community, 1969–1984* (Oxford: Clarendon, 1985). For an analysis that incorporates a focus on Britain, see Taylor, *European Integration*, 60–92, 162–95. For discussions of the current political process by which the EC countries develop their joint positions on trade matters, see John H. Jackson, *Implementing the Tokyo Round: National Constitutions and International Economic Rules* (Ann Arbor: University of Michigan Press, 1984); R. C. Hine, *The Political Economy of European Trade: An Introduction to the Trade Policies of the EEC* (Brighton, Sussex: Wheatsheaf, 1985); and Ernst-Ulrich Petersmann, *The European Community and GATT* (Boston: Kluwer, 1986).

shorthand term for the consensus view of the major EC member-states.

International cooperation may be defined as the voluntary adjustment by states of their policies so that they manage their differences and reach some mutually beneficial outcome.[62] This concept of international cooperation comprises a number of elements. First, cooperation involves efforts by states to work together voluntarily: states must be able to choose not to join or to exit from a cooperative arrangement. Second, international cooperation involves the specification by states of some common or at least compatible end to which they devote their combined efforts. Third, cooperation in this study signifies not a one-time interaction but rather a longer-term engagement by states, typically associated, in differing degrees and forms, with the establishment and operation of an international regime in the issue-area in which joint action is undertaken.[63] Regimes are the norms, principles, rules, and decision-making procedures that shape, guide, and constrain state policies in such a way as to promote common or compatible ends in a particular issue-area.[64] Useful work has been done recently on the influence of regime norms and principles as characteristics of cooperation and as forces shaping state action.[65] In this study, however, special attention is devoted to what may be the key element of regime-based cooperation, namely, the acceptance and development by governments of common rules.

62. This definition of cooperation is based on Keohane, *After Hegemony*, 12, 51–52. Policy entails the specification by states of goals (or the ends of policy) and the development and implementation of programs of actions (or the means) to achieve these goals. For a discussion of policy in these terms, see Peter J. Katzenstein, "Introduction: Domestic and International Forces and Strategies of Foreign Economic Policy," and "Conclusion: Domestic Structures and Strategies of Foreign Economic Policy," in Katzenstein, ed., *Between Power and Plenty*, 3–22, 295–336.

63. In recent years scholars have absorbed the concept of "international regimes" into the concept of "international institutions"; the latter may be defined as international "practices composed of recognized roles coupled with sets of rules or conventions governing relations among occupants of these roles." See Oran Young, "International Regimes: Toward a New Theory of Institutions," *World Politics* 39 (October 1986), 108.

64. See Stephen D. Krasner, "Structural Causes and Regime Consequences: Regimes as Intervening Variables," in Krasner, ed., *International Regimes*, 2–5; and Keohane, *After Hegemony*, 57–59, 61. For critiques of this formulation, see Friedrich Kratochwil, "The Force Of Prescriptions," *International Organization* 38 (Autumn 1984), 685–708; Young, "International Regimes"; and Kratochwil and John Gerard Ruggie, "International Organization: A State of the Art on an Art of the State," *International Organization* 40 (Autumn 1986), 764–771.

65. Studies of regimes—all in Krasner, ed., *International Regimes*—that emphasize norms and principles include Donald J. Puchala and Raymond F. Hopkins, "International Regimes: Lessons from Inductive Analysis," 61–91; John Gerard Ruggie, "International Regimes, Transactions, and Change: Embedded Liberalism in the Postwar Economic Order," 195–232; and Finlayson and Zacher, "GATT and Trade Barriers," 273–314.

Rules in an international regime or institution are "specific prescriptions or proscriptions for action" and as such are injunctions about state behavior.[66] Scholars in recent years appear to be reaching a consensus that international cooperation cannot be separated from rule-governed state behavior and that rules may in fact be the most important element of international regimes or institutions. For example, in their review of regimes theory, Stephan Haggard and Beth Simmons conclude that they prefer to think of regimes as "multilateral agreements among states which aim to regulate national actions within an issue area" insofar as they undertake to "define the range of permissible state action by outlining *explicit* injunctions."[67] A focus on rules also ensures that this book concentrates on the same aspects of cooperation that are emphasized by neoliberal theory. For example, in his most recent work, Keohane drops norms, principles, and procedures from his definition of regimes and instead suggests that we think of them as "institutions with explicit rules, agreed upon by governments, which pertain to particular sets of issues in international relations." He also observes that "extensive terminological discussion of regimes has convinced me that it is clearest to limit the term 'regimes' to institutions with explicit rules, negotiated by states."[68]

Rules are important for interstate cooperation for a number of reasons. First, they provide standards of behavior by which states may legitimize their own actions or challenge those of their partners. In addition, rules often induce transparency in the actions of states and thereby enhance the confidence of each partner that the others are complying with their commitments.[69] Third, by providing standards of behavior, rules inform and guide states in resolving disputes with one another.[70] Finally, by providing standards of behavior and channels of communication, regime rules help states solve problems that were unforeseen or unresolved at the time the cooperative endeavor was undertaken.

To understand U.S.-EC trade relations and the Tokyo Round NTB

66. Krasner, "Regimes as Intervening Variables," 2.

67. See Haggard and Simmons, "Theories of International Regimes," *International Organization* 41 (Summer 1987), 495.

68. See Keohane, "Neoliberal Institutionalism," 17, fn. 5. It should be noted that realists also recognize that rules are the core ingredient of international cooperation. For example, Carr suggested that "no political society, national or international, can exist unless people submit to certain rules of conduct. The problem why people should submit to such rules is the fundamental problem of political philosophy." See Carr, *Twenty Years' Crisis*, 41.

69. Transparency is observed by Kratochwil and Ruggie to be a "core requirement" of regimes: see their "International Organization," 772–73.

70. The more general legitimation function of regimes is noted by Kratochwil and Ruggie, "International Organization," 773.

regime, this book starts with the state (or, in the case of the EC, an association of states expressing the preferences of its major members) and the political system formed by states.[71] One likely result of such a systemic-level focus is that some important aspects of the NTB code experience will be overlooked, for there is no doubt that domestic political institutions and dynamics also shape a nation's foreign economic goals and strategies and especially its foreign trade policies.[72] Similarly, the cognitive frameworks and ideological values of officials who set national policy importantly influence and constrain the latter's perceived range of options in the international political economy.[73] However, a systemic-level focus can be justified on two grounds. First, the discussion will demonstrate that, even in an arena such as trade where domestic factors are unquestionably operating, systemic-level factors still show themselves to be very important. Second, a systemic-level focus is necessary in order to address the problem of interest to me—the debate between realism and neoliberalism on the question of international cooperation.

At the same time, I would not argue that approaching the problem of cooperation from a systemic perspective precludes attention to the impact of internal attributes and dynamics of states on their preferences and actions.[74] As already noted, the agreements on technical

71. A state may be defined as those institutions and roles within a nation that are responsible for foreign policies. This conceptualization of the state as a set of roles and institutions follows the discussion provided by Krasner, *Defending the National Interest*, 10.

72. That insight has informed and directed the research program of such scholars as Katzenstein, Gourevitch, Zysman, and, in some measure, Krasner: see their work cited in footnotes 23 and 24. It also informs the work of Joanne Gowa in *Closing the Gold Window: Domestic Politics and the End of Bretton Woods* (Ithaca: Cornell University Press, 1982); and G. John Ikenberry in *Reasons of State: Oil Politics and the Capacities of American Government* (Ithaca: Cornell University Press, 1987). For recent studies of the impact of domestic interest groups and governmental structures on foreign-trade policy, see I. M. Destler, *American Trade Politics: System under Stress* (Washington, D.C.: Institute for International Economics, 1986); Destler and John S. Odell, *Anti-Protection: Changing Forces in American Trade Politics* (Washington, D.C.: Institute for International Economics, 1987); Helen V. Milner, *Resisting Protection: Global Industries and the Politics of International Trade* (Princeton: Princeton University Press, 1988); and Henry R. Nau, ed., *Domestic Trade Politics and the Uruguay Round* (New York: Columbia University Press, 1989).

73. Major studies on the impact of person-level forces on foreign policy have been provided by such scholars as Holsti, George and George, Steinbruner, and Jervis: for citations, see footnote 13. On the significance of cognitive frameworks of national decision makers as they formulate foreign economic objectives and strategies, see John S. Odell, *U.S. International Monetary Policy* (Princeton: Princeton University Press, 1982); Judith Goldstein, "The Political Economy of Trade: Institutions of Protection," *American Political Science Review* 80 (March 1986), 161–84; and Goldstein, "The Impact of Ideas on Trade Policy: The Origins of U.S. and Agricultural Policies," *International Organization* 43 (Winter 1989), 31–71.

74. As Keohane explains, in systemic theory "*the internal attributes of actors are given by*

barriers and government procurement, and in some measure the subsidy rules in the code on subsidies and countervailing measures, generated relative-gains problems for the EC during the 1980s. Accounting for those relative-gains concerns on the part of the EC, Chapter 7
demonstrates, requires an analysis of the differences between European and American institutions and policies in the issue-areas covered
by the two agreements, and European perceptions of the likely impact
of those institutional differences on the distribution of gains generated by the two accords. It also requires an analysis of European
perceptions about the strategic significance of those issue-areas for
Europe's economic independence. Hence this study argues that it is
sometimes fruitful and even necessary to combine systemic and unit-
level explanations of state preferences. It also suggests that a realist-
oriented systemic focus, informed by an awareness of the impact of
domestic institutional conditions on the interpretation by states of
their position in the international system, can help us understand
important elements of the Tokyo Round NTB code experience and,
more generally, the politics of international economic cooperation.

Overview of the Book

This first chapter has provided an outline of the major theoretical
perspectives to be explored in the book and a preview of its main
empirical findings. The next chapter presents the argument that realism has a stronger logical grasp of the implications of anarchy for
states than does neoliberal institutionalism. Attention then shifts in
Chapters 3–7 to a competitive testing of the two perspectives through
their application to the Tokyo Round NTB code experience. The first
of these empirical chapters describes the background to the NTB
codes and their main objectives, and it reports how the trade policy
community evaluated the performance of the codes after they had
been in operation for several years. These summary assessments of

---

assumption rather than treated as variables." See Keohane, "Theory of World Politics: Structural Realism and Beyond," in Ada W. Finifter, ed., *Political Science: The State of the
Discipline* (Washington, D.C.: American Political Science Association, 1983), 508–9, emphasis in original; also see Keohane, "The Demand for International Regimes," in
Krasner, ed., *International Regimes*, 143, and Keohane, *After Hegemony*, 25–26. However,
Keohane acknowledges that variation in the internal characteristics of states may cause
systemically based constraints and inducements on policy to affect states in different
degrees and in different ways. For example, he argues that "open" states may find it
easier than "closed" states to persuade partners that they keep their promises in spite of
the opportunities afforded by international anarchy to cheat. See "Demand for Regimes," 163; and *After Hegemony*, 94–95.

the codes are then buttressed through a detailed empirical review in Chapters 4 and 5 of the operation of the NTB codes from 1980 through 1987. The former reports on the relative effectiveness of the NTB codes in terms of rule compliance and, when necessary, the successful settlement of disputes among code signatories, and the latter assesses the capacity of the various committees of signatories to undertake different types of rule construction in the face of problems and opportunities encountered while administering the agreements.

Chapters 4 and 5 demonstrate that the codes varied in effectiveness and that this variance was largely a function of the level of U.S.-EC cooperation. Chapters 6 and 7 seek to account for the variance in European-American cooperation across the different codes through the application, respectively, of neoliberal institutionalism and realism. They yield the finding that the latter offers the more complete explanation for U.S.-EC policy interactions regarding the codes and thus of the NTB code experience. Chapter 8 summarizes the book's major findings, demonstrates that its theoretical conclusions are not built on anomalous empirical observations, and highlights some of the lines of future research and the possible policy implications that are produced by a realist-based focus on defensive state positionalism and the relative-gains problem for international cooperation.

Chapter Two

Realism, Neoliberal Institutionalism, and the Problem of International Cooperation

Realist theory argues that international anarchy inhibits the willingness of states to work together even when they have common interests, and that international institutions are largely unable to mitigate the constraining effects of anarchy on interstate cooperation. Realism presents a fundamentally pessimistic analysis of the prospects for international cooperation and the capabilities of international institutions.[1] Earlier variants of liberal institutionalism—functionalism, neofunctional regionalism, and interdependence theory—all rejected realism's gloomy understanding of world politics and argued that international institutions can help states cooperate. International tensions during the 1970s undermined liberal institutionalism and reconfirmed realism in large measure. Yet that difficult decade did not witness a collapse of the international system, and, in the light of continuing modest levels of interstate cooperation, a new liberal institutionalist challenge to realism came forward during the 1980s.

What is distinctive about this newest liberal institutionalism is its claim that it accepts a number of core realist propositions, including, apparently, the realist argument that anarchy impedes the achievement of cooperation. However, the core liberal arguments—that realism overemphasizes conflict and underestimates the capacities of international institutions to promote cooperation—remain firmly intact. The new liberal institutionalists basically argue that even if the realists are correct in believing that anarchy constrains the willingness

---

1. This pessimistic outlook in realist theory is most clearly evident in Hans J. Morgenthau, *Scientific Man vs. Power Politics* (Chicago: University of Chicago Press, 1946), 187–203.

of states to cooperate, they nevertheless can work together and can do so especially with the assistance of institutions.

This point is crucial for students of international relations. If neo-liberal institutionalists are correct, they have dealt realism a major blow while providing the intellectual justification for treating their own approach, and the tradition from which it emerges, as the most effective for understanding world politics.

The key argument in this chapter is that neoliberal institution-alism misunderstands the realist analysis of international anarchy and therefore misconstrues the realist analysis of the impact of anarchy on the preferences and actions of states. The new liberal institutionalism fails to identify a major effect of anarchy on states stressed in realist theory—the recognition by states that others might seek to destroy or enslave them. Because of this fundamental flaw in its understanding of anarchy, neoliberalism is unable to identify a major constraint on the willingness of states to cooperate, one which is generated by anar-chy and which is identified by realism: the concern of states that others may achieve relatively greater gains.

Neoliberalism claims that it employs the same definition of anarchy as does realism, namely the absence of centralized authority among states. It then argues that states in such an environment are atomistic "rational egoists." It argues that states seek to maximize their individ-ual absolute gains and are indifferent to the gains achieved by others. Cheating, the new theory suggests, is the greatest impediment to co-operation among rationally egoistic states facing mixed interests, but international institutions, the new theory also suggests, can help states overcome this barrier to joint action. Realists understand that states seek absolute gains and worry about compliance. However, realists do not believe that anarchy causes states to be rational egoists, but instead to be defensive positionalists. Realists consequently argue that states, in addition to their concerns about cheating, worry that their partners might gain more than they from their joint endeavors. Realism, then, finds that there are at least two major barriers to international cooper-ation: state concerns about cheating and state concerns about relative achievements of gains. Neoliberal institutionalism pays attention ex-clusively to the former and is unable to identify, analyze, or account for the latter.

Realism's identification of defensive state positionalism and the relative-gains problem for cooperation is based on its insight that states in anarchy must fear for their survival and their independence. According to realists, states in such circumstances worry at the ex-

28

treme that today's friend may be tomorrow's enemy in war, and thus states fear that achievements of joint gains that advantage a friend in the present might produce a more dangerous potential foe in the future. Moreover, states worry that even if they remain on good terms with their partners and indeed even if they are allies, they will inevitably find themselves in disagreements with those partners and in varying types of bargaining encounters in which relative (non-military) power may be brought to bear. For all these reasons, states must give serious attention to the gains of partners. Neoliberals fail to consider the threat of war and the threats to one's autonomy arising from international anarchy, the fundamental awareness on the part of states that relative capabilities will determine bargaining outcomes even with the best of friends, and the core desire of states to retain a margin of independence even from the closest of allies. This allows them to ignore the matter of relative gains, but, in doing so, they fail to identify a major source of state inhibitions about international cooperation. As a result, the new liberal institutionalists' optimism about international cooperation is likely to be wrong.

From a logical viewpoint, realism offers a more complete understanding than neoliberalism of the effects of anarchy on states and, by consequence, the problem of international cooperation. The chapters that follow address the empirical question of whether realism also allows us to understand the actual behavior of states regarding cooperation more fully than does neoliberalism through analysis of the Tokyo Round NTB regime and European-American cooperation and discord in the context of that regime. Before turning to the empirical test, however, it is necessary—especially in light of claims by neoliberals to have co-opted major elements of realist theory—to demonstrate that the two schools of thought differ profoundly and to show that the analysis by realism of the effects of anarchy on states allows it to provide a better understanding than neoliberalism of the problem of international cooperation.

The Newest Liberal Challenge to Realism

In contrast to earlier versions of liberal institutionalism, the newest liberalism accepts realist arguments that states are the major actors in world affairs and are unitary-rational agents. It also claims to accept realism's emphasis on anarchy to explain the preferences and actions of states. Robert Axelrod, for example, seeks to address this question:

"Under what conditions will cooperation emerge in a world of egoists without central authority?"[2] Similarly, Axelrod and Robert Keohane observe of world politics that "there is no common government to enforce rules, and by the standards of domestic society, international institutions are weak."[3] Arthur Stein also claims to begin his analysis with realism's emphasis on states and anarchy, suggesting that his theory of international regimes "is rooted in the classic characterization of international politics as relations between sovereign entities dedicated to their own self-preservation, ultimately able to depend only upon themselves, and prepared to resort to force."[4] Finally, Charles Lipson notes that he wishes to employ Axelrod's arguments in his own analysis of international cooperation because they "obviously bear on a central issue in international relations theory: the emergence and maintenance of cooperation among sovereign, self-interested states, operating without any centralized authority."[5]

Yet neoliberals argue that realists are wrong to discount the possibilities for international cooperation and the capacities of international institutions. Neoliberals claim that, contrary to realist arguments and in accordance with traditional liberal views, such institutions can help states work together in spite of their anarchical context.[6] Thus, neoliberals argue, the prospects for international cooperation are better than realism allows.[7] These points of convergence and

2. Robert Axelrod, *The Evolution of Cooperation* (New York: Basic, 1984), 3; also see 4, 6.

3. Robert Axelrod and Robert O. Keohane, "Achieving Cooperation under Anarchy: Strategies and Institutions," *World Politics* 38 (October 1985), 226.

4. See Arthur Stein, "Coordination and Collaboration: Regimes in an Anarchic World," in Stephen D. Krasner, ed., *International Regimes* (Ithaca: Cornell University Press, 1983), 116.

5. See Charles Lipson, "International Cooperation in Economic and Security Affairs," *World Politics* 37 (October 1984), 6.

6. Robert Keohane notes, "I begin with Realist insights about the role of power and the effects of hegemony," but, "my central arguments draw more on the Institutionalist tradition, arguing that cooperation can under some conditions develop on the basis of complementary interests, and that institutions, broadly defined, affect the patterns of cooperation that emerge." See Keohane, *After Hegemony: Cooperation and Discord in the World Political Economy* (Princeton: Princeton University Press, 1984), 9. Keohane also notes (26), "What distinguishes my argument from structural Realism is my emphasis on the effects of international institutions and practices on state behavior."

7. Keohane indicates in *After Hegemony* (14, 16) that he does not seek the wholesale rejection of realism, but on the issue of the prospects for cooperation, like the question of international institutions, he does seek to refute realism's conclusions while employing its assumptions. He notes (29), "starting with similar premises about motivations, I seek to show that Realism's pessimism about welfare-increasing cooperation is exaggerated," and he proposes (67) "to show, on the basis of their own assumptions, that the characteristic pessimism of Realism does not follow." Keohane also suggests (84) that rational-choice analysis "helps us criticize, in its own terms, Realism's bleak picture of

divergence among the three perspectives are summarized in Table 2.1.

Neoliberalism and International Institutions

Neoliberals begin with assertions of acceptance of several key realist arguments; however, they end with a rejection of realism and with claims of affirmation of the central tenets of the liberal institutionalist tradition. To develop this argument, neoliberals first observe that states in anarchy often face common but mixed interests and, in particular, situations that they believe can be depicted by conventional versions of the game of Prisoner's Dilemma.[8] In the game, each state prefers mutual cooperation to mutual noncooperation ($CC > DD$), but also successful cheating to mutual cooperation ($DC > CC$) and mutual defection to victimization by another's cheating ($DD > CD$); overall, then, $DC > CC > DD > CD$. In these circumstances, and in the absence of a centralized authority or some other countervailing force to bind states to their promises, each defects regardless of what it expects the other to do.

However, neoliberals stress that countervailing forces often do exist—forces that cause states to keep their promises and thus to resolve the Prisoner's Dilemma. They argue that states may pursue a strategy of tit-for-tat and cooperate on a conditional basis—that is, each adheres to its promises so long as partners do so. They also suggest that conditional cooperation is more likely to occur in Prisoner's Dilemma if the game is highly iterated, since states that interact repeatedly in either a mutually beneficial or harmful manner are likely to find that mutual cooperation is their best long-term strategy. Finally, conditional cooperation is more attractive to states if the costs of verifying one another's compliance, and of sanctioning cheaters, are low compared with the benefits of joint action. Thus conditional cooperation among states may evolve in the face of international anar-

---

the inevitability of either hegemony or conflict." Finally, he asserts (84) that rational-choice theory, "combined with sensitivity to the significance of international institutions," allows for an awareness of both the strengths and weaknesses of realism, and in so doing "we can strip away some of the aura of verisimilitude that surrounds Realism and reconsider the logical and empirical foundations of its claims to our intellectual allegiance."

8. On the importance of Prisoner's Dilemma in neoliberal theory, see Axelrod, *Evolution of Cooperation*, 7; Keohane, *After Hegemony*, 66–69; Axelrod and Keohane, "Achieving Cooperation," 231; Lipson, "International Cooperation," 2; and Stein, "Coordination and Collaboration," 120–24.

Table 2.1. Summary of major propositions in liberal institutionalism, neoliberal institutionalism, and realism

Proposition	Liberal institutionalism	Neoliberal institutionalism	Realism
States are the only major actors in world politics	No; other actors include: —specialized international agencies —supranational authorities —interest groups —transgovernmental policy networks —transnational actors	Yes (but international institutions play a major role)	Yes
States are unitary-rational actors	No; state is fragmented	Yes	Yes
Anarchy is a major shaping force for state preferences and actions	No; additional salient forces include: —technology —knowledge —welfare-orientation of domestic interests	Yes (apparently)	Yes
International institutions are an independent force facilitating cooperation	Yes	Yes	No
Theory is optimistic/pessimistic about prospects for cooperation	Optimistic	Optimistic	Pessimistic

chy and mixed interests through strategies of reciprocity, extended time horizons, and reduced verification and sanctioning costs.

Neoliberals find that one way states manage verification and sanctioning problems is to restrict the number of partners in a cooperative arrangement.[9] With a smaller number of partners, neoliberals argue, the range of behavior that must be monitored by each goes down, and this reduces verification costs. In addition, with a smaller number of partners, the collective-action costs of organizing retaliation against defectors will be lower, and as a result the implicit credibility of small-group threats to punish cheaters will be higher and more effective.

However, neoliberals place much greater emphasis on a second factor—international institutions. In particular, neoliberals argue that institutions reduce verification costs, make relationships more iterated, and facilitate punishment of cheaters. As Keohane suggests, "in general, regimes make it more sensible to cooperate by lowering the likelihood of being double-crossed."[10] Similarly, Axelrod and Keohane assert that "international regimes do not substitute for reciprocity; rather, they reinforce and institutionalize it. Regimes incorporating the norm of reciprocity delegitimize defection and thereby make it more costly."[11] In addition, finding that "coordination conventions" are often an element of conditional cooperation in Prisoner's Dilemma, Lipson suggests that "in international relations, such conventions, which are typically grounded in ongoing reciprocal exchange, range from international law to regime rules."[12] Finally, Stein argues that, just as societies "create" states to resolve problems of collective action among individuals, so too "regimes in the international arena are also created to deal with the collective suboptimality that can emerge from individual [state] behavior."[13] Hegemonic power may be necessary to establish cooperation among states, neoliberals argue, but it may endure after hegemony with the aid of institutions. As Keohane concludes, "when we think about cooperation after hegemony, we need to think about institutions."[14]

9. See Keohane, *After Hegemony*, 77; Axelrod and Keohane, "Achieving Cooperation," 234–38. For a demonstration, see Charles Lipson, "Bankers' Dilemmas: Private Cooperation in Rescheduling Sovereign Debts," *World Politics* 38 (October 1985), 200–225.

10. Keohane, *After Hegemony*, 97.

11. Axelrod and Keohane, "Achieving Cooperation," 250.

12. Lipson, "International Cooperation," 6.

13. Stein, "Coordination and Collaboration," 123.

14. Keohane, *After Hegemony*, 246.

Neoliberalism and Rational State Egoism

The new liberals claim that they can accept key realist views about states and anarchy and still substantiate classic liberal arguments about institutions and international cooperation. To do this, they make a number of important assumptions. First, they assume that states have only one goal in mixed-interest interactions: to achieve the greatest possible individual gain. For example, Axelrod suggests that the key issue in selecting a "best strategy" in Prisoner's Dilemma— offered by neoliberals as a powerful model of the problem of state cooperation in the face of anarchy and mixed interests—is to determine "what strategy will yield a player the highest possible score."[15] Similarly, Lipson observes that cheating is attractive in a single play of Prisoner's Dilemma because each player believes that defecting "can maximize his own reward," and, in turning to iterated plays, Lipson retains the assumption that players seek to maximize individual payoffs over the long run.[16] Indeed, reliance upon conventional Prisoner's Dilemma to depict international relationships and upon iteration to solve the dilemma unambiguously requires neoliberalism to adhere to an assumption of individualistic payoff maximization, for a player (state) responds to an iterated conventional Prisoner's Dilemma with conditional cooperation *solely out of a desire to maximize its individual long-term total payoffs.*

Moreover, neoliberal institutionalists assume that states define their interests in strictly individualistic terms. Keohane, for example, notes that his work is based on the assumption that states are "rational utility maximizers," and that this means that, in his view, states "display consistent tendencies to adjust to external changes in ways that are calculated *to increase the expected value of outcomes to them.*"[17] Similarly, Axelrod indicates that his objective is to show how actors "who pursue their own self-interest" may nevertheless work together.[18] He also notes that Prisoner's Dilemma helps us understand states in anarchy because it is assumed in the game that "the object is to do as well as possible, regardless of how well the other player does."[19] And, in the same vein, Lipson suggests that Prisoner's Dilemma "clearly parallels the Realist conception of sovereign states in world politics" because

15. Axelrod, *Evolution of Cooperation*, 14.
16. Lipson, "International Cooperation," 2, 5.
17. Robert O. Keohane, "The Demand for International Regimes," in Krasner, ed., *International Regimes*, 151, emphasis added.
18. Axelrod, *Evolution of Cooperation*, 6.
19. Ibid., 22.

each player in the game "is assumed to be a self-interested, self-reliant maximizer of his own utility."[20]

It is now possible to isolate the core of the neoliberal perspective. For neoliberal institutionalists, states are assumed to be fundamentally atomistic actors that are interested only in their own individual situation. This is quite evident from the commentary, cited above, by Robert Axelrod, Arthur Stein, and Charles Lipson. It is also absolutely central to the analysis of states and cooperation provided by Robert Keohane in his seminal work, *After Hegemony: Cooperation and Discord in the World Political Economy*. In it, Keohane argues that states in the anarchical context of the international political system are, as microeconomic theory assumes with respect to business firms in the context of markets, "rational egoists." Rationality, Keohane explains, means that states possess "consistent, ordered preferences, and . . . calculate costs and benefits of alternative courses of action in order to maximize their utility in view of those preferences." In turn, state egoism, he suggests, "means that their [that is, state] utility functions *are independent of one another;* they do not gain or lose utility simply because of the gains or losses of others."[21]

Overall, neoliberal theory argues that anarchy causes states to be "rational egoists" and, as such, to care only about their own situation and to be indifferent to the circumstances of others. Neoliberals believe that in any particular relationship—and especially in situations characterized by common but mixed interests—states do not care whether partners achieve or do not achieve gains from the relationship, or whether those gains are large or small, or whether such gains are greater or less than the gains they themselves achieve. So if states were to attain utility, U, in direct proportion to their receipt of an absolute payoff, V, the utility function attributed by neoliberal theory to states would be simply $U = V$. Given this assumed absolute-gains orientation of states, the major constraint on their cooperation in mixed-interest international situations is cheating. Institutions, however, can help reduce cheating and thus can help facilitate international cooperation.

Such is the neoliberal understanding of states, anarchy, and the beneficent effect of international institutions on the willingness of states to cooperate. If it were validated, neoliberal theory would lead us to conclude that realism had become bankrupt. This is because the

20. Lipson, "International Cooperation," 2.
21. Keohane, *After Hegemony*, 27, emphasis added.

main point of neoliberalism is that realist expectations about the limited effectiveness of international institutions and the fragile bases for international cooperation do not necessarily follow from realist arguments about states and anarchy. If validated, neoliberal institutionalism would have strong grounds to claim that it had displaced realist political theory as the most effective approach to the study of international politics.

THE REALIST RESPONSE TO NEOLIBERALISM

Realist theory rejects the exclusive focus of neoliberalism on cheating as the principal inhibitory effect of anarchy on the willingness of states to cooperate. It does so because, contrary to the claims of neoliberals, realists do not argue that anarchy causes states to be rational egoists but, instead, to be what I shall term "defensive positionalists."

Differences in realist and neoliberal understandings of the problem of cooperation result from a fundamental divergence in their interpretations of the basic meaning of international anarchy. Neoliberal institutionalism offers a well-established definition of international anarchy, specifying that it "refers to a lack of common government in world politics."[22] Within such a realm, according to neoliberalism, actors believe that no agency is available to "enforce rules," or to "enact and enforce rules of behavior," or to "force them to cooperate with each other."[23] In the international sphere this generates the problem of state compliance, for as Axelrod and Keohane observe, "cheating and deception are endemic" in international relations.[24] Similarly, Keohane emphasizes that "many situations—both in game theory and in world politics—are characterized by conflicts of interests as well as common interests. In such situations, actors have to worry about being deceived and double-crossed, just as the buyer of a used car has to guard against purchasing a 'lemon.'"[25] Lipson offers a similar argument, noting that whereas institutionalized mechanisms (such as governments) that guarantee the enforcement of contracts are available in civil society, "the absence of reliable guarantees is an essential feature of international relations and a major obstacle to

22. Axelrod and Keohane, "Achieving Cooperation," 226; see also Keohane, *After Hegemony*, 7; Lipson, "International Cooperation," 1–2; Axelrod, *Evolution of Cooperation*, 3–4; and Stein, "Coordination and Collaboration," 116.

23. See Axelrod and Keohane, "Achieving Cooperation," 226; Keohane, *After Hegemony*, 7; and Axelrod, *Evolution of Cooperation*, 6.

24. Axelrod and Keohane, "Achieving Cooperation," 226.

25. Keohane, *After Hegemony*, 93.

concluding treaties, contracts, and agreements." The essential problem in the international arena, according to Lipson, is that "constraints on opportunism are weak."[26]

Associated with and driven by the problem of cheating in neoliberal theory are the problems of uncertainty and transaction costs. That is, because of the uncertainty about a partner's compliance and, for the most part, because of the transaction costs of ensuring that promises are kept, cooperation may be difficult to achieve even when partners have common interests. With regard to uncertainty, for example, Keohane argues that "awareness that others have greater information than oneself, and are therefore capable of manipulating a relationship or even engaging [in] successful deception and double-cross, is a barrier to making agreements. . . . This problem of asymmetrical information only appears when dishonest behavior is possible."[27] Keohane also states that "under conditions of uncertainty and decentralization, governments will decide whom to make agreements with, and on what terms, largely on the basis of their expectations about their partners' willingness and ability to keep their commitments."[28] Similarly, Keohane views transaction costs of reaching agreement among states in the absence of international institutions as arising fundamentally from the need to ensure compliance; as a result, according to Keohane, "International regimes reduce transaction costs of legitimate bargains and increase them for illegitimate ones."[29]

From the neoliberal institutionalist viewpoint, then, anarchy means that states may wish to cooperate, but, aware that cheating is both possible and profitable, are reticent about doing so since they lack a central agency to enforce promises. Given this understanding of the meaning of anarchy for states, neoliberalism correctly identifies the problem of cheating and then proceeds to investigate how institutions can help states manage that particular problem.

Realism and Defensive State Positionalism

For realists, as for neoliberals, international anarchy means the absence of a common interstate government. Yet, according to realists, states do not believe that the lack of a common government only

---

26. See Lipson, "International Cooperation," 4. For a similar argument by Stein, see "Coordination and Collaboration," 123–24.

27. Keohane, *After Hegemony*, 93.

28. Ibid., 105. Similar statements can be found on 100, 114–15, and 126.

29. Keohane, *After Hegemony*, 90; also see 89. According to Keohane, regimes also reduce transaction costs of interstate agreements by bringing governments together efficiently: see *After Hegemony*, 90–91.

means that no agency can reliably enforce promises. Instead, realists stress, states recognize that in anarchy there is no overarching authority to prevent others from using violence, or the threat of violence, to dominate or even to destroy them. This is in fact the core insight of realism concerning international politics: as E. H. Carr observes, war "lurks in the background of international politics just as revolution lurks in the background of domestic politics"; as Raymond Aron suggests, international relations "present one original feature which distinguishes them from all other social relations: they take place within the shadow of war"; and as Kenneth Waltz argues, wars can occur in anarchy "because there is nothing to prevent them," and therefore "in international politics force serves, not only as the *ultima ratio*, but indeed as the first and constant one."[30] Realists thus argue that certain states may sometimes be driven by greed or ambition, but anarchy and the resulting danger of war and domination cause all states always to be motivated in some measure by fear and distrust.[31]

Neoliberal theory does not give evidence of an awareness of the existence or impact of these perceived dangers for states attributed to anarchy by realism. Indeed one key assumption underlying Axelrod's analysis appears positively to exclude such an awareness by states of their fundamental vulnerability in the context of international anarchy. That is, in his discussion of Prisoner's Dilemma, Axelrod posits as an initial condition the view that each player believes "there is no way to eliminate the other player or run away from the interaction. Therefore each player retains the ability to cooperate or defect on each move."[32] This initial condition means that each player by definition continues to operate as an agent in the game, and each retains a capacity for independent judgment: each player can choose on the basis of individual calculations to cooperate or to defect. Realists argue in contrast that states cannot assume that they necessarily will remain as agents in international affairs or that they will retain independence of choice; instead, realists argue, states believe that their

30. See Carr, *The Twenty Years' Crisis, 1919–1939: An Introduction to the Study of International Relations* (New York: Harper Torchbooks, 1964), 109; Aron, *Peace and War: A Theory of International Relations*, trans. Richard Howard and Annette Baker Fox (Garden City, N.Y.: Doubleday, 1973), 6; Waltz, *Man, the State, and War: A Theoretical Analysis* (New York: Columbia University Press, 1959), 232; and Waltz, *Theory of International Politics* (Reading, Mass.: Addison-Wesley, 1979), 113.

31. See Robert Gilpin, "The Richness of the Tradition of Political Realism," in Robert O. Keohane, ed., *Neorealism and Its Critics* (New York: Columbia University Press, 1986), 304–5.

32. Axelrod, *Evolution of Cooperation*, 12.

survival and independence will continue and be ensured only as a result of their continuous efforts and sustained vigilance.

By consequence, realism argues that individual well-being is not the key interest of states; instead it finds that survival and independence constitute their core interest. Aron, for example, suggests that "politics, insofar as it concerns relations among states, seems to signify—in both ideal and objective terms—simply the survival of states confronting the potential threat created by the existence of other states."[33] Similarly, Robert Gilpin observes that individuals and groups may seek truth, beauty, and justice, but he emphasizes that "all these more noble goals will be lost unless one makes provision for one's security in the power struggle among groups."[34] And, in the same vein, Waltz teaches us that "in anarchy, security is the highest end. Only if survival is assured can states safely seek such other goals as tranquility, profit, and power."[35]

Driven by an interest in survival and independence, states are acutely sensitive to any erosion of their relative capabilities. Capabilities are economic, military, and political resources whose employment permits a state to induce changes it desires in the behavior of other states or to resist what it views as undesirable changes in its own behavior sought by others. Capabilities—and especially their amount and quality compared to others—are the ultimate basis for state security and independence in the self-help context of international anarchy. As a result, realists find that the fundamental goal of states in any relationship is not to attain the highest possible individual gain or payoff; instead, it is to prevent others from achieving advances in their relative capabilities. For example, Carr suggests that "the most serious wars are fought in order to make one's own country militarily stronger or, *more often*, to prevent another from becoming militarily stronger."[36] Along the same lines, Gilpin finds that the international system "stimulates, and may compel, a state to increase its power; at the least, it necessitates that the prudent state prevent relative increases in the power of competitor states."[37] Indeed, states may even forgo increases in their absolute capabilities if doing so prevents others from

33. Aron, *Peace and War*, 7; also see 64–65.
34. Gilpin, "Political Realism," 305.
35. See Waltz, *Theory of International Politics*, 126, and see 91–92; also see Waltz, "Reflections on *Theory of International Politics*: A Response to My Critics," in Keohane, ed., *Neorealism*, 334.
36. Carr, *Twenty-Years' Crisis*, 111, emphasis added.
37. Robert Gilpin, *War and Change in World Politics* (Cambridge: Cambridge University Press, 1981), 87–88.

achieving even greater gains. This is because, as Waltz suggests, "the first concern of states is not to maximize power but to maintain their positions in the system."[38]

Wishing to remain independent agents, states always assess relationships—including cooperative arrangements based on common interests—in terms of their impact on relative capabilities. As Gilpin observes, "The essential fact of politics is that power is always relative; one state's gain in power is by necessity another's loss. Thus, even though two states may be gaining absolutely in wealth, in political terms it is the *effect of these gains on relative power positions* which is of primary importance." Gilpin argues further that "changes in the relative distribution of power are of fundamental significance politically. Though all may be gaining or declining in absolute capability, what will concern states principally are the effects of these absolute gains or losses on relative power."[39] States, then, worry about and seek to prevent increases in others' relative capabilities. States are defensive positionalists.

Realism and the Relative-Gains Problem for Cooperation

Most significant for the present discussion, defensive positionalism may act as a constraint on the willingness of states to work together even in the face of common interests. This is because states fear that partners may achieve relatively greater gains; that, as a result, the partners could surge ahead of them in relative capabilities; and, finally, that these increasingly powerful partners in the present could use their additional power to pressure them or, at the extreme, to become all the more formidable foes at some point in the future.[40]

38. Waltz, *Theory of International Politics*, 126; see also Waltz, "Response to My Critics," 334.

39. See Robert Gilpin, *U.S. Power and the Multinational Corporation: The Political Economy of Foreign Direct Investment* (New York: Basic, 1975), 34, 36, emphasis added. On the tendency of states to compare performance levels, also see Oran Young, "International Regimes: Toward a New Theory of Institutions," *World Politics* 39 (October 1986), 118. Young suggests that realists assume that states are "status maximizers" and attribute to states the tendency to compare performance levels because each seeks "to attain the highest possible rank in the hierarchy of members of the international community." I offer a different understanding of realism: while realism acknowledges that *some* states may be aggressively or offensively positional in the sense noted by Young, its fundamental insight is that *all* states are defensively positional and compare performance levels out of a fear that *others* may attain a higher ranking in the issue-area in question.

40. As Waltz suggests, "When faced with the possibility of cooperating for mutual gains, states that feel insecure must ask how the gain will be divided. They are compelled to ask not 'Will both of us gain?' but 'Who will gain more?' If an expected gain is to be divided, say, in the ratio of two to one, one state may use its disproportionate gain

Realism, by virtue of the line of analysis sketched in this chapter, would characterize a state's utility function as incorporating not one but *two* distinct terms. It would include the state's individual payoff, V, reflecting the realist view that states are motivated by absolute gains. Yet it would also include a term integrating both the state's individual payoff and the partner's payoff, W, in such a way that gaps favoring the state add to its utility whereas, more important, gaps favoring the partner detract from it. One function that depicts this realist understanding of state utility is:

$$U = V - k(W - V) \text{ where } k > 0, \tag{1}$$

with k representing the state's coefficient of sensitivity to gaps in payoffs either to its advantage or disadvantage.[41]

This realist specification of state utility can be contrasted with that inferred from neoliberal theory, namely $U = V$. In both cases the state obtains utility from the receipt of absolute payoffs. However, whereas neoliberal institutionalist theory assumes that state utility functions are independent of one another (see Keohane's statement above) and that states are indifferent to the payoffs of others, realist theory argues that state utility functions are at least partially interdependent and that one state's utility can affect another's.[42] We may also observe that this realist-specified function does not suggest that any payoff attained by a partner detracts from the state's utility. Rather, only gaps in payoffs to the advantage of a partner do so.

Gaps in gains favoring partners may reduce the utility a state enjoys from cooperation. Indeed, an amended version of the game of Prisoner's Dilemma illuminates the possibility that such a relatively disadvantaged state may conclude that it would be better off not cooperating even if joint action offered it the promise of absolute gains. To observe this, we first note that statement (1) may be reformulated as:

---

to implement a policy intended to damage or destroy the other." See Waltz, *Theory of International Politics*, 105.

41. Similar to the concept of a state "sensitivity coefficient" to gaps in jointly produced gains is the concept of a "defense coefficient" in Lewis Richardson's model of arms races. The latter serves as an index of one state's fear of another: the greater the coefficient, the stronger the state's belief that it must match increases in the other's weapons inventory with increases in its own. See Richardson, *Arms and Insecurity: A Mathematical Study of the Causes and Origins of War*, ed. Nicolas Rachevsky and Ernesto Trucco (Pittsburgh: Boxwood, 1960), 14–15.

42. Robert Jervis also argues that realist theory posits at least partially interdependent state utility functions. See Jervis, "Realism, Game Theory, and Cooperation," *World Politics* 40 (April 1988), 334–36.

$$U = (1 + k)V - kW \quad \text{where } k > 0 \tag{2}$$

Employing this general function, and substituting V and W for their corresponding labels in a 2×2 matrix, it is possible to recast the game matrix for Prisoner's Dilemma in the form depicted in Table 2.2, where R, S, T, P, and $R*$, $S*$, $T*$, and $P*$ are the classic Rapoport payoff-ranges for referent state A and for any other, B, respectively, and k and $k*$ are their respective sensitivity coefficients to gaps in gains.[43]

Moreover, the characteristic ranking of outcomes by players in Prisoner's Dilemma, using state A as an example, may be restated as:

$$[(1 + k)T - kS*] > [(1 + k)R - kR*] > [(1 + k)P - kP*] >$$
$$[(1 + k)S - kT*] \tag{3}$$

Statement (3) defines the characteristic inequality for an Amended Prisoner's Dilemma game model, incorporating and making explicit the impact of state A's defensive positionalism and its concerns about relative achievements of gains on its interdependent calculus of choice between cooperation and defection. Likewise, if the distribution of payoffs, or the value of k, or some combination of the two leads state A to conclude that no collective action problem exists because it is better

---

43. In his "games of anti-difference," Michael Taylor presents a game matrix composed of utility functions for which it is assumed that actors seek their highest possible payoffs and the smallest gap in payoffs favoring partners: see Taylor, *Anarchy and Cooperation* (London: Wiley, 1976), 73–74, and in the revised version, *The Possibility of Cooperation* (Cambridge: Cambridge University Press, 1987), 117–18. However, Taylor assumes that Prisoner's Dilemma is perfectly symmetric insofar as both players achieve the same payoff in the mutual cooperation and mutual noncooperation outcomes. On the use by Taylor of the symmetry convention in Prisoner's Dilemma, see *Possibility of Cooperation*, 113–14. He also assumes that unless actors are "sophisticated altruists" and are concerned not with others' payoffs but their *utility*, they will be concerned about gaps in payoffs but only in the two possible unilateral-defection outcomes, that is, CD* and DC*. In contrast, the present discussion suggests that relative-gains concerns will also operate on states in the CC* and DD* outcomes. Furthermore, while providing a very useful inventory of games involving inter-player sensitivities to payoffs, Taylor does not offer a theoretically grounded argument to account for the circumstances that would induce one type of sensitivity to payoffs on the part of players as opposed to another. Thus the present discussion differs from Taylor insofar as it argues that "games of anti-difference" are played by states in all four possible outcomes of Prisoner's Dilemma *because, as in the CD* and DC* outcomes, payoffs within CC* and DD* may also differ in magnitude*, and insofar as it suggests there is a particular logic, captured by realist political theory, that leads states to approach mixed-interest situations with the objective of minimizing gaps in gains in all possible outcomes produced by their interactions.

Table 2.2. An Amended Prisoner's Dilemma game

		Player B	
		$C*$	$D*$
Player A	C	$(1 + k)R - kR*, (1 + k*)R* - k*R$	$(1 + k)S - kT*, (1 + k*)T* - k*S$
	D	$(1 + k)T - kS*, (1 + k*)S* - k*T$	$(1 + k)P - kP*, (1 + k*)P* - k*P$

Assumptions
$T > R > P > S$
$R > (T + S)/2$

off in mutual noncooperation than in mutual cooperation, then the game for state A is Deadlock, in which:

$$[(1 + k)T - kS*] > [(1 + k)P - kP*] > [(1 + k)R - kR*] > [(1 + k)S - kT*] \tag{4}$$

Statement (4) defines an Amended Deadlock game. As required by the definitions of Prisoner's Dilemma and Deadlock, the essential difference between statements (3) and (4) lies in the reversal of the middle terms in the two statements of inequality.

Whether state A finds that the game is Amended Prisoner's Dilemma (3), where cooperation is difficult but possible, or Amended Deadlock (4), where cooperation is impossible, depends on state A's sensitivity to gaps in gains (k) and on the difference in R and P payoffs achieved by itself and state B. This may be clarified if Amended Prisoner's Dilemma and Amended Deadlock are reformulated as, respectively:

$$[(1 + k)T - kS*] > (R + k\Delta R) > (P + k\Delta P) > [(1 + k)S - kT*] \tag{5}$$

and

$$[(1 + k)T - kS*] > (P + k\Delta P) > (R + k\Delta R) > [(1 + k)S - kT*] \tag{6}$$

where $\Delta R = R - R*$ and $\Delta P = P - P*$, and thereby denote gaps in payoffs from mutual cooperation and mutual noncooperation.

The direct effect of defensive state positionalism and the relative-gains problem for international cooperation can now be seen by solving for k in the two terms that distinguish these inequalities. For instance, solving statement (6) for k, we observe that state A will define the situation as Amended Deadlock if:

$$k > (R - P)/(\Delta P - \Delta R) \tag{7}$$

Given a particular level of state sensitivity to gaps in gains, and its estimation of the maximum gap favoring state B that might arise from mutual noncooperation, the likelihood that statement (7) will be true for state A escalates as ΔR declines—that is, as estimated gaps in gains from mutual cooperation turn progressively against state A and in favor of state B. If ΔR declines sufficiently to validate statement (7), state A will define itself to be in Amended Deadlock and unambiguously will choose defection. Thus gaps in mutual-cooperation gains may result in the breakdown of a cooperative arrangement.

Defensive state positionalism, then, engenders a "relative-gains problem" for cooperation. That is, a state will decline to join, will leave, or will sharply limit its commitment to a cooperative arrangement if it believes that gaps in gains will substantially favor partners. It will so eschew cooperation even if participation in the arrangement was providing it, or would have provided it, with large absolute gains. Moreover, a state concerned about relative gains may decline to cooperate even if it is confident that partners will keep their commitments. Indeed, if a state believed a proposed arrangement would provide all parties absolute gains but would also generate gaps in gains favoring partners, greater certainty that partners would adhere to the terms of the arrangement would only accentuate its concerns about relative gains. For such a state, greater certainty about the faithfulness of partners might induce a lower, rather than a higher, willingness to cooperate!

I must stress that realists do not believe that states are positionalists in the sense of always trying to maximize to their own advantage differences in gains arising from cooperation. Realists do not, in other words, attribute to all states what Stein correctly calls a mercantilist definition of self-interest.[44] Instead, realists argue that most states

44. Stein acknowledges that he employs an absolute-gains assumption and that the latter "is very much a liberal, not mercantilist, view of self-interest; it suggests that actors focus on their own returns and compare different outcomes with an eye to maximizing their own gains." See Stein, "Coordination and Collaboration," 134. Stein does not explain how he can employ a "liberal" assumption of state interest and assert

concentrate on the danger that relative gains from joint action may advantage partners and may thus foster the emergence of what at best might be a potentially more domineering friend and at worst could be a potentially more powerful future adversary.[45] For realists, state positionalism is typically more defensive than offensive in nature.

In addition, realists find that defensive state positionalism and the relative-gains problem for cooperation essentially reflect the persistence of uncertainty in international relations. States are uncertain about one another's future *intentions*; thus they pay close attention to how cooperation might affect relative *capabilities* in the future.[46] This uncertainty results from the inability of states to predict or readily to control the future leadership or interests of partners. As Robert Jervis notes, "Minds can be changed, new leaders can come to power, values can shift, new opportunities and dangers can arise."[47]

It should also be emphasized that, from a realist viewpoint, the coefficient for a state's sensitivity to gaps in payoffs—k—can be expected to vary but always to be greater than zero. In general, k is likely to increase as a state transits from relationships in what Karl Deutsch terms a "pluralistic security community" to those approximating a state of war.[48] The level of k, for example, will be lower if a state's

that his theory of regimes, as cited above in footnote 4, is based on the "classic characterization" of international politics.

45. In her review of Axelrod, Joanne Gowa cites the 1979 Waltz passage employed above in footnote 40 and, following Taylor's terminology in *Anarchy and Cooperation* (73–74), suggests that a state may display "negative altruism." Furthermore, according to Gowa, a state "may seek to maximize a utility function that depends both on increases in its own payoffs *and* on increases in the difference between its payoffs and those of another state." See Gowa, "Anarchy, Egoism, and Third Images: *The Evolution of Cooperation* and International Relations," *International Organization* 40 (Winter 1986), 178. This portrays realist thinking in a manner similar to that suggested by Young and cited above in footnote 39. However, this understanding of state utility cannot be readily based on Waltz, for his core insight, and that of the realist tradition, is not that all states necessarily seek a balance of advantages in their favor (although some may do this) but rather that all fear relative gains may favor and thereby strengthen others. From a realist viewpoint, some states may be negative altruists, but *all* states will be defensive positionalists. Waltz emphasizes that he does not believe that all states necessarily seek to maximize their power; see his statement cited above in footnote 38 and see especially his "Response to My Critics," 334.

46. Waltz, for example, observes that "the impediments to collaboration may not lie in the character and the immediate intention of either party. Instead, the condition of insecurity—at the least, the uncertainty of each about the other's future intentions and actions—works against their cooperation." See *Theory of International Politics*, 105.

47. Robert Jervis, "Cooperation under the Security Dilemma," *World Politics* 30 (January 1978), 168.

48. A pluralistic security community, according to Deutsch and his associates, "is one in which there is real assurance that the members of that community will not fight each other physically, but will settle their disputes in some other way," and in which the

partner is a long-term ally rather than a longtime adversary. To the degree that there is a common enemy posing a clear and present danger, a state may actually welcome increases in an ally's capabilities.[49] However, as that common threat becomes less severe, a state's tolerance for gaps in gains favoring allies will probably decrease.[50]

A state's sensitivity coefficient to gaps in gains is also likely to be greater if a cooperative venture involves security matters rather than economic well-being. In addition, and with the exception of military allies facing an imminent common threat, the level of k for a given state is likely to increase if its relative power has been on the decline rather than on the rise. The level of k is also likely to increase if payoffs in a particular issue-area are more rather than less easily converted into capabilities within that issue-area, or if those capabilities and the influence associated with them are more rather than less readily transferred to other issue-areas.

Finally, states of differing levels of power may experience differing levels of sensitivity to gaps in gains. Very powerful states may believe that, at least in the short run, gaps in gains arising from any particular relationship will have little impact on their position of preeminence. Very weak states may believe that they cannot in any event ensure their security through their own efforts and thus can largely ignore shifts in relative capabilities arising from gaps in cooperatively generated gains. In contrast, middle-range states may be extremely sensitive to gaps in gains, for they must simultaneously fear the strong and aspire to their status *and* they must worry that they might slip down into ranks of the weak.

A state's sensitivity coefficient to gaps in gains may vary according to its partners, its own circumstances, and the type of cooperative endeavor to which it has committed itself. Yet given the uncertainties of international politics, and of the importance of relative power in interstate relations, realist theory would expect every state's level of k

---

members retain separate governments; the examples they provide are Canada-United States and Norway-Sweden. See Karl Deutsch et al., *Political Community and the North Atlantic Area* (Princeton: Princeton University Press, 1957), 5–7.

49. Jervis, for example, observes that "when a state believes that another not only is not likely to be an adversary, but has sufficient interests in common with it to be an ally, then it will actually welcome an increase in the other's power." Jervis cites the positive interdependence of utility for Britain and France during the interwar years in the face of the threat posed to both by Germany. See Jervis, "Cooperation under the Security Dilemma," 175.

50. Examples might include Soviet-American relations toward the end of World War II, Franco-American relations during the 1960s, and U.S. relations with Germany and Japan during the 1980s.

to be greater than zero in virtually all its cooperative relationships. This is likely to hold even in interactions with allies except in the face of clear, immediate threats. This, again, is because the state may believe the possibility always exists that, were friends to become relatively stronger by virtue of their enjoyment of disproportionate gains from joint action, they might use that relatively greater power to seek to restrict its independence or to force it to accept a progressively less favorable set of terms in the joint arrangement. There is even the danger, however remote, that today's ally will become tomorrow's enemy. Thus gaps in payoffs favoring partners will always detract from a state's utility to some degree.[51]

Faced with both potential problems—cheating and gaps in gains—states seek to ensure that partners comply with their promises *and* that their collaborative arrangements produce "balanced" or "equitable" achievements of gains. According to realists, states define balance and equity as a distribution of gains that roughly maintains pre-cooperation balances of capabilities. To attain this, Hans Morgenthau suggests, states offer their partners "concessions"; in exchange, they expect to receive approximately equal "compensations." As an example of this balancing tendency in joint endeavors, Morgenthau offers the case of "cooperation" among Prussia, Austria, and Russia in their partitions of Poland in 1772, 1793, and 1795. He indicates that in each case, "the three nations agreed to divide Polish territory in such a way that the distribution of power among themselves would be approximately the same after the partitions as it had been before."[52] For Morgenthau, state balancing of joint gains is a universal characteristic of the diplomacy of cooperation. He attributes this characteristic to the firmly grounded practice of states to balance power and argues that "given such a system, no nation will agree to concede political advantages to another nation without the expectation, which may or may not be well founded, of receiving *proportionate* advantages in return."[53]

To attain balanced distributions of gains, realists would expect states to include mechanisms in their cooperative arrangements that allow otherwise disadvantaged partners to enjoy preferential treat-

---

51. In contrast, Keohane asserts that relative-gains concerns may impede cooperation only in cases in which states pursue "positional goods" such as "status"; see Keohane, *After Hegemony*, 54. Similarly, Lipson expects that states will be sensitive to relative gains only in security relationships; see Lipson, "International Cooperation," 14–16.

52. Hans J. Morgenthau, *Politics among Nations: The Struggle for Power and Peace*, 5th ed. (New York: Knopf, 1973), 179.

53. Ibid., 180, emphasis added.

47

ment, or programs whereby stronger partners compensate weaker participants. Moreover, realists would predict that disputes and strains within international institutions, and indeed the outright collapse of international arrangements, may be rooted in their failure to bring about a balanced sharing among partners of the gains and costs arising from joint action. Thus, from a realist viewpoint, the politics of international cooperation and of international institutions frequently revolve around the articulation by defensively positional states of relative-gains concerns; of attempts by partners in joint arrangements to resolve such concerns; and, if these concerns are not managed or mitigated, of strains developing among the partners so severe that they hamper or cripple the arrangement.

In sum, neoliberals find that anarchy impedes cooperation through its generation of uncertainty in states about the compliance of partners. For neoliberals, the outcome a state most fears in mixed-interest situations is to be cheated. Yet successful unilateral cheating is difficult to execute, and the more probable neoliberal "worst case" is for all states to defect and to find themselves less well off than if they had all worked together. For neoliberal institutionalists, anarchy and mixed interests often cause states to suffer the opportunity costs of not achieving an outcome that is mutually more beneficial. Keohane and Axelrod argue that games like Prisoner's Dilemma, Stag Hunt, Chicken, and Deadlock illustrate how many international relationships simultaneously offer both the danger that "the myopic pursuit of self-interest can be disastrous" and the prospect that "both sides can potentially benefit from cooperation—if they can only achieve it."[54]

Realists identify additional uncertainties for states considering cooperation: which among them might achieve the greatest gains, and would imbalances in gains affect relative capabilities? In addition, even if cheating is controlled, states perceive yet another serious risk in cooperative ventures: perhaps a partner will achieve greater gains, and, thus strengthened, might seek to exert undue influence or to extract progressively more concessions or, at the extreme, it might even become a dangerous potential adversary. For neoliberal theory, then, the problem of cooperation under anarchy is that states may fail to achieve it and thus may suffer a lost opportunity. For realist theory, cooperation entails these dangers for states plus the much greater risk that cooperation might someday result in lost independence or se-

---

54. Axelrod and Keohane, "Achieving Cooperation," 231; see also Stein, "Coordination and Collaboration," 123–24.

curity. Realism and neoliberalism thus present markedly opposed views about states and their inhibitions about cooperation: these are summarized in Table 2.3.

THE ANALYTICAL SUPERIORITY OF REALISM OVER NEOLIBERALISM

Realism offers an understanding of anarchy as a force shaping the preferences of states that is analytically superior to neoliberal institutionalism. Although both approaches define international anarchy as the absence of centralized authority among states, realism identifies an absolutely necessary effect of anarchy that is ignored by neoliberalism, that is, the danger states perceive that others might seek to de-

Table 2.3. Summary of neoliberal and realist views on states and international cooperation

Basis of comparison	Neoliberal institutionalism	Political realism
Meaning of anarchy	No central agency is available to enforce promises	No central agency is available to enforce promises *or* to provide protection
State properties		
Core interest	To advance in utility defined individualistically	To enhance prospects for survival and independence
Main goal	To achieve greatest possible absolute gains	To achieve greatest gains *and* smallest gap in gains favoring partners
Basic character	Atomistic ("rational egoist")	Defensively positional
Utility function	Independent: $U = V$	Partially interdependent: $U = V - k(W - V)$
State inhibitions concerning cooperation		
Range of uncertainties associated with cooperation	Partners' compliance	Compliance *and* relative achievement of gains *and* uses to which gaps favoring partners may be employed
Range of risks associated with cooperation	To be cheated and to receive a low payoff	To be cheated *or* to experience decline in relative power if others achieve greater gains
Barriers to cooperation	State concerns about partners' compliance	State concerns about compliance *and* partners' relative gains

stroy or enslave them. As a result, when states have common interests and could all gain through collaborative action, their anarchical context causes each to fear that the other might achieve relatively greater gains. This is understood by realists and missed by neoliberals. From a logical viewpoint, then, realism has a firmer grasp than neoliberalism of the full range of implications for states of finding themselves co-situated in an anarchical context, and realism consequently provides a more complete and compelling understanding than neoliberalism of the inhibitory effects of anarchy on the willingness of states to work together.

Realism and neoliberal institutionalism, by virtue of their differing conceptualizations of anarchy and states, also present very different expectations about the conditions that must be satisfied if international cooperation is to be achieved and maintained. The next task, then, is to determine whether one or the other is more useful empirically as we analyze efforts of states to work together. The Tokyo Round NTB codes, and U.S.-EC cooperation and discord regarding them, may provide important leverage on that question. As noted in Chapter 1, the NTB codes would appear to be almost tailor-made for neoliberal theory. That makes it all the more remarkable that realism ends up providing a better understanding of the NTB code experience than does neoliberal institutionalism.

CHAPTER THREE

The Tokyo Round Regime on Non-tariff Barriers to Trade

This chapter focuses attention on the Tokyo Round regime on non-tariff barriers to trade. The first section highlights the reasons that the United States, the EC, and other GATT partners decided by the 1970s that such a regime was necessary. This is followed by a synopsis of the major elements of the six codes that emerged from the Tokyo Round of 1973–79 and that constituted the new NTB regime. The last section presents the views of outside observers and of code participants on the effectiveness achieved by the agreements after they had been in operation for several years. These views are largely confirmed by a detailed review in Chapters 4 and 5 of code activities during the 1980s.

BACKGROUND TO THE TOKYO ROUND NTB REGIME

The major trading nations had reason to believe at the outset of the 1970s that they had made good progress in constructing a more open international economy. The number of states adhering to the General Agreement on Tariffs and Trade increased from twenty-three in 1947 to seventy-seven in 1970; the value of commerce covered by GATT-sponsored negotiations increased from $10 billion in the first round in 1947 to $40 billion in the sixth (the Kennedy Round) conducted during 1964–67; and as a result of these rounds the average tariff rates of major trading countries such as the United States and the EC member-states fell below 10 percent by the late-1960s.[1] GATT-

1. See John H. Jackson, *Legal Problems of International Economic Relations: Cases,*

sponsored tariff cuts helped spur dramatic increases in world trade: the value of the latter more than doubled during 1960–70, and increased an additional 85 percent between 1970 and 1973.[2]

In spite of these favorable developments, however, by the early 1970s there was growing discontent within the community setting international trade policy, especially in the United States. American dissatisfaction with the international economic order expressed itself most dramatically on August 15, 1971, when President Richard Nixon renounced convertibility of the dollar on official accounts and imposed an emergency 10 percent surcharge on virtually all dutiable imports. The immediate cause of the U.S. actions was the acceleration in the erosion of the American balance of payments during 1970 and especially the first part of 1971.[3] However, the "Nixon shocks" of 1971 were fundamentally an effort by the United States to compel its major trading partners—Japan and the EC—to undertake negotiations aimed at the reversal of an increasingly serious deficit in U.S. payments.[4]

American officials recognized that the deterioration in the U.S. balance of payments after 1965 had largely been caused by domestically induced inflation and the resulting erosion of the international competitiveness of U.S. industry.[5] However, American officials argued that their efforts to reduce the U.S. external deficit had been hampered by an overvalued dollar (owing to the evolution of the Bretton Woods monetary system into a dollar-specie system) and by

Materials, and Text (St. Paul: West Publishing, 1977), 473. Also see Gilbert R. Winham, *International Trade and the Tokyo Round Negotiation* (Princeton: Princeton University Press, 1986), 19–20; and Commission on International Trade and Investment Policy (Williams Commission), *United States International Economic Policy in an Interdependent World* (Washington, 1971), 372.

2. See General Agreement on Tariffs and Trade, *International Trade 1973/74* (Geneva, 1974), 1.

3. The basic balance-of-payments deficit in the United States totaled $3.0 billion in 1970; this grew by $7.1 billion during the first nine months of 1971. See United States, Office of the President, *Economic Report of the President* (Washington, D.C., 1972), 142–55.

4. See Hugh Corbet, "Commercial Diplomacy in an Era of Confrontation," in Hugh Corbet and Robert Jackson, eds., *In Search of a New World Economic Order* (New York: Wiley, 1974), 18–25. Also see Andrew Shonfield, "International Economic Relations of the Western World: An Overall View," in Shonfield, ed., *Politics and Trade*, vol. 2 of *International Economic Relations of the Western World, 1959–1971*, ed. Shonfield (London: Oxford University Press for the Royal Institute of International Affairs, 1976), 72–92; Winham, *Tokyo Round*, 22–27; and Stephen D. Krasner, "The Tokyo Round: Particularistic Interests and Prospects for Stability in the Global Trading System," *International Studies Quarterly* 23 (December 1979), 493–500.

5. See Office of the President, *Economic Report*, 151.

discriminatory trade practices of a number of states, especially those of the EC.[6] The United States criticized not European economic integration itself—which the United States had supported as part of its strategy of containment of the Soviet Union—but instead selected EC activities that it believed harmed American trading interests. These included the Common Agricultural Policy (CAP) of the EC, its network of preferential trading arrangements with developing countries, and what the U.S. viewed as a widening range of EC non-tariff barriers.[7] Thus the United States linked resolution of the 1971 crisis to the EC's acceptance of a new GATT round to address these issues.[8]

The United States was not alone in its desire to take action against non-tariff barriers. For example, during the 1960s, member-states of the European Free Trade Association (EFTA) sought to establish rules to mitigate trade-distorting effects of national policies concerning subsidies, government procurement, and technical standards.[9] In addition, the member-states of the EC agreed to its directives in 1971 to liberalize government contracts for public works and accepted directives in 1969 and 1976 to liberalize other public-supply contracts.[10] Third, under the auspices of the Organization for Economic Cooperation and Development (OECD), governments of advanced countries pooled information in the mid-1960s on their public-purchasing practices, and the OECD member-states formulated a draft agreement by

6. Ibid., 144.

7. See Williams Commission, *U.S. International Economic Policy*, 12–13, 199–200; Commission of the European Communities, *The European Community's External Trade, 1958–1974* (Brussels, 1975), 4; Gerald Curzon, "Crisis in the International Trading System," in Corbet and Jackson, eds., *New World Economic Order*, 38–39; Hugh Corbet, "Industrial Tariffs and Economic Spheres of Influence," in Corbet and Jackson, eds., *New World Economic Order*, 178–82; and Gerald Curzon and Victoria Curzon, "The Management of Trade Relations in the GATT," in Shonfield, ed., *Politics and Trade*, 230–32.

8. In January 1971 the EC Commissioner for External Relations, Ralf Dahrendorf, indicated that "a fresh comprehensive 'round' would probably not accomplish much at the moment"; see "Community, United States, Japan: Trade Policy—Problems and Outlook," *Bulletin of the European Communities* 4, no. 2 (1971), 29. However, in January 1972 the EC reported that the U.S. actions in August had created "new facts, the most important of which were the fixing of new exchange rates . . . and the preparation of discussions on trade problems between the Community and the United States." See "International Monetary and Commercial Events (IV) and the Organization of Monetary and Financial Relations within the Community," *Bulletin of the European Communities* 5, no. 1 (1972), 15. Also see Winham, *Tokyo Round*, 77–78. On the importance attached by the United States to NTBs in the proposed round, see Williams Commission, *U.S. International Economic Policy*, 12–14, 85–102.

9. See Victoria Curzon, *The Essentials of Economic Integration: Lessons of EFTA Experience* (London: Macmillan for the Trade Policy Research Center, 1974), 90–146.

10. Commission of the European Communities, *Public Supply Contracts: Conclusions and Perspectives* Com (84), 14 (Brussels, 1984), 6.

the early 1970s for a code of conduct in the field of government procurement.[11] Finally, the OECD served during the 1960s and 1970s as the venue for the negotiation of a series of international arrangements to begin to regulate the terms of member-states' various programs for subsidized export-credits.[12]

In addition to these efforts, the General Agreement itself articulated a number of rules relating to non-tariff barriers.[13] Article VI established rules for signatories regarding anti-dumping and countervailing duties. Article VII specified that customs-valuation systems should not be based "on arbitrary or fictitious values" assigned to imports.[14] Article VIII sought to limit administrative fees assigned to imports and tried to specify the types of documentation required of importers by customs officials.[15] Further, Article IX sought to prevent discriminatory restraints on imports through the use of marks of origin, and Article XX exempted from GATT jurisdiction most national measures concerning health and safety standards *except* if they "constitute a means of arbitrary or unjustifiable discrimination . . . or a disguised restriction on international trade."[16] Article XI called for the abolition of existing quantitative restrictions (QRs) and prohibited the imposition of most new QRs unless the GATT member was experiencing difficulties with its balance of payments.[17] Finally, Article XVI required states to notify their trade-impacting subsidies to the

11. See Organization for Economic Cooperation and Development, *Government Procurement in Europe, North America, and Japan* (Paris, 1966); also see Robert E. Baldwin, *Nontariff Distortions of International Trade* (Washington, D.C.: Brookings Institution, 1970), 58–83.

12. On the OECD credit arrangements, see John M. Duff, Jr., "The Outlook for Official Export Credits," *Law and Policy in International Business* 13, no. 4 (1981), 891–959; Steven P. Buffone, "Subsidized Export Credits and the 1983 Amendments to the Export-Import Bank Act," *Cornell Journal of International Law* 17 (Summer 1984), 303–8; and Andrew M. Moravcsik, "Disciplining Trade Finance: The OECD Export Credit Arrangement," *International Organization* 43 (Winter 1989), 173–205.

13. Fourteen articles of the General Agreement prohibit or regulate NTBs: see John W. Evans, *The Kennedy Round in American Trade Policy: Twilight of the GATT?* (Cambridge: Harvard University Press, 1971), 88.

14. See "General Agreement on Tariffs and Trade," reprinted in United States, Senate, Committee on Finance, *Executive Branch GATT Studies* (Washington, D.C., March 1974), hereafter cited as General Agreement, 234–35. Also see John H. Jackson, *World Trade and the Law of the GATT* (Indianapolis: Bobbs-Merrill, 1969), 446–54.

15. See General Agreement, 236; also see Jackson, *World Trade,* 454–59; Evans, *Kennedy Round,* 92; and Kenneth W. Dam, *The GATT: Law and International Economic Organization* (Chicago: University of Chicago Press, 1970), 181–86. Article VIII was supplemented with the 1952 GATT-sponsored Code of Standards for Documentary Requirements.

16. See General Agreement, 237, 259–60; also see Jackson, *World Trade,* 459–61, 742–45; Dam, *GATT,* 186–87, 192–95; also see Evans, *Kennedy Round,* 92–93.

17. See General Agreement, 238–48; Jackson, *World Trade,* 305–27; and Dam, *GATT,* 19–20, 148–57.

GATT, prohibited export subsidies resulting in lower prices for exported as opposed to domestically consumed nonprimary products, and sought to restrict export subsidies for primary products to such a level that recipients would not attain "more than an equitable share" of world trade.[18]

The above provisions were supplemented by two accords negotiated during the Kennedy Round. The first was the Anti-Dumping Agreement of 1967, which called for speedier, more transparent national anti-dumping procedures. The second was the American Selling Price (ASP) agreement, according to which the United States would have ended its use of a valuation system for benzenoid chemicals incompatible with the GATT and the EC would have provided additional tariff reductions on chemicals and other trade concessions.[19]

Thus, prior to the Tokyo Round, the GATT had articulated obligations for member-states concerning subsidies, countervailing duties, dumping, anti-dumping duties, customs valuation, customs procedures, and, at least indirectly, national health and sanitary standards. In addition, GATT-sponsored negotiations had sought to address non-tariff distortions involving anti-dumping rules and customs-valuation practices in the chemicals sector. Finally, efforts to regulate or reduce non-tariff barriers had been undertaken in such international forums as EFTA, the EC, and the OECD.

Yet these efforts had been largely ineffective. One problem was that many states were pursuing trade policies in 1947 at great variance with the obligations contained in Part II of the GATT, which includes all the provisions concerning NTBs. To address this problem, a "Protocol of Provisional Application" was formulated that committed the contracting parties fully to Part I (on the most-favored-nation principle and tariff bindings) and to Part III (on procedures and regional trade arrangements), but to Part II only "to the fullest extent not inconsistent with existing legislation."[20] As a result, non-tariff barriers that could be related to national legislation in existence prior to accep-

18. See Jackson, *World Trade*, 365–99; Dam, *GATT*, 142; and Gary Clyde Hufbauer and Joanna Shelton Erb, *Subsidies in International Trade* (Washington, D.C.: Institute for International Economics, 1984), 45–47, 192–94.

19. On the negotiation of the two accords, see Jackson, *World Trade*, 401–38; Dam, *GATT*, 186–95; Evans, *Kennedy Round*, 89–93, 106–10, 227–29, 272–73, 285–86, and 301–5; and Ernest H. Preeg, *Traders and Diplomats: An Analysis of the Kennedy Round of Negotiations under the General Agreement on Tariffs and Trade* (Washington, D.C.: Brookings Institution, 1970), 127–28, 134–35, 166–76, 179–91. On the operation of the anti-dumping agreement, see Curzon and Curzon, "Management of Trade Relations," 246–52.

20. See United States, *Executive Branch GATT Studies*, 299–300; also see Jackson, *World Trade*, 60–63, 74–75; Jackson, *International Economic Relations*, 401–4; and Dam, *GATT*, 341–44.

tance of the GATT were protected by the Protocol and effectively escaped GATT jurisdiction. In addition, the GATT often failed to give sufficiently precise guidance for the international regulation of NTBs.[21] A third problem was that the GATT explicitly allowed for the use of one major non-tariff barrier, namely discriminatory government procurement.[22]

Finally, many pre-Tokyo Round efforts regarding NTBs failed to attain international acceptance, or, when they did so, they generated new difficulties related to trade policy. The Kennedy Round's anti-dumping and ASP agreements both constituted important potential progress in the field of NTBs; however, the U.S. Congress declined to accept either of them.[23] EC and EFTA efforts to remove their respective intraregional NTBs constituted progress for trading interests within the regions. However, enhanced intra-European discipline over NTBs, when combined with retention of these barriers with respect to nonregional partners, only exacerbated the concern of the United States that Europe was becoming an inward-looking trade bloc.[24] Lastly, efforts were made during the Kennedy Round to construct new rules not just in the areas of customs valuation and anti-dumping, but also in government procurement, administrative and technical regulations (i.e., standards), internal taxes, and quantitative restrictions. However, as one observer reported, except for the anti-dumping and ASP agreements, "the negotiations for the most part did not progress beyond the agreement to establish negotiating groups."[25]

By the early 1970s the international trading community had

21. This was especially true in regard to Article XVI's standard of a "more than an equitable share." See Dam, *GATT*, 142–44, and Hufbauer and Erb, *Subsidies in International Trade*, 47–48. For an analysis of three GATT panel reports that have tried to deal with this problem, see Colin Phegan, "GATT Article XVI.3: Export Subsidies and 'Equitable Shares,'" *Journal of World Trade Law* 16 (May--June 1982), 255–61, and Balayneh Seyoum, "Export Subsidies under the MTN: An Analysis with Particular Emphasis on Developing Countries," *Journal of World Trade Law* 18 (November–December 1984), 513–15.

22. See General Agreement, 229, 249–50; Jackson, *World Trade*, 290–93, 359–61; also see Dam, *GATT*, 199–209.

23. On the failure of the U.S. Congress to accept the ASP accord, see Winham, *Tokyo Round*, 67–68, 70–71, 107; and on its rejection of the anti-dumping agreement, see Winham, ibid., 69, and Shelly A. Lorenzen, "Technical Analysis of the Antidumping Agreement and the Trade Agreements Act," *Law and Policy in International Business* 12 (1979), 1414–15.

24. See Williams Commission, *U.S. International Economic Policy*, 12–13, 101–2, 199–214.

25. Evans, *Kennedy Round*, 260. Also see Preeg, *Traders and Diplomats*, 135; and Robert E. Baldwin, *Nontariff Distortions of International Trade* (Washington, D.C.: Brookings Institution, 1970), 2.

achieved only limited success in regulating or reducing non-tariff barriers. At the same time, the relative significance of NTBs as impediments to trade and as a possible source of disputes over trade policy became more evident to the trade community as tariff rates were progressively reduced as a result of successful GATT-sponsored trade negotiations.[26] The two political giants of the GATT during the early 1970s—namely the United States and the EC—agreed that the time had come to deal with non-tariff barriers. For example, having accepted the American proposal in December 1971 for a new multilateral trade round, the EC indicated in a preparatory statement in 1972 that "the growing importance of non-tariff barriers throws particular light on the advisability of new international measures in this field."[27] Similarly, in requesting congressional authority in 1973 to undertake negotiations in the new round, the U.S. Special Trade Representative, William Eberle, reported that "the forthcoming trade negotiations must differ substantially from those in the past. . . . The negotiations must cover all barriers which distort trade and as they pertain to both agriculture and industry."[28] This interest in constructing new rules on NTBs extended to the September 1973 Ministerial Declaration formally initiating the Tokyo Round. It asserted that, in addition to achieving further reductions of tariffs, the new trade round should aim to "reduce or eliminate non-tariff measures or, where this is not appropriate, to reduce or eliminate their trade restricting or distorting effects, and to bring such measures under more effective international discipline."[29] With the Tokyo Round, then, non-tariff barriers had moved to the center of international commercial diplomacy.

SYNOPSIS OF THE TOKYO ROUND NTB CODES

The Tokyo Round, completed in April 1979, produced several types of trade agreements. The 1979 Protocol to the General Agree-

26. On the linkage between success in tariff negotiations and heightened awareness of the importance of non-tariff barriers, see Baldwin, *Nontariff Distortions*, 1–2; Preeg, *Traders and Diplomats*, 267; Evans, *Kennedy Round*, 309; and GATT, *GATT Activities 1967/68* (Geneva, March 1969), 10.

27. See Commission of the European Communities, "Preparation of Trade Negotiations between the Community and the United States," *Bulletin of the European Communities* 5, no. 1 (1972), 16.

28. See United States, House, Committee on Ways and Means, "Prepared Testimony by Ambassador William Eberle, United States Special Representative for Trade Negotiations," *Prepared Statements of Administration Witnesses*, (Washington, D.C., 1973), 134.

29. See "Ministerial Meeting Tokyo, 12–14 September 1973: Declaration," in Gener-

ment reduced tariffs on industrial goods by an average of 33 percent on an import-weighted basis.[30] In one industrial sector—civil aircraft—an accord was reached to eliminate tariffs and to reduce non-tariff barriers.[31] Two other agreements established consultative bodies concerning trade in bovine meat and in dairy products, and additional protocols to the dairy accord established minimum prices for milk powder, butter, and selected cheese products.[32] Moreover, a set of "Framework" agreements codified preferences and rules within the GATT for developing countries, articulated an agreed interpretation of the dispute-settlement provisions of the GATT (Articles XXII and XXIII), and reemphasized GATT rules on export restrictions.[33]

Although these agreements were significant, the key accomplishment of the Tokyo Round was its development of a comprehensive regime for non-tariff barriers to trade.[34] The bargaining agenda in this area had been determined in large measure well before the Tokyo Declaration of 1973. In November 1967 (i.e., within six months of the close of the Kennedy Round), the CONTRACTING PARTIES authorized the GATT secretariat to develop an inventory of non-tariff measures for a newly formed Committee on Trade in Industrial Products based on notifications of such measures that member-states believed to be in use by their GATT trading partners. The GATT secretariat presented the resulting eight hundred notifications in terms of five categories of NTBs: "government participation in trade," such as subsidies and government procurement practices; "customs and administrative entry procedures," such as valuation and anti-dumping procedures and documentation requirements; "standards" involving health and safety requirements and packaging rules; "specific limita-

---

al Agreement on Tariffs and Trade, *The Tokyo Round of Multilateral Trade Negotiations: Report by the Director General of GATT* (Geneva, 1979), 186.

30. See GATT, *Tokyo Round*, 119–20.

31. See GATT, *Tokyo Round*, 180; the text of the Civil Aircraft Arrangement can be found in GATT, *Basic Instruments and Selected Documents*, Twenty-Sixth Supplement (Geneva, 1980), 162–70. Hereafter, the latter series of documents will be cited as *BISD* and supplement number.

32. For the texts, see GATT, *BISD* 26, 84–115. For an analysis of these agreements, see GATT, *Tokyo Round*, 143–47.

33. For the texts, see United States, House and Senate, Committee on Ways and Means and Committee on Finance, *Multilateral Trade Negotiations: International Codes Agreed to in Geneva, Switzerland, April 12, 1979* (Washington, 1979), 361–401. An analysis is provided in Bela Balassa, "The Tokyo Round and the Developing Countries," *Journal of World Trade Law* 14 (March–April 1980), 112–15.

34. The most complete history of the negotiations is provided by Winham, *Tokyo Round*. For general overviews of the major elements of the NTB codes, also see Krasner, "Tokyo Round," 511–18; and Balassa, "The Tokyo Round and the Developing Countries," 102–12.

tions" and notably quantitative requirements; and, finally, "restraints on imports through the price mechanism," such as prior deposits and variable levies.[35] By 1971 the Committee on Trade had established three working groups to construct codes relating to customs valuation, standards, and import licensing.[36] By the end of 1972 tentative accords had been drafted in the areas of customs valuation and import licensing, and a code on technical standards was nearing completion.[37] In addition, groups were formed in 1972 in the areas of import documentation requirements, packaging and labeling requirements, export subsidies, countervailing duties, quantitative restrictions, and export restraints.[38] Finally, in early 1977 the OECD provided the GATT those elements of a draft code on government procurement that the OECD members had formulated up to that time.[39]

Working with these materials, the Tokyo Round negotiators produced six codes on non-tariff barriers. Each specified rules, rights, and obligations for signatories. In addition, each required code participants to establish a Committee of Signatories. These were to serve as the principal ongoing institutional mechanism by which signatories could work together to oversee and verify one another's implementation of code obligations, to facilitate the resolution of disputes among them, and to authorize retaliation against a signatory if they found it to be in noncompliance with its code obligations.[40]

The first of the Tokyo Round NTB arrangements concerned customs valuation. The Agreement on Implementation of Article VII, or the Customs Valuation Code (CV code), sought to expand on the GATT's general injunction that values assigned to imported goods for customs purposes should be the "actual value" of the goods, and not artificially inflated so as to increase customs duties and restrict trade. According to the CV code, "actual value" should normally be the "transaction value" of the goods, with transaction value defined as "the price actually paid or payable for the goods."[41] The CV code signatories recognized that the transaction value—the price listed in

35. See *GATT Activities, 1969/70*, 13–15.
36. *GATT Activities, 1970/71*, 14–16.
37. *GATT Activities, 1972*, 13–14.
38. Ibid., 14.
39. On the transfer of the OECD draft agreement to the GATT in January 1977, see GATT, *Tokyo Round*, 76–78, and Winham, *Tokyo Round*, 138–41.
40. For a discussion of the Tokyo Round code committees, see John H. Jackson, "GATT Machinery and the Tokyo Round Agreements," in William R. Cline, ed., *Trade Policy in the 1980s* (Washington, D.C.: Institute for International Economics, 1983), 176–80.
41. See "Agreement on Implementation of Article VII of the General Agreement on Tariffs and Trade," cited hereafter as CV code, in *BISD* 26, 117.

the sales invoice—might sometimes need to be adjusted for the purposes of customs assessment. They agreed, however, that when they do not accept the transaction value as the basis for customs valuation, they must employ, in a fixed order specified by the code, a hierarchy of five methods by which they may make such valuation adjustments.[42]

Another of the Tokyo Round NTB codes was the Agreement on Import Licensing Procedures (LIC code). Signatories to this code committed themselves to ensure that their import-licensing systems would not create distortions to trade that would be in addition to or that would compound those resulting from the original imposition of an import quota. For example, they agreed that import applications should not be refused as a result of minor documentation errors.[43] Insofar as signatories operated automatic import-licensing systems— i.e., licensing procedures for imports for which approval is "freely granted"—they promised they would avoid administering them in ways that cause undue delays, expense, or inconvenience for importers.[44] Of greater importance were the commitments by signatories on nonautomatic licensing systems. These are created to administer quotas resulting from the imposition of quantitative restrictions by an importing country, and the LIC signatories committed themselves to administer them in such a way that they "shall not have trade restrictive effects on imports additional to those caused by the imposition of the restriction."[45]

Another NTB code that emerged from the Tokyo Round was the Agreement on the Implementation of Article VI of the GATT, or the Code on Anti-Dumping Practices (ADP code).[46] This code is essentially the Anti-Dumping Agreement of 1967 modified to conform with the new Code on Subsidies and Countervailing Measures. For example, the negotiators of the revised ADP code retained the material-injury test for applying anti-dumping duties that appeared in the 1967 Agreement but dropped the requirement of the latter that dumping had to be the "principal cause" of such injury in order to justify anti-dumping charges.[47] In addition, the code negotiators

42. See CV code, Articles 2–5, in *BISD* 26, 72–80.
43. See "Agreement on Import Licensing Procedures," hereafter cited as LIC code, Article 1:7, in *BISD* 26, 155. For an overview of the LIC code, see Balassa, "The Tokyo Round and the Developing Countries," 107–8.
44. LIC code, Article 2, *BISD* 26, 156–57.
45. LIC code, Article 3, *BISD* 26, 157–58.
46. For a review of the major provisions of the ADP code, and its incorporation into American law, see Lorenzen, "Antidumping Agreement," 1416–36.
47. See "Agreement on Implementation of Article VI," in *BISD* 26, Article 3, fn. 21,

specified that a wide range of indicators can be examined in national assessments of whether material injury has occurred and thus may warrant anti-dumping duties.[48]

The fourth NTB code produced by the Tokyo Round—the Code on Technical Barriers to Trade (TBT code)—was directed toward ameliorating trade distortions arising from national health, safety, and other technical standards and regulations whose satisfaction is required by governments as a condition of sale.[49] Its principal obligation for signatories is to ensure that their national technical standards or regulations "are not prepared, adopted, or applied with a view to creating obstacles to trade." The signatories further agreed that imported products would receive nondiscriminatory treatment as regards standards and regulations, and that neither their content nor their application would create "unnecessary obstacles to trade."[50] Signatories also committed themselves to adhere to international technical standards whenever possible and to participate in international standards-setting bodies.[51] Signatories further promised to publicize their intent to introduce technical regulations, to notify them to the GATT secretariat, to share information on them with other signatories in order to allow the latter the opportunity to offer comments, and to establish a national "enquiry point" that would share information regarding their standards, testing, and certification systems with fellow signatories.[52] Another obligation undertaken by signatories was that their testing and certification systems would be operated on a nondiscriminatory basis.[53] Finally, the signatories undertook to take "such reasonable measures as may be available to them" to bring local governments and nongovernmental standards bodies, as well as regional intergovernmental bodies of which they are members, into compliance with the TBT code.[54]

173, for the material-injury standard, and Article 3:4, 174, for the language that no longer requires dumping to be the "principal cause" of injury.

48. See Article 3:3, in ADP code, *BISD* 26, 174.

49. For an overview of the TBT code, see R. W. Middleton, "The GATT Standards Code," *Journal of World Trade Law* 14 (May–June 1980), 201–19, and, from the viewpoint of a GATT official, see Jacques Nusbaumer, "The GATT Standards Code in Operation," *Journal of World Trade Law* 18 (November–December 1984), 542–52. For an EC analysis of the TBT and GPR codes, see J. H. J. Bourgeois, "The Tokyo Round Agreements on Technical Barriers and on Government Procurement in International and EEC Perspective," *Common Market Law Review* 19 (1982), 5–33.

50. See Article 2.1, TBT code, in *BISD* 26, 9–10.

51. TBT code, Articles 2.3, *BISD* 26, 10.

52. TBT code, Articles 2.5, 10, *BISD* 26, 10–11, 17–18.

53. TBT code, Articles 5, 7, *BISD* 26, 13–15.

54. TBT code, Articles 3, 4, 6, 8, and 9, in *BISD* 26, 12, 14, 16–17.

Prior to the Tokyo Round, it was noted above, government purchases had been largely exempt from the GATT. With the fifth NTB agreement—the Government Procurement Code (GPR code)—signatories reversed this position and committed themselves to apply the GATT's national treatment and most-favored-nation obligations to purchases made by designated central-government entities above a certain monetary value (the national equivalent of SDR 150,000).[55] To ensure compliance and to liberalize government contracts, the GPR code obligates signatories to publicize and to provide specific information on code-covered contracts in a predesignated official journal or digest, and to employ tendering procedures that do not discriminate against foreign suppliers.[56] Signatories also promised to provide information on winners of competitions for contracts, and to report statistics annually to the GPR committee of signatories on recipients of national and foreign contracts.[57]

The sixth Tokyo Round NTB agreement—and the accord that was most difficult to negotiate between the United States and the EC—was the Code on Subsidies and Countervailing Measures (SCM code).[58] In the negotiations, the EC achieved its principal objective of attaining U.S. acceptance of a material-injury test when applying countervailing duties as specified in Article VI of the GATT. The United States, under the protection of the Protocol of Provisional Application, had been operating on the basis of pre-GATT legislation not requiring a demonstration of material injury, but would do so in adhering to the SCM code. In turn, the United States attained EC

55. See "Agreement on Government Procurement," hereafter cited as GPR code, Articles I and II, in *BISD* 26, 35. For analyses of the code, see Morton Pomeranz, "Toward a New International Order in Government," *Law and Policy in International Business* 12, no. 4 (1979), 1263–1300; David V. Anthony and Carol K. Hagerty, "Cautious Optimism as a Guide to Foreign Government Procurement," *Law and Policy in International Business* 12, no. 4 (1979), 1301–43; Richard A. Horsch, "Eliminating Non-tariff Barriers to International Trade: The MTN Agreement on Government Procurement," *New York University Journal of International Law and Politics* 12 (Fall 1980), 31–42; and M. L. Jones, "The GATT-MTN System and the European Community as International Frameworks for the Regulation of Economic Activity: The Removal of Barriers to Trade in Government Procurement," *Maryland Journal of International Law and Trade* 8 (Spring–Summer 1984), 52–121.

56. GPR code, Articles V, *BISD* 26, 39–46.

57. GPR code, Article VI, *BISD* 26, 46–48.

58. See Krasner, "Tokyo Round," 515. For a detailed review by Americans involved in the negotiations, see Richard R. Rivers and John D. Greenwald, "The Negotiation of a Code on Subsidies and Countervailing Measures: Bridging Fundamental Policy Differences," *Law and Policy in International Business* 11 (1979), 1447–95. For a review of the major elements of the code, see, in addition to Rivers and Greenwald, Phegan, "GATT Article XVI:3," 261–64; and Seyoum, "Export Subsidies," 515–28.

agreement that the SCM code would not require signatories to find that subsidies were the "principal cause" of material injury to a home industry in order to impose countervailing duties.[59] The U.S. also obtained EC acceptance of a wide range of indicators of material injury, thus reducing the difficulty of proving such an injury.[60]

The SCM agreement also articulated—at U.S. insistence—what appeared to be substantially stricter rules on the use by signatories of subsidies. In particular, Article 9 of the SCM code appeared to strengthen the ban in Article XVI:4 of the GATT on export subsidies on nonprimary products. For example, Article 9, in contrast to Article XVI:4, includes in its ban on export subsidies those bounties that do not result in lower export than domestic prices for the subsidizing country. Second, Article 9 includes an illustrative list of twelve types of export subsidies coming under its ban, an increase by four over the list developed by the GATT Working Group in 1960.[61] In addition, in seeking to clarify the standard in Article XVI:3 of the GATT that export subsidies for a primary product should not result in the subsidizing country achieving "more than an equitable share" of the market for that product, Articles 10:2(a) and 10:3 of the SCM code specify that important indicators of such a "more than an equitable share" will be displacement of nonsubsidized exports by subsidized exports or price undercutting by the latter.[62] Moreover, the SCM signatories acknowledged for the first time that the domestic subsidy programs in one state can harm industries in other signatory states or "nullify or impair" benefits that, in the absence of the subsidies, they would have enjoyed by virtue of their adherence to the GATT.[63]

Overall, the six NTB codes constructed during the 1970s offered the promise that the 1980s would be characterized by a new regime regulating several important classes of non-tariff barriers to trade.[64]

59. The material-injury standard is specified in the code in Part I, Article 2, footnote 4: see "Agreement on Implementation of Application of Articles VI, XVI, and XXIII of the General Agreement on Tariffs and Trade," hereafter cited as SCM code, in GATT, *BISD* 26, 57; the language on causality and material injury is found in Article 6:4, 65. For an analysis of the negotiation of this language, see Rivers and Greenwald, "Code on Subsidies," 1483–84.

60. The price-undercutting and market-loss criteria are specified in Article 6:1 and 6:2; the additional criteria are listed in Article 6:3, in SCM code, *BISD* 26, 64–65.

61. See SCM code, *BISD* 26, 68–69, 80–82; the list developed by the Working Group in 1960 may be found in Hufbauer and Erb, *Subsidies in International Trade*, 192–93.

62. SCM code, *BISD* 26, 69.

63. See Articles 8:3, 12:3, 13:2, 13:4, and especially 11:2, in SCM code, *BISD* 26, 67–72; also see Rivers and Greenwald, "Code on Subsidies," 1473–74.

64. However, efforts failed during the Tokyo Round to negotiate codes for two major classes of state practices that could constitute non-tariff barriers—quantitative

Expectations were very high that the NTB codes would give new significance to the GATT. However, by the mid-1980s, the next section suggests, it became clear that the codes had not met these expectations in equal measure.

PERFORMANCE OF THE TOKYO ROUND NTB CODES

As noted in Chapter 1, the community involved with international trade policy was generally unenthusiastic by the mid-1980s in its assessment of the Tokyo Round NTB regime. Yet that community recognized there was significant variation in the effectiveness achieved by the different codes constituting the new regime. For example, Gilbert Winham observed in 1986 that "the codes that were technical in nature, namely customs valuation, standards, and import licensing, have all been brought into force with a minimum of difficulty and appear to be operating effectively," that "worthwhile progress has been made on the government-procurement code," but that "the subsidy/countervail code has the reputation of being the least effective of the Tokyo Round codes."[65]

This assessment was shared by the GATT Wisemen in their 1985 review of the international trading system. They noted in their report that, in spite of their deficiencies, "most of the codes . . . have clearly established their value, clarifying the international trade rules, opening up new opportunities, and making trade fairer." They also specified that "examples are the codes on customs valuation, import licensing and technical standards."[66] In contrast, the Wisemen said that many elements of the codes were inadequate and stressed that they had in mind "notably those [provisions] of the subsidy code."[67] Similarly, Michael Aho and Jonathan Aronson observed in 1985 that "the subsidies, government procurement, and standards codes negotiated during the Tokyo Round need to be fully implemented, enforced and

restrictions and safeguard actions. See Winham, *Tokyo Round,* 110–25, 197–200, and 240–47. Also on the safeguard negotiations, see Victoria Curzon Price, *Industrial Policies in the European Communities* (New York: St. Martins, 1981), 1–16; and Leslie Alan Glick, *Multilateral Trade Negotiations: World Trade after the Tokyo Round* (Totowa: Rowman & Allanheld, 1984), 113–20.

65. For these comments, see Winham, *Tokyo Round,* 357, 358, 359, respectively; also see 362.

66. See GATT, *Trade Policies for a Better Future: Proposals for Action* (Geneva, 1985), 41.

67. Ibid.

extended. To some degree, these codes were oversold to the legislatures and parliaments which ratified the agreements."[68]

This understanding of the relative effectiveness of the codes was shared during the 1980s by the committees responsible for administering the accords. They were instructed by the CONTRACTING PARTIES on two occasions—in the final communiqué of the special GATT Ministerial Meeting in November 1982, and the joint statement produced by the regular GATT annual session in 1984—to report on the overall effectiveness of their respective codes.[69] In response to these two requests, the Committee on Customs Valuation offered the most positive self-assessment. Its response in 1983, for example, was that "the experience of the Parties applying the Agreement with its implementation has been very positive. All Parties recognize that the new valuation system has resulted in a uniform, fair, and greatly simplified system for the valuation of imported products." The CV committee went on to note that "a significant benefit of the new valuation system, to both customs authorities and to traders, has been greater certainty in determining the customs value of imported products and thus of duties payable," and observed that "experience indicates that the new valuation system has saved time and money, and improved the efficiency of the preparation and processing of customs entries."[70] In its second assessment, conducted in May 1985, the CV committee simply stated that the signatories had "agreed that these assessments of the adequacy and effectiveness of the Agreement were still valid."[71]

The Committee on Import Licensing offered reviews of its work almost as positive as those submitted by the CV committee. The LIC committee's response in 1983 to the Ministerial Declaration was that "the work carried out so far under the Agreement has permitted a marked improvement in transparency with regard to import licensing procedures and their operation." In addition, the committee con-

68. See C. Michael Aho and Jonathan David Aronson, *Trade Talks: America Better Listen!* (New York: Council on Foreign Relations, 1985), 29, 50.

69. See GATT, "Ministerial Declaration," Thirty-Eighth Session at Ministerial Level, Adopted November 29, 1982, reprinted in *BISD* 30, 18, and GATT, Working Group on MTN Agreements, "Adequacy and Effectiveness of the MTN Agreements and Arrangements and Obstacles to Their Acceptance: Consolidation of the Observations Made and Conclusions Reached in the Committees and Councils: Note by the Secretariat," GATT Doc. MDF/12, June 11, 1985, 2.

70. See Committee on Customs Valuation, "Report (1983) Presented to the CONTRACTING PARTIES at Their Thirty-Ninth Session," in *BISD* 30, 58.

71. MDF/12, 8.

cluded in 1983, "In the light of the experience to date, the Parties consider that the Agreement is adequate to ensure the discipline necessary to prevent trade distortions arising from the operation of licensing procedures."[72] In April 1985 the LIC committee met in response to the request of the 1984 annual session for code assessments. It recalled its 1983 findings and stated that they "remained basically valid."[73]

A positive self-assessment—although not as enthusiastic as that produced by the LIC and CV committees—was also offered by the Committee on Technical Barriers to Trade. It reported in 1983 that "the work carried out so far under the Agreement has permitted a marked improvement in transparency with regard to technical regulations, standards, and certification systems adopted at [the] national level." The committee also "noted with satisfaction that the Agreement had been accepted by a large and growing number of contracting parties."[74] Then, in response to the 1984 GATT request for a code review, the TBT committee agreed in May 1985 that "the Agreement was considered to have operated adequately and to have met initial expectations."[75]

In regard to the anti-dumping code, its committee of signatories reported in 1983 that "in general, the Agreement continued to be perceived by Parties to be balanced between rights and obligations and provided a satisfactory framework for the implementation of Article VI of the General Agreement." However, the report stated that "the Committee also noted that some specific problems had arisen in relation to the application of the Agreement and agreed that these problems should continue to be discussed in the Committee with a view to resolving them in accordance with the letter and spirit of the Agreement."[76] As a result of its review in April 1985, the ADP committee decided simply to reiterate this assessment of performance.[77]

The 1983 report by the Committee on Government Procurement stated that the signatories had found the GPR code to be "a significant first step to reducing protection to domestic products and suppliers,

72. See Committee on Import Licensing, "Report (1983) Presented to the CONTRACTING PARTIES at Their Thirty-Ninth Session," *BISD* 30, 64.
73. MDF/12, 9.
74. See Committee on Technical Barriers to Trade, "Report (1983) to the CONTRACTING PARTIES at Their Thirty-Ninth Session," *BISD* 30, 33.
75. MDF/12, 3.
76. See Committee on Anti-Dumping Practices, "Report (1983) to the CONTRACTING PARTIES at Their Thirty-Ninth Session," *BISD* 30, 69.
77. MDF/12, 10.

to reducing discrimination among foreign products and suppliers, to providing transparency and to establishing international procedures on consultations, surveillance and dispute settlement." Thus the signatories found that the code "[had] served and continues to serve the objectives of the GATT" and that "on the whole [it had] worked satisfactorily." However, the GPR committee report went on to observe that "the commercial impact of the Agreement will materialize only gradually," and that although some data on foreign purchases by member-governments had been exchanged, it "did not consider it appropriate to draw substantive conclusions from data available to it so far."[78] Not much progress was made in the two years following the presentation by the GPR committee of this mixed assessment of its code, for at its special review meeting in May 1985, it simply reported that "the Committee recalled these observations and conclusions."[79]

Several GPR code problems were also identified in 1986 by a special Working Group of the International Chamber of Commerce (ICC). Its report noted that there were "very substantial differences between the level of effort made and the degree of observance of the Code among governments," and that "our enquiries suggest that the business community in general feels that the Code has not made a significant change in the buying patterns of entities covered by it."[80] It argued further that "in some cases there has been deflection in the channelling of contracts from covered entities to those not covered, and redefinition as strategic of [*sic*] goods not previously so regarded, in order to avoid the Code being applicable," and that "there is also concern about the use of derogations and, in particular, that the rapid procedure provisions [of the code] may give undue advantage to domestic suppliers, who are in a position to have better advance information."[81]

Finally, the Committee on Subsidies and Countervailing Measures reported that the two major parts of the SCM code—Part I on countervailing measures and Part II on the use of subsidies—had attained very different levels of effectiveness during the 1980s. In 1983 the committee noted that Part I "had contributed to greater transparency

78. Committee on Government Procurement, "Report (1983) to the CONTRACTING PARTIES at Their Thirty-Ninth Session," *BISD* 30, 37.

79. MDF/12, 4.

80. See Aldo Frignani, Chair, ICC Working Group on the GATT Government Procurement Code, "The GATT Agreement on Government Procurement: ICC Symposium," *Journal of World Trade Law* 20 (September–October 1986), 568.

81. Ibid. The ICC also found that signatories were providing insufficient statistical information on their code-covered purchases to the GPR committee, and that the code was not sufficiently publicized either within industry or within government.

regarding the imposition of countervailing duties." Regarding Part II, "The Committee felt that there was greater transparency and compliance with the obligations concerning the notifications of subsidies granted or maintained" but cautioned that "there was room for improvement." The SCM committee then reported severe dispute-settlement problems regarding the subsidies side of the code, stating that "some fundamental issues have emerged, bearing upon the interpretation and application of important provisions of the Agreement." The committee concluded by saying that there was "an urgent need to examine these issues with a view to arriving at a uniform interpretation and effective application of the provisions in question."[82] However, this consensus was not attained in the following two years: the SCM committee reported in April 1985 that "certain fundamental issues relating to the interpretation and application of the Agreement had not yet been resolved."[83] The SCM code had proven itself effective in regulating signatories' procedures for countervailing measures, but not in providing discipline over their use of subsidies.

By the mid-1980s some of the Tokyo Round NTB codes were viewed by GATT participants and outside experts as having been more successful than others. This variation in code performance is confirmed in the next two chapters, which provide an in-depth analysis of the operation of the agreements from 1980 until 1987. These chapters also reveal that the performance of each code was largely a reflection of the level of cooperation or discord between the United States and the EC concerning the agreement in question. The discussion sets the stage for Chapters 6 and 7, which consider whether realism or neoliberal institutionalism is better able to account for the variation in code performance.

82. Committee on Subsidies and Countervailing Measures, "Report (1983) to the CONTRACTING PARTIES at Their Thirty-Ninth Session," *BISD* 30, 47–48.
83. MDF/12, 5.

CHAPTER FOUR

Rule Compliance and Dispute Settlement in the Tokyo Round NTB Regime, 1980–1987

The Tokyo Round was successful in constructing a new regime on non-tariff barriers to trade. Yet the long-term significance of that new regime would depend on the capacity of its six constituent codes to facilitate trade and to foster order in the international trade system. By the mid-1980s, GATT member-states and outside experts had reached a tentative assessment of the performance of six accords in meeting these objectives. The agreements on customs valuation and import licensing were viewed as effective, as were the countervail rules contained in the subsidies/countervail code; those on technical barriers and government procurement were seen as having attained a mixed level of success, and I would add the anti-dumping code to that intermediate category; the subsidy rules in the subsidies/countervail code were considered to have been markedly unsuccessful.

The actual course of developments involving the codes confirm these summary judgments. In this chapter and the next I review the administrative history of the codes and assess their relative effectiveness during the 1980s. The key challenge in undertaking such an analysis is to select measures that remain faithful to the diversity of the content and goals of the different agreements. To meet this challenge, it is useful to recall John Jackson's observation that "two problems that repose behind every international obligation . . . are the twin ones of how to achieve a reasonable degree of *compliance* with the obligation and how to *settle disputes* about it."[1] Drawing upon Jackson, then, I take one basic measure of effectiveness to be the level of rule

1. John H. Jackson, *World Trade and the Law of the GATT* (Indianapolis: Bobbs Merrill, 1969), 163, emphasis added.

compliance each agreement attained during the 1980s. Rule compliance in the present context is defined as the initiation, modification, or cessation of some form of behavior by signatories so that they are in accord with injunctions articulated in code rules. I also follow Jackson's suggestion of a second basis for comparison of the NTB codes: the efficacy of dispute-settlement efforts undertaken within the context of the codes and their committees of signatories. This second standard is especially useful in estimating the impact of the codes on U.S.-EC trade relations.

The two standards are employed in the present chapter to estimate what might be called the comparative administrative effectiveness of the Tokyo Round NTB agreements. Since rules often require interpretation or refurbishment, in the next chapter a third criterion is employed: rule construction, or the capacity of signatories to reconfigure codes in the light of problems and opportunities encountered while administering them.

RULE COMPLIANCE

Each of the Tokyo Round NTB codes requires signatories to enhance the transparency of those national policies and practices that are covered by the codes. This has been attempted through two types of rules. First, when the agreements first came into effect, signatories were required to submit information on their implementation of code obligations for review by fellow code participants. Second, the codes have obliged signatories to report on an ongoing basis on their national policies and practices covered by the agreements. Such rules serve two purposes: they allow signatories to verify that partners are complying with their code obligations, and they reduce uncertainty in the expectations of traders and thereby liberalize trade.

The Codes on Customs Valuation and Import Licensing

The signatories to the Code on Customs Valuation rapidly achieved heightened transparency of laws and regulations. In compliance with Article 25 of the CV code, they agreed at their first meeting in January 1981 that all would submit their customs-valuation legislation to the committee for review, and they decided in May 1981 that all would provide written responses to a questionnaire on customs-valuation practices drawn up by the GATT secretariat.[2] Of the eleven original signatories applying the code in January 1981, eight—including the United States and the EC—submitted their legislation by May 1981, and the remaining three did so by November 1981.[3] In addition, eight of the nine original signatories that needed to submit responses to the GATT questionnaire—including the United States and the EC—did so by November 1981, and the ninth submitted its response by May 1982.[4]

The CV code also quickly attained very high levels of compliance with its rules concerning methods of customs valuation. As previously noted, the CV code establishes a hierarchy of six valuation methods and specifies that the first and preferred method is the transaction value of imported goods. The signatories agreed in May 1981 to conduct studies of the incidence of their employment of the six valuation methods; the results are presented in Table 4.1.

The data indicate that, by the end of 1981, CV code participants overwhelmingly employed the transaction value of imported goods for the purposes of customs valuation. Data on different valuation methods employed by all signatories prior to 1981 are unavailable, and therefore it cannot be said that the code induced the signatories' high level of convergence regarding customs-valuations methods. However, at the very least it may be observed that the principal rule of the code enjoyed a very high level of compliance from 1981. In addition, by 1986 the CV committee could report that "some two-thirds of international trade is already subject to the provisions of the agree-

2. See "Agreement on Implementation of Article VII," in GATT, *Basic Instruments and Selected Documents*, Twenty-Sixth Supplement (Geneva, 1980), 132. Hereafter, all such citations will identify the NTB agreement, the *BISD* supplement number, and the page number. The committee decision on national legislation is reported in Committee on Customs Valuation, "Minutes of Committee Meeting of January 31, 1981," GATT Doc. VAL/M/1, February 27, 1981, 8–9, 11. Hereafter, the first citation of the minutes of an NTB code committee meeting will be reported by the code committee, date of the committee meeting, the GATT document designation for the minutes of the committee meeting, the publication date for the minutes, and the page number. Subsequent citation of those minutes will refer simply to the GATT document designation and page number. For the decision on the CV questionnaire, see CV committee, "Minutes," May 5, 1981, GATT Doc. VAL/M/2, June 17, 1981, 12.

3. Spain and five developing countries were signatories, but by invoking a clause in Article 21 of the agreement permitting postponement of implementation of the agreement, they were not required to submit their legislation. See VAL/M/1, 9; on the submissions, see VAL/M/2, 4; and CV committee, "Minutes," November 4–5, 1981," GATT Doc. VAL/M/3, January 29, 1982, 3.

4. See VAL/M/3, 3, and CV committee, "Minutes," May 4–5, 1982, GATT Doc. VAL/M/4, July 19, 1982, 6.

Table 4.1. Valuation methods of signatories to the Code on Customs Valuation (as percentage of import entries covered by CV code article—not trade-weighted)

Country/ country group	Article 1	Article 2	Article 3	Article 5	Article 6	Article 7
Original Signatories						
Austria	87.0	2.0	1.0	–	–	10.0
EC	95.4	0.3	0.2	2.1	–	2.0
Finland	93.1	0.3	0.1	–	–	6.5
Hungary	86.8	10.9	2.3	–	–	–
Japan	96.6	1.4	0.1	0.3	0.5	1.1
Norway	98.5	0.4	–	–	–	1.0
Romania	100.0	–	–	–	–	–
Sweden	99.0	–	–	–	–	–
United States	94.0	1.0	0.5	1.0	2.0	1.5
Later signatories						
Australia	96.5	0.1	–	1.3	0.1	2.0
Canada	95.0	0.5	0.5	0.5	2.0	1.5

Note: Figures for the original signatories were reported by national delegations to the Committee on Customs Valuation on the basis of samples of import entries, typically during the period July–September 1981. The Norwegian sample was drawn from entries during January 1982. The Australian sample is from the period April–August 1983, and the Canadian figure is based on an estimate by the Canadian delegation for 1985.

Sources: GATT, *Basic Instruments and Selected Documents,* Twenty-Eighth Supplement (Geneva, 1982), 42; Committee on Customs Valuation, "First Annual Review of the Implementation and Operation of the Agreement: Background Document by the Secretariat," GATT Doc. VAL/W/4/Rev. 1, November 17, 1981, 8; also Committee on Customs Valuation, "Use of Valuation Methods by Parties," Addendum for Norway, GATT Doc. VAL/W/5/Add. 8; also Committee on Customs Valuation, "Minutes of the Meeting Held on 10–11 November 1983," GATT Doc. VAL/M/8, January 18, 1984, 5, 14–15; and "Minutes of the Meeting Held on 13 November 1985," GATT Doc. VAL/M/14, January 17, 1985, 6–7.

ment."[5] It will also be recalled that CV code signatories had reported in 1983 that the code had liberalized trade by reducing uncertainty about the valuation of customs.[6] Thus by the mid-1980s the customs code appeared to enjoy high levels of compliance and a capacity to liberalize trade.

As with the CV code, the Code on Import Licensing Procedures contains several transparency requirements, including the publication of laws and regulations, the notification of these materials to the LIC

5. CV committee, "Report (1986) to the CONTRACTING PARTIES at Their Forty-Second Session," *BISD* 33, 217.
6. CV committee, "Report (1983) Presented to the CONTRACTING PARTIES at Their Thirty-Ninth Session," *BISD* 30, 58.

code committee, and the submission of additional information at biennial LIC committee reviews.[7] In November 1981, at the first such review, the committee chair reported that all twenty-seven signatories had notified the required materials. The chair observed further that "the process of collection of information had on the whole been satisfactory."[8] At the second review, in October 1983, the chair reported that the committee had made "considerable progress in improving the transparency of licensing systems through the collection and exchange of information" and suggested that the committee "may not need, in the future, to give as much attention to collecting the basic documentation."[9] Hence by late 1983 the transparency obligations of the LIC code had been largely fulfilled by the participants.

The LIC committee also offers an example of signatories pressuring a fellow code participant into compliance with its transparency obligations. In February 1981 Japan's delegate acknowledged that, in spite of a code obligation that import quotas be published, "there still remained a few exceptional items for which the total amounts of quotas were not open to the public."[10] From April 1981 until October 1985, Japan was sharply questioned and criticized about this practice by the United States, the EC, and several other signatories.[11] In the face of these pressures, Japan slowly altered its quota-publication practices.[12] By October 1985 the Japanese delegate provided specific figures for the disputed quotas in leather and a number of agricultural and fisheries products, and also reported that all such figures would be published in the future. These actions largely satisfied Japan's code partners: the committee chair reported for the record that "one major problem which had arisen in the past concerning Japan's non-compliance with certain provisions of the Agreement concerning the publication of quotas had now more or less been settled."[13]

7. See "Agreement on Import Licensing Procedures," Articles 1:4, 5:4(b), and 5:5, in *BISD* 26, 154–61; and LIC committee, "Minutes," April 29, 1980, GATT Doc. LIC/M/2, June 12, 1980, 2–3.

8. LIC committee, "Minutes," November 9–10, 1981, GATT Doc. LIC/M/5, February 18, 1982, 2–3.

9. LIC committee, "Minutes," October 6, 1983, GATT Doc. LIC/M/9, November 1, 1983, 4.

10. See LIC/M/5, 4; and LIC committee, "Minutes," April 6, 1981, GATT Doc. LIC/M/4, May 25, 1981.

11. See LIC committee, "Minutes," May 10, 1982, GATT Doc. LIC/M/6, July 9, 1982, 5–6; also see LIC/M/9, 2; and LIC committee, "Minutes," December 13, 1982, GATT Doc. LIC/M/7, February 18, 1983, 4.

12. LIC/M/6, 5; LIC/M/7, 3.

13. LIC committee, "Minutes," October 9, 1985, GATT Doc. LIC/M/14/Rev. 1, November 19, 1985, 3–4.

*The Codes on Anti-Dumping Practices, Technical Barriers,
and Government Procurement*

The Code on Anti-Dumping Practices contains both initial and ongoing transparency requirements. Concerning the former, the ADP signatories agreed in January 1980 that they would submit their respective anti-dumping legislation to the ADP committee for mutual review and evaluation. By May 1980, seven of the seventeen original signatories had notified their legislation; three more did so by the end of 1980, and four others did so by the end of 1982. The long-term transparency requirement of the ADP code, contained in Article 14:4, obliges signatories to notify the ADP committee biannually of all their anti-dumping actions (including the finding that they had taken no actions). Adherence to this requirement was uniformly very high during the 1980s. For example, all seventeen signatories submitted notifications for July–December 1980, twenty-one of twenty-two did so for January–June 1985, and twenty of twenty-two met the requirement for January–June 1987.[14]

In addition to fostering greater transparency, the ADP code articulates a number of standards and procedural rules to be followed by signatories in their anti-dumping proceedings. Clearly, the frequency of such anti-dumping actions in signatory-states increased dramatically during the 1980s. For example, seventy-one actions were initiated by ADP signatories in July 1980–June 1981; this increased to 116 during 1983–84, and 379 during 1985–86.[15] In spite of this upsurge in anti-dumping activity, signatories rarely invoked the ADP code's dispute-settlement provisions during the 1980s. This suggests that the anti-dumping activities of the signatories were in substantial compliance with the code.

There is at least one instance in which the ADP committee brought about a modest change in a signatory's anti-dumping procedures. In November 1983 the EC representative complained that Australia's practice of making preliminary determinations as to the imposition of anti-dumping duties within forty-five days of the initiation of an investigation "was too short. . . . This procedure was not fair to exporter

14. See ADP committee, "Minutes," April 27–28, 1981, GATT Doc. ADP/M/5, June 11, 1981, 4; ADP committee, "Report (1985) Submitted to the CONTRACTING PARTIES at Their Forty-First Session," in GATT, *BISD* 32, 185–86; and ADP committee, "Minutes," October 26–28, 1987, GATT Doc. ADP/M/20, January 15, 1988, 14–15.

15. For these data on the initiation of anti-dumping actions, see *BISD* 30, 70–71; *BISD* 31, 289–90; *BISD* 32, 188–90; and *BISD* 33, 211–12.

nor in conformity with the Code."[16] After additional statements of concern during 1984 by the EC, the United States, Canada, and the Nordic countries, the Australian representative reported in October 1985 that "his authorities had carefully examined the cases where extensions were granted and had decided to increase the period in which preliminary findings should be made from 45 to 55 days."[17]

Compliance with the ADP code appears to have been quite good during 1980–87. However, there were a number of problems regarding implementation of the agreement, suggesting that it did not enjoy the same high level of consensus that characterized the CV and LIC agreements. For example, at three ADP committee meetings during 1980–82, the EC complained that a U.S. practice of assuming an 8 percent profit margin when establishing the "constructed value" of an exporting firm's home-market price did not comply with Article 2:4 of the ADP code. The ADP committee urged the United States in October 1980 to review that practice; the United States resisted, arguing that the practice conformed with the GATT and that, in any event, changing the rule would require congressional approval which the U.S. administration was reluctant to seek. As a result, the issue ceased to be discussed after April 1982.[18] Similarly, Japan complained at the October 1982 ADP meeting that U.S. "best information available" rules had recently produced an "arbitrary" material-injury determination against Japanese firms, and that a U.S. requirement that responses to its anti-dumping questionnaire be placed on magnetic tapes caused Japanese firms undue difficulties and expenses. Japan further complained that an EC rule that anti-dumping questionnaires be returned within thirty days of the opening of an investigation gave insufficient time to targeted firms. The EC for its part complained that Australia and Canada had not provided Community-based firms "appropriate prior notice" for on-the-spot visits undertaken in anti-dumping investigations of such firms.[19] Thus compliance with the

16. ADP committee, "Minutes," November 15, 1983, GATT Doc. ADP/M/11, February 7, 1984, 4.

17. See ADP committee, "Minutes," May 8, 1984, GATT Doc. ADP/M/12, July 25, 1984, 3–4; and ADP committee, "Minutes," October 21, 24, 1985, GATT Doc. ADP/M/16, January 9, 1986, 4–5.

18. See ADP committee, "Minutes," October 20–22, 1980, GATT Doc. ADP/M/3, January 7, 1981, 8–10; ADP/M/5, 3; and ADP committee, "Minutes," April 26–27, 1982, GATT. Doc. ADP/M/7, June 28, 1982, 3.

19. ADP committee, "Minutes," October 25–26, 1982, GATT Doc. ADP/M/9, December 22, 1982, 6–7, 13–14.

revised ADP code was high overall during the 1980s, but only after some initial turbulence and controversy.

In the case of the Agreement on Technical Barriers to Trades, signatories were required by Article 15:7 to submit statements on implementation.[20] Compliance with this obligation, and a committee agreement that signatories would submit responses to a common checklist, occurred more slowly than in the cases of the CV and LIC codes.[21] The TBT signatories agreed in March 1980 to submit materials by the following month, but only seven—including the United States but none of the EC states—did so at that time. The United Kingdom, Belgium, Japan, and three other signatories submitted materials in June 1980, but by the end of the year only sixteen of the original twenty-nine signatories, and only four of the nine EC member-states, had submitted information. Ten more signatories (including the EC and four of its member-states) submitted materials by early 1981; nevertheless, it was not until January 1982 that all the original signatories had submitted the information required by Article 15:7.[22]

The major ongoing transparency obligation of the TBT code is that signatories notify one another through the GATT secretariat of all proposed technical regulations (that is, mandatory standards) or rules for product certification having a significant effect on trade. In this regard, the TBT committee has enjoyed success but of a mixed character. This can be observed in Table 4.2, which presents the annual total number of technical measures notified by TBT signatories to the GATT from 1980 until 1986. Throughout the period, approximately 1500 technical measures were notified, and as the table indicates, annual notifications more than doubled from 130 in 1980 to almost 300 in 1981. However, notifications then dropped to a total of about 200 in 1982 and remained in the range of 200–250 notifications annually through 1986. This suggests a limitation on the effectiveness of the TBT code and its standards-notification obligation, for notifications remained basically constant throughout the period despite

20. *BISD* 26, 27.
21. TBT committee, "Minutes," January 28, 1980, GATT Doc. TBT/M/1, March 13, 1980, 2.
22. Ibid.; TBT committee, "Minutes," April 24, 1980, GATT Doc. TBT/M/2, June 6, 1980, 4–7; TBT committee, "Minutes," June 19, 1980, GATT Doc. TBT/M/3, July 18, 1980, 2–5; TBT committee, "Minutes," July 22, 1980, GATT Doc. TBT/M/4, September 30, 1980, 2–3; TBT committee, "Minutes," November 4–6, 1980, GATT Doc. TBT/M/5, January 16, 1981, 9–11; TBT committee, "Minutes," February 4–5, 1981, GATT Doc. TBT/M/6, March 27, 1981, 4–5; and TBT committee, "Minutes," October 20–22, 1981, GATT Doc. TBT/M/8, January 7, 1982, 5–7.

Table 4.2. Notifications of measures under the Code on Technical Barriers to Trade, 1980–86

Notifications and Signatories	1980	1981	1982	1983	1984	1985	1986
Total notifications	130	295	201	255	223	196	215
Total signatories	29	32	35	37	37	38	38
Total signatories making notifications	13	20	20	22	22	20	19
Notifications/total signatories	4.5	9.2	5.7	6.9	6.0	5.2	5.6
Notifications/signatories making notifications	10.0	14.8	10.0	11.6	10.1	9.8	11.3

Source: Committee on Technical Barriers to Trade, "Eighth Annual Review of the Implementation and Operation of the Agreement: Basic Document of the Secretariat," GATT Doc. TBT/28, October 5, 1987, 7.

the fact that there were eight more code signatories in 1986 than in 1981.

The TBT code also stipulates that notifications of proposed technical measures be made sufficiently ahead of the date these measures are to go into effect so that fellow code participants can offer comments in time for the latter to be taken into account by the issuing agency of the notifying signatory.[23] The TBT signatories agreed in June 1980 that this "comment period" should be a minimum of six weeks, and they extended it to sixty days in May 1983.[24] Data on the compliance of signatories with these two comment periods during the 1980s are presented in Table 4.3. It suggests that compliance with the TBT committee's comment-period recommendations was good but not complete, exceeding 50 percent only once (in 1985). However, in response to the TBT committee's two comment-period decisions, compliance increased over time, although this progress was reversed in 1986.

Finally, the signatories to the Code on Government Procurement agreed in January 1981 that they would notify the GPR committee of both their legislation and regulations implementing the code and their

23. The obligation to provide notification of regulations, standards, or rules of certification is contained in Articles 2, 3, 4, and 7 of the TBT code: see *BISD* 26, 9–16.

24. See TBT/M/3, 5, 12; also TBT committee, "Minutes," May 17–18, 1983, GATT Doc. TBT/M/13, July 15, 1983, 4–5.

Table 4.3. Compliance with comment periods recommended by the Committee on Technical Barriers to Trade, 1980–86

Notifications	1980	1981	1982	1983		1984	1985	1986
				Up to May 18	After May 18			
Total	130	295	201	97	158	223	196	215
With recommended comment period	33	116	85	36	55	92	106	68
With recommended comment period/total notifications (%)	25.4	39.3	42.2	37.1	34.8	41.2	54.1	31.6

Note: From January 1, 1980 until May 18, 1983, the recommended comment period was six weeks; thereafter it was sixty days.

Sources: Committee on Technical Barriers to Trade, "Fifth Annual Review of the Implementation and Operation of the Agreement: Basic Document by the Secretariat," GATT Doc. TBT/18, September 28, 1984, 9–10; "Sixth Annual Review of the Implementation and Operation of the Agreement: Basic Document by the Secretariat," GATT Doc. TBT/22, October 16, 1985, 8; "Seventh Annual Review of the Implementation and Operation of the Agreement: Basic Document by the Secretariat," GATT Doc. TBT/25, September 25, 1986, 9; and "Eighth Annual Review of the Implementation and Operation of the Agreement: Basic Document by the Secretariat," GATT Doc. TBT/28, October 5, 1987, 9.

responses to a checklist of code-related issues prepared by the GATT secretariat.[25] Compliance with these requirements was very prompt: nineteen code participants (including the United States, the EC, and eight of the latter's member-states) submitted their replies to the checklist by April 1981 (Italy and Singapore did so in October), and nineteen submitted their legislation and regulations by July (Singapore did so in October, and Austria had no new legislation or regulations arising from the code).[26]

Several signatories also made modest changes in their procurement practices as a result of their adherence to the GPR code. For example, in response to criticisms from fellow signatories, Japan revised its certification procedures for potential government contractors so that foreign firms could be certified as possible suppliers during the entire year rather than only at the beginning of the Japanese fiscal year, as had been previous practice.[27] In addition, the United States, responding to EC criticisms during 1981, changed its contract advertisements in early 1982 so as to highlight contracts covered by the code.[28] Similarly, in response to U.S. concerns, the French delegation reported in February 1983 that it would assign a special marker to contract advertisements falling between the EC Directive on Public Supplies and the GPR code (that is, contracts from covered entities between the EC threshold of 1,100,000 French francs and the GATT threshold of 800,000 francs).[29] Finally, and in response to mutual criticism, both the United States and the EC undertook in February 1983 and in June 1985, respectively, to ensure that bid-times on contracts covered by the code would be at least thirty days as required by the agreement.[30]

25. GPR committee, "Minutes," January 15, 1981, GATT Doc. GPR/M/1, March 11, 1981, 4.

26. See GPR committee, "Minutes," April 4, 1981, GATT Doc. GPR/M/2, June 5, 1981, 4–11; GPR committee, "Minutes," July 8–9, 1981, GATT Doc. GPR/M/3, June 29, 1981, 3–16; and GPR committee, "Minutes," October 13–15, 1981, GATT Doc. GPR/M/4, December 17, 1981, 2–10.

27. See GPR/M/2, 8; GPR/M/3, 11; GPR committee, "Minutes," February 2–3, 1982, GATT Doc. GPR/M/5, April 19, 1982, 7; and GPR committee, "Minutes," December 16, 1982, GATT Doc. GPR/M/6, February 14, 1983, 4.

28. GPR/M/1, 16; GPR/M/2, 15; GPR/M/3, 12; GPR/M/4, 12; GPR/M/5, 12.

29. See GPR/M/5, 12; for the U.S. questions to the EC concerning French contract identification practices, see GPR/M/6, 5, and GPR committee, "Minutes," February 24, 1983, GATT Doc. GPR/M/7, April 22, 1983, 12.

30. EC criticism of U.S. bid-times is noted in GPR/M/6, 2–3; the U.S. commitment was made at the next meeting; see GPR/M/7, 4. According to figures reported by the EC, 90 percent of U.S. contracts covered by the code had bid-times of less than twenty-nine days during the first ten months of 1982 (GPR/M/6, 2); by January–April 1983, between 40 and 50 percent of these contracts had bid-times of less than thirty days,

On the other hand, there were many indications of non-compliance with the GPR code during the 1980s. For example, at the GPR committee meeting in February 1985, the EC complained that one-half of Japan's contract announcements in December 1984 had bid-times of less than two weeks; when Japan's representative responded that the purchases in question were of a recurring nature not requiring a thirty-day bid period, the U.S. representative replied that the Japanese "had discovered a loophole in the Agreement which they were making extensive use of."[31] In addition, the United States argued during the 1980s that several EC member-states had not fulfilled important obligations under the GPR code. In May 1983, for example, the U.S. representative charged that Italy had only advertised twenty-eight contracts during January–April of that year, whereas West Germany, Great Britain, and France had advertised 124, 104, and 85 contracts, respectively. The United States also complained that more than one-half of the Italian contract notices during that period had not "allowed sufficient time for bidding."[32] Further, the United States noted in February 1987 that Italy had failed to submit code-required contract statistics for 1984 and that its 1985 statistics, as well as Ireland's, were incomplete.[33] The United States also complained during the 1980s that EC members in general made unwarranted use of single-tendering procedures—the granting of contracts with little or no bidding—which almost always result in the exclusion of foreign suppliers. In February 1985, for example, the United States recalled that, under the code, single-tendering "was intended to be used only in exceptional cases" but that, in the case of the EC during 1983, single-tendering "accounted for 54% of all above-threshold purchases with virtually no improvement over previous years" [the figure was 55 percent in 1982 and 51 percent in 1981].[34] Finally, the United States directed pointed questions to the EC concerning the latter's "large decreases in the value and share of above-threshold contracts in spite of a significant increase in announced Code-covered procurement."[35]

---

leading the EC to observe that "an improvement had taken place in the United States with regard to bid deadlines." See GPR committee, "Minutes," May 25–26, 1982, GATT Doc. GPR/M/8, July 27, 1983, 6. U.S. criticism of EC bid-deadlines is noted in GPR committee, "Minutes," February 13, 1985, GATT Doc. GPR/M/15, April 22, 1985, 10, and the EC commitment to extend deadlines is noted in GPR committee, "Minutes," June 19, 1985, GATT Doc. GPR/M/18, August 23, 1985, 7.

31. The EC supported the U.S. criticisms of Japan: see GPR/M/15, 9.

32. GPR/M/8, 4.

33. GPR committee, "Minutes," February 12, 1987, GATT Doc. GPR/M/25, April 9, 1987, 6.

34. GPR/M/15, 2.

35. Ibid.

From the U.S. viewpoint, then, EC members had attained only a highly imperfect level of compliance during the 1980s with their GPR code commitments.

The Code on Subsidies and Countervailing Measures

The GATT secretariat, on the basis of Article 19:5 of the Code on Subsidies and Countervailing Measures, circulated a request in early 1980 that participants provide the SCM committee with their legislation, regulations, and administrative practices relating to the imposition of countervailing measures.[36] By May 1980, six advanced-country signatories had submitted these materials, and by the end of the year all advanced-country signatories except Canada (which was preparing new legislation) had met this requirement. By the end of 1986, only two original developing-country signatories (Brazil and Yugoslavia) and two newer developing-country members (Egypt and Turkey) had not done so.[37] Thus compliance with the transparency provisions of the SCM code was very prompt among the advanced countries but less so among the developing countries.

The SCM code also specifies (in Article 2:6) that signatories notify the committee on a biannual basis of any countervailing-measure action they had taken in the previous six months, including the finding that they had not taken any such action. For the first reporting period (January–June 1980), only the eight advanced-countries signatories presented countervail notifications. However, transparency improved very quickly: sixteen signatories presented reports for the second period (July–December 1980), and by the seventh reporting period (January–June 1983) the chair of the committee noted that "all Signatories had submitted their notifications."[38]

In contrast to the high levels of compliance relating to countervailing measures, enhanced transparency of national subsidy programs (required both by Article XVI:1 of the General Agreement and by Article 7:1 of the code) was not attained and in fact revealed a severe division between the United States and the EC. In October 1980 the SCM committee chair reminded code signatories that they were

36. See *BISD* 26, 79; and SCM committee, "Minutes," May 8, 1980, GATT Doc. SCM/M/3, June 27, 1980, 9-10.

37. *BISD* 27, 31–32; ADP committee, "Minutes," February 2–3, 1981, GATT Doc. ADP/M/4, March 19, 1981, 4–6. Also see *BISD* 32, 158–59; *BISD* 33, 197–98; and SCM committee, "Minutes," October 23–24, 1985, GATT Doc. SCM/M/30, January 10, 1986, 8.

38. SCM committee, "Minutes," November 17, 1983, GATT Doc. SCM/M/19, February 21, 1984, 8.

obliged to provide notifications of their subsidy programs and to submit responses to a questionnaire on subsidies by January 1981.[39] By April, however, only three responses had been submitted (by Finland, Luxembourg, and Romania), and by October 1981 only one additional signatory—the EC—had submitted a notification, and its report failed to identify any EC industrial subsidies.[40] The signatories agreed to hold a special meeting in early 1982 on subsidy notifications.[41] At that meeting, in March 1982, the SCM chair reported that twelve of twenty signatories (including the EC, the United States, and all other developed-country members except New Zealand) had submitted notifications; among the eight developing-country members, only two (Hong Kong and Chile) had done so.[42]

Of much greater concern to the United States and other code participants were EC arguments about its obligation to notify subsidies. The EC argued that the notification obligations arising from Article 16:1 of the General Agreement needed "to be reconsidered in the light of the new provisions of the Code," and the EC's essential argument was that the code required *less* transparency with respect to subsidies than had been required by the General Agreement.[43] Based on this interpretation, the EC reported no industrial subsidies in any detail, and no EC member-state submitted a notification of its national subsidies, to the SCM committee at its March 1982 meeting.[44] In addition, the EC notification failed to report the estimated trade impact of Community-wide industrial subsidy programs.[45] Finally, the EC argued that the code allowed it not to notify its members' export credit programs, although such programs were notified by the United States, Canada, Finland, and Korea.[46]

The same EC minimalist understanding of subsidy transparency

39. SCM committee, "Minutes," October 23–24, 1980, GATT Doc. SCM/M/4, December 11, 1980, 8.
40. See SCM committee, "Minutes," April 29, 1981, GATT Doc. SCM/M/6, June 24, 1981, 3–4; and SCM committee, "Minutes," October 28–30, 1981, GATT Doc. SCM/M/9, December 22, 1981, 4–5.
41. SCM/M/9, 4–6.
42. See SCM committee, "Minutes," March 28, 1980, GATT Doc. SCM/M/Spec/2, May 8, 1980, 3; SCM committee, "Minutes," April 29, 1982, GATT Doc. SCM/M/11, July 7, 1982, 5.
43. SCM committee, "Minutes," May 19, 1983, GATT Doc. SCM/M/17, July 12, 1983, 1.
44. Ibid; also see SCM/Spec/2, 3–5. Japan also argued that it operated no industrial subsidy program that needed to be notified: see SCM committee, "Minutes," April 21, 1983, GATT Doc. SCM/M/16, July 25, 1983, 3.
45. SCM/M/16, 6–7.
46. See SCM committee, "Minutes," July 15, 1982, GATT Doc. SCM/M/12, August 11, 1982, 5; and SCM committee, "Minutes," October 27, 1982, GATT Doc. SCM/M/13, January 6, 1983, 4–6; and SCM/M/16, 6.

obligations in the code was evident when the SCM committee under-took a second major review of subsidy notifications in December 1984. At that time, the United States, Canada, and Sweden notified their export credit programs; however, the EC (as well as Japan and Norway) continued to decline to do so.[47] The EC did notify its agri-cultural subsidies and subsidies for shipbuilding, steel, and textiles, and three member-states (Britain, West Germany, and Belgium) also notified their national subsidies both for agriculture and for industry; yet all other EC member-states declined to provide subsidy notifica-tions either for agriculture or for industry.[48] These EC actions were criticized by the United States, Canada, and Australia.[49] In response to U.S. questions, the EC did provide in April 1985 some information on French and Italian subsidy programs (but did not provide a com-prehensive notification for either), as well as information on subsidy programs not contained in the original German, British, and Belgian notifications. The U.S. representative argued that the EC response was inadequate and that there were in fact EC subsidy programs against which there had been countervailing duty actions by other countries but which had still not been notified by the EC.[50] Finally, in December 1986, and during another committee notification exercise, the SCM chair reported that the EC had provided materials on its subsidy programs, and that Belgium, Germany, and the United King-dom had provided information on their respective national pro-grams, but that "no notifications had ever been received regarding measures applied at the national level in the other member States."[51] Thus, while enjoying consensus on the countervail side of the SCM code, the United States (and a number of other signatories) differed sharply with the EC on SCM rules aimed at enhanced international transparency of subsidies.

SETTLEMENT OF DISPUTES

The Tokyo Round NTB codes can be assessed in terms of their comparative capacity to help signatories resolve trade disputes. Five of

47. Norway indicated that it would notify its programs if other signatories did so: see SCM committee, "Minutes," December 4–5, 1984, GATT Doc. SCM/M/24, Febru-ary 14, 1985, 8, 10, 12; and SCM committee, "Minutes," April 25, 1985, GATT Doc. SCM/M/27, July 25, 1985, 10.
48. SCM/M/24, 15–19.
49. Ibid., 18.
50. SCM/M/27, 12–15.
51. See SCM committee, "Minutes," October 27–31, November 13, 1986, GATT Doc. SCM/M/32, January 27, 1987, 15; the full review by the SCM chair is reported on 12–15.

the six agreements mandate that disputes be handled by their respective Committees of Signatories. The exception is the LIC accord, which mandates that disputes be addressed through the GATT's conflict-resolution mechanisms outlined in Articles XXII and XXIII of the General Agreement. Following precedents developed in the GATT, the NTB codes call on signatories to seek resolution of disputes through a progression of steps, beginning with bilateral consultations, moving through committee-sponsored investigations and conciliation meetings or the formation of working parties, and, finally, the establishment of ad hoc panels that are tasked to receive information from the disputants and to offer judgments about the relative merits of the positions of the conflicting parties under relevant code provisions. The codes also provide that committees of signatories may authorize retaliatory actions that may be taken by a code member that believes the code-based benefits it is due are impaired by another's violation of code provisions.[52] Because all codes specify institutionalized remedies for the settlement of disputes, a particular code's effectiveness in resolving disputes, and its capacity to provide remedies that are faithful to its rules and procedures, can serve as an indicator of that code's relative effectiveness during the 1980s.

The Codes on Customs Valuation and Import Licensing

In the case of the customs code, no signatory had invoked its dispute-settlement procedures through 1987.[53] Indeed, signatories pointed to this absence of disputes as evidence of the code's success. For example, the CV committee reported in 1984 that "the experience of Parties applying the Agreement had led to general satisfaction on their part" and suggested that "one indication of this was that no substantial difficulties had been encountered by Parties in applying the Agreement and that no use had yet been made of the consultation and dispute settlement provisions of the Agreement."[54]

The dispute-settlement provisions of the import-licensing code

52. On GATT dispute-settlement provisions and procedures, see Jackson, *Law of the GATT*, 163–87; Kenneth W. Dam, *The GATT: Law and International Economic Organization* (Chicago: University of Chicago Press, 1970), 351–75; William J. Davey, "Dispute Settlement in GATT," *Fordham International Law Journal* 11 (1987), 51–109; Julia Christine Bliss, "GATT Dispute Settlement Reform in the Uruguay Round: Problems and Prospects," *Stanford Journal of International Law* 23 (Spring 1987), 31–55; and Rosine Plank, "An Unofficial Description of How a GATT Panel Works and Does Not," *Journal of International Arbitration* 4 (December 1987), 53–102.

53. *BISD* 26, 128–29.

54. See *BISD* 31, 278–79. This had also been noted by the CV committee in its 1985 response to the CONTRACTING PARTIES: see Working Group on MTN Agreements, "Adequacy and Effectiveness of the MTN Agreements and Arrangements and

were not formally invoked until the end of 1987, when the United States requested that the LIC committee establish a panel to examine India's import-licensing regime for almonds.[55] Although formal proceedings were not required among the advanced-country signatories of the LIC code during the 1980s, informal efforts were undertaken in 1984–85 to settle a dispute between the EC and the United States over the latter's administration of an import quota for specialty steel. The U.S. Customs Service had required steel importers to complete a "Specialty Steel Summary Invoice" (SSSI) upon landing shipments, and, if the quota for a particular period had been filled, these "excess" steel shipments had to be warehoused until the next quota period. The EC complained in June 1984 that the SSSI was an import-licensing system and that warehousing of steel shipments violated code obligations.[56] The United States responded that the SSSI did not constitute an import-licensing system and thus did not come under the jurisdiction of the LIC code.[57] The EC then relented, indicating in October 1985 that there was indeed a question as to whether the U.S. steel procedures constituted an import-licensing system. It therefore "requested that the Committee include with a degree of priority in its Work Programme [discussed in Chapter 5] the question of what was and what was not an import licensing procedure," and noted that "pending successful work on the more general question raised by this problem [the SSSI] in the context of the Work Programme, it could be dropped from the regular meetings of the Committee."[58] Finally, the EC reported to the LIC committee in March 1986 that as part of the new U.S.-EC agreement on quotas for specialty steel, "the specific bilateral problem with the United States concerning specialty steel had been resolved."[59]

The Codes on Anti-Dumping Practices, Technical Barriers, and Government Procurement

Only one dispute was brought to the committee of signatories for the ADP code by advanced-country participants during the 1980s, but

---

Obstacles to Their Acceptance—Note by the Secretariat," GATT Doc. MDF/12, November 6, 1985, 8.

55. LIC/M/9, passim.

56. See LIC committee, "Minutes," June 12, 1984, GATT Doc. LIC/M/10, August 8, 1984, 4–5; LIC committee, "Minutes," October 4, 1984, GATT Doc. LIC/M/11, December 14, 1984, 4; for the relevant provisions of the LIC code, see *BISD* 26, 157.

57. See LIC/M/10, 4–5; and LIC/M/11, 4.

58. LIC/M/14/Rev.l, 4.

59. LIC committee, "Minutes," March 11, 1986, GATT Doc. LIC/M/15, May 7, 1986, 3.

the committee was unable to help resolve it. In October 1980 the EC complained that Canada had initiated an anti-dumping investigation against an Italian firm not for actually dumping products (large hydroelectric generators) but rather for placing bids on contracts that Canadian producers alleged were set at artificially low levels.[60] The EC raised the issue again in April 1983 and requested formal conciliation in November 1983; this special conciliation meeting of the committee was held in March 1984.[61] The EC, noting that the code referred to a dumped good in terms of "the product exported," argued that a good had to be exported to a country before the latter could undertake a dumping investigation. Canada, noting that the code also referred to dumped goods as those "introduced into the commerce of another country," argued that goods with very long delivery times such as large generators effectively entered into world commerce once foreign bids were placed on contracts for such goods.[62] The EC reported at the end of the March meeting that it believed conciliation had failed and that it might request a panel.[63] However, as in the SSSI case, the EC decided not to call for a panel but instead requested in May 1984 that the committee's ad hoc group (discussed in Chapter 5) "urgently examine the question of definition of sale," a request accepted by the ADP committee.[64]

The Committee on Technical Barriers to Trade experienced both success and failure in its dispute-settlement efforts during its first decade of operation. The most important example of success involved the United States and Japan. The case appeared to be a minor trade dispute—the export to Japan of American metal baseball bats. The Japanese government had refused to grant American manufacturers access to Japan's safety certification system for athletic equipment and instead had wanted to use safety inspection checks that would have created uncertainty and additional costs for American producers. According to the United States, this was in violation of Article 7:2 of the TBT code, and in September 1982 the United States requested a committee investigation. The Japanese requested bilateral consultations. These resulted in an agreement guaranteeing U.S. access to Japan's certification system, and the United States reported to the TBT committee in March 1983 that it wished to withdraw its request

60. ADP/M/3, 24.
61. See ADP committee, "Minutes," April 26–27, 1983, GATT Doc. ADP/M/10, July 27, 1983, 13; ADP/M/11, 10–12; and ADP committee, "Minutes," January 22, 1980, GATT Doc. ADP/M/Spec/1, March 6, 1980, passim.
62. ADP/M/3, 24; ADP/M/10, 13; also see *BISD* 26, 172.
63. ADP/M/Spec/1, 3.
64. ADP/M/12, 11.

for a committee investigation.[65] This U.S.-Japanese agreement led to a review by Japan of its standards and certification system and the amendment of parts of sixteen Japanese laws in this issue-area.[66] The Office of the U.S. Trade Representative would report later that these revisions had the potential of liberalizing as much as five billion dollars in U.S. exports to Japan, and that they constituted "the most significant development in the [United States-Japan] bilateral relationship since the conclusion of the Tokyo Round."[67]

Another example of successful TBT dispute settlement involved Spain and the EC prior to the former's joining the latter in January 1986. In October 1983 the EC reported bilateral consultations with Spain over the latter's new type-approval certification rules for heating radiators.[68] The following February the EC requested a TBT committee investigation of these rules and similar rules for electrical medical equipment. The EC argued that Spain had applied its new certification rules in a discriminatory fashion and had been unduly slow in processing the certification applications of EC producers.[69] In July 1984 the TBT committee adopted a recommendation calling on Spain to change its testing procedures.[70] In October the EC noted that Spain had not made substantial progress in processing EC applications and warned that it would soon call for a special meeting of the committee if the issue were not resolved.[71] However, the EC did not call for such a meeting, suggesting that Spanish authorities had begun to process EC applications. Similarly, in October 1984 the United States reported bilateral consultations with Spain concerning type-approval procedures for medical equipment but reported in May 1985 that these were no longer necessary since the application of an American firm had been approved.[72]

---

65. TBT committee, "Request for Initiation of Dispute Settlement Procedures under Article 14.4 of the Agreement—Communication from the United States," GATT Doc. TBT/Spec/8, March 24, 1983.

66. TBT/M/13, 2.

67. Fred J. Coccodrilli, "Dispute Settlement Pursuant to the Agreement on Technical Barriers to Trade: The United States-Japan Metal Bat Dispute," *Fordham International Law Journal* 7, no. 3 (1983–84), 157; the U.S. estimate of $5 billion in affected trade is noted at 158.

68. A type-approval is based on testing a sample of products to be imported, rather than every unit of the shipment.

69. TBT committee, "Request for Initiation of Dispute Settlement Procedures under Article 14.4 of the Agreement—Communication from the European Economic Community," GATT Doc. TBT/Spec/9, February 20, 1984.

70. See *BISD* 31, 236–37.

71. TBT committee, "Minutes," October 16–17, 1984, GATT Doc. TBT/M/17, December 17, 1984, 10.

72. TBT committee, "Minutes," May 6–10, 1985, GATT Doc. TBT/M/19, August 1, 1985, 11.

Finally, in October 1986 the EC, Austria, Switzerland, and the United States reported consultations with Japan on new standards for ski equipment adopted by that country's Consumer Product Safety Association (CPSA). The new standards, according to the EC representative, "deviated considerably from the standards existing at the international level and their application would have adverse effects on the market penetration that had been achieved by exporters."[73] At the October meeting the Japanese representative stated that the CPSA would review the new standards.[74] In March 1987 the Japanese representative reported that CPSA had decided "to harmonize the SG [safety goods] mark system on ski equipment with the relevant international standards and to simplify the inspection and certification procedures within the system."[75] In response, the EC, Austria, and Switzerland "thanked the Japanese authorities for their efforts in finding a satisfactory solution to the matter," and the U.S. representative added that "his authorities appreciated the commitment by the Japanese authorities to keep under survey the smooth operation of the revised system."[76]

In contrast to these instances of success, two U.S.-EC disputes ended in failure.[77] In June 1980 the United States complained that Britain's proposed manner of implementating a 1978 EC directive on the preparation of fresh poultry for market would discriminate against non-EC suppliers, thus violating Article 2:1 of the code.[78] The standard involved processing and production methods (PPMs), which are not covered by the code. However, Article 14:2.5 stipulates that a signatory may invoke the dispute-settlement provisions of the code if it believed "that obligations under this agreement are being circumvented" by another signatory's formulation of standards in terms of PPMs.[79] The United States argued that Britain was trying to circum-

73. TBT committee, "Minutes," October 13–14, 1986, GATT Doc. TBT/M/23, December 12, 1986, 2.

74. Ibid., 3.

75. TBT committee, "Minutes," March 9–10, 1987, GATT Doc. TBT/M/24, June 3, 1987, 3.

76. Ibid., 4.

77. One other dispute involving the EC began to develop at the end of the period under review. In March 1987 Japan complained that Spain had adopted and was implementing new standards for metallic tableware in a manner contravening the TBT code. In October 1987 the EC representative reported that "his authorities were still reviewing the problem with the Spanish authorities." See TBT committee, "Minutes," October 12–14, 1987, GATT Doc. TBT/M/26, February 2, 1988, 6.

78. See TBT/M/3, 8–10; BISD 26, 9; and TBT committee, "The United States' Complaint Concerning the United Kingdom's Application of EC Directive 78/50," GATT Doc. TBT/Spec/4, July 1, 1980, 7–10.

79. See BISD 26, 26.

vent the code, thus justifying its request for an investigation.[80] The EC responded that the new standard had been formulated before the code had been in force and that, as a result, Britain's actions could not be brought to the committee.[81]

At the July 1980 meeting of the TBT committee, only New Zealand and Brazil supported the U.S. interpretation of Article 14:2.5. Austria, Canada, Switzerland, and the Nordics did not, but they indicated that they were willing to discuss the more general question of whether PPMs should be covered more fully by the code.[82] The U.S. representative then dropped the UK poultry complaint and requested that the general issue of PPMs be examined at subsequent committee meetings.[83] In February 1981 the United States proposed that PPMs be a regular agenda item of the committee, that the GATT secretariat prepare an inventory of PPMs and case studies of their impact on trade, and that PPMs be addressed in the committee's three-year review of the TBT code.[84] Brazil, Canada, Chile, Romania, and Switzerland declined to support the full U.S. proposal but agreed to a PPM inventory and to inclusion of PPMs in the three-year review. However, the EC opposed *every* element of the U.S. proposal.[85]

In October 1982, when the three-year review commenced, the United States proposed a working party on PPMs. Australia, Brazil, Canada, New Zealand, Romania, and Switzerland supported this proposal, and Japan indicated it would accept a committee consensus. Austria and the EC flatly opposed the U.S. proposal. The EC delegate noted that PPMs were not part of the code and that the U.S. proposal involved an issue that "was not one of interpretation of the Agreement, but one of extension of its coverage." The idea of extending the code to PPMs was unacceptable to the EC, whose representative said that "he saw no usefulness in establishing a working party when the positions of the members of the Committee remained as far apart as they had always been on this subject," and that "as long as this was the

---

80. TBT/M/3, 6, and TBT/Spec/4, 7–10.
81. See TBT/M/3, 9; also see TBT/M/4, 5; and TBT committee, "Statement of the European Communities on the Coverage and Applicability of the Agreement on Technical Barriers to Trade," GATT Doc. TBT/Spec/5, July 17, 1980.
82. TBT/M/4, 5–8.
83. TBT/M/5, 10.
84. TBT committee, "The Agreement's Applicability to Processes and Production Methods—Paper by the Delegation of the United States," GATT Doc. TBT/W/24, February 3, 1981, 6.
85. For statements in support of the U.S. proposals, see TBT/M/7, 11; on their rejection by the EC, see TBT/M/6, 3; and TBT committee, "Minutes," June 12, 1981, GATT Doc. TBT/M/7, August 5, 1981, 12.

case, his delegation therefore opposed the establishment of a working party to discuss PPMs."[86] No working party on PPMs was ever established. All that the United States could obtain was a TBT committee statement in October 1983 that "the Parties agree to cooperate in the process of dispute settlement" in instances covered by Article 14:2.5.[87]

This failure came back to hamper U.S.-EC relations at the end of the period under review. In March 1987 the U.S. representative complained that revised EC certification rules—adopted in December 1985 and then scheduled for implementation in January 1988—concerning the use of hormones in animals raised for meat products "would create an unnecessary obstacle to international trade that would nullify or impair benefits accruing to the United States under the Agreement."[88] The United States also charged that the EC had intended to circumvent the TBT code since it had relied on PPMs in the directive. The U.S. delegate reported that the two partners had had bilateral consultations in February, that these had been unsuccessful, and that the United States therefore requested a committee investigation.[89] The EC representative suggested that bilateral talks continue but also made it clear that, should these fail, the EC would not accept TBT committee jurisdiction over the case.[90]

The bilateral discussions did not resolve the dispute. At two special committee meetings in July and August 1987, the United States requested the formation of a group of experts in the field, as provided for in Article 14:9 of the TBT code; this the EC refused. The EC proposed instead that the committee establish an informal ad hoc group on PPMs; this the United States declined. The United States then invoked Article 301 of the U.S. trade law on unfair practices and positioned itself to impose trade restrictions in response to the implementation of the Animal Hormone Directive. The EC and the United States then agreed that the former would delay implementation until 1989 while the latter would rescind its 301 sanctions, and that the two sides would continue negotiations. These discussions were unsuccessful. In January 1989 the EC banned U.S. meat imports valued at about $100 million; the United States retaliated by imposing tariffs of 100 percent on EC imports of comparable value; and, in spite of

86. TBT committee, "Minutes," October 29, 1982, GATT Doc. TBT/M/11, January 25, 1983, 7.
87. TBT committee, "Minutes," October 4–5, 1983, GATT Doc. TBT/M/14, November 1, 1983, 3.
88. Ibid., 11.
89. Ibid., 11–12.
90. Ibid., 12–15.

ongoing negotiations, the EC and the United States had not resolved the dispute as of mid-1989.[91]

Finally, the two major conflicts within the Committee on Government Procurement during the 1980s both involved the United States and the EC and both ended either without a code-based solution or without any solution at all.[92] At the first meeting of the GPR committee, in January 1981, the United States complained that one party excluded taxes from its estimates of contract values and that this "effectively raised the threshold value of the Agreement with respect to that Party."[93] The United States was referring to the EC, which allowed member-states to exclude value-added taxes (VAT) from their calculation of the cost of contracts issued by entities covered by the code; this omission obviously affected the determination whether those contracts exceeded SDR 150,000 and thereby came under the jurisdiction of the code. In April 1981 most signatories reported that they included national taxes in estimating the value of such contracts.[94] Austria reported in July 1981 that it had decided not to include taxes, but indicated that it would do so if this reflected the consensus of the committee.[95] Only the EC argued that the GPR code did not require the inclusion of taxes in determining the value and code applicability of government contracts.[96] In July and December 1982 the committee sought to conciliate U.S.–EC differences on the VAT issue, and in February 1983 the committee established a panel to examine the dispute.[97] The panel issued its report in January 1984 and found that the EC practice of excluding VAT "was not in conformity" with the code.[98]

---

91. Interview Materials, U.S. official, Washington, D.C., September 1, 1988; "U.S., EC Officials Fail to Resolve Dispute over Beef Hormones, Agree to Pursue Talks," *International Trade Reporter*, July 5, 1989, 859.

92. In addition to these cases, the U.S. reported in November 1984 that it had undertaken consultations with Japan: see GPR committee, "Minutes," November 14–15, 1984, GATT Doc. GPR/M/14, January 30, 1985, 12; also GPR/M/15, 17. However, as of May 1985, the only information available from GATT sources was that the United States and Japan had had two rounds of consultations and expected to undertake a third: see GPR committee, "Minutes," May 1–2, 1985, GATT Doc. GPR/M/16, June 14, 1985, 13.

93. GPR/M/1, 15.

94. GPR/M/2, 16.

95. GPR/M/3, 20–21.

96. GPR/M/2, 16–17.

97. See GPR committee, "Minutes," January 15, 1981, GATT Doc. GPR/Spec/M/1, March 11, 1981; GPR committee, "Minutes," April 9, 1981, GATT Doc. GPR/Spec/M/2, June 5, 1981; GPR committee, "Minutes," July 8–9, 1981, GATT Doc. GPR/Spec/M/3, June 29, 1981, all passim.; and GPR/M/7, 10–11.

98. See *BISD* 31, 247–56, and especially 257.

In January and February 1984 the EC challenged the panel's findings but reported in April that it was "working on a formula" by which it could accept the panel report.[99] In May the committee adopted the report without the EC indicating how it would bring itself into conformity with the panel's recommendation.[100] In June 1985 the EC offered to reduce its community-wide threshold by 6.5 percent in exchange for the right to keep VAT out of contract valuations; this proposal was rejected by the United States in September.[101] In June 1986 the United States indicated that the VAT issue was "a matter of extreme urgency" and warned that it was "considering taking alternative actions." In October the United States repeated its warning and obtained the support of Canada and the Nordics for the following U.S. proposal: if the EC did not present a solution to the VAT problem by February 1987, the GPR committee would adopt a recommendation that the EC bring its practices into conformity with the VAT panel report.[102]

Finally, the EC came forward in February 1987 with a new proposal that all its members would reduce the threshold of code-covered purchases by 13 percent, instead of the original offer of 6.5 percent. The former, according to the EC representative, "was equivalent to the average effective rate of the different VAT regimes in the Community." The United States reported to the GPR committee that it had accepted the EC offer. However, the U.S. representative also emphasized to the committee that the offer "was a compromise practical solution, and not the preferred legal solution."[103] Hence, after trying for six years to resolve the conflict, the VAT issue was brought to a conclusion, although one that could not be readily grounded in the language of the GPR code itself.

The second major attempt at dispute settlement in the GPR committee occurred in 1985. In May the United States complained that code-covered French educational authorities were planning to purchase approximately 120,000 micro- and minicomputers for a national "Computer Literacy Program" in a manner that precluded foreign bidding and contravened the code.[104] The United States requested

99. GPR committee, "Minutes," May 25–26, 1983, GATT Doc. GPR/M/Spec/8, July 27, 1983, 6–7.

100. GPR committee, "Minutes," November 3, 1983, GATT Doc. GPR/M/Spec/9, January 10, 1984.

101. GPR committee, "Minutes," September 26, 1985, GATT Doc. GPR/M/19, November 22, 1985, 9.

102. See GPR committee, "Draft Minutes," June 19, 1986, GATT Doc. GPR/Spec/53, July 2, 1986, 1. Also see GPR committee, "Minutes," October 15–16, 1986, GATT Doc. GPR/M/23, November 21, 1986, 2.

103. GPR/M/25, 14.

104. GPR/M/16, 1–2.

"the immediate establishment" of a panel or working group even though it had not, as required by the code, undertaken prior bilateral consultations with France or the EC.[105] The EC responded that the French government had not violated the code and that it would not accept establishment of a panel or working group until bilateral consultations had been completed.[106] The GPR committee agreed that bilateral consultations had to precede formation of a panel and that, after such consultations were completed, it would examine the matter again at its meeting in June.

At that time the United States reported that it had consulted with the EC but that, because the French government had already awarded the contracts to French computer firms, "dispute settlement seemed of little use since all commercial opportunities had been lost."[107] The United States thus requested that a working party be established "to examine the implications for the Agreement of the questions raised by this case."[108] The EC delegate agreed that a working party should be established but that it should not examine the French case. The working party's report, accepted by the committee in December 1985, made no mention of the computer procurement practices of any state, although it did indicate that some signatories believed that "the Code has not worked well" in the field of computer procurement and that relevant amendments of the code were under review (these are discussed in the next chapter).[109] For the time being, however, the United States could obtain no redress in its dispute with the EC over the French computer contracts of 1985.

The Code on Subsidies and Countervailing Measures

The SCM code was the least successful of the Tokyo Round agreements in the field of dispute settlement during the 1980s. During that period, only the United States and Canada were able to resolve an SCM-related conflict. During 1982 and 1983, Canada requested SCM committee conciliation regarding U.S. countervailing measures taken against Canadian softwood exports. However, Canada requested that this be deferred pending U.S.-Canadian bilateral consultation. Canada returned to the SCM committee in August 1986 and requested the formation of a panel. This occurred in October; however, in January

105. GPR/Spec/53, 1.
106. GPR/M/16, 3–4.
107. GPR/M/18, 8.
108. Ibid., 8.
109. *BISD* 32, p. 147; GPR committee, "Minutes," December 12, 1985, GATT Doc. GPR/M/20, February 17, 1986, 8; and *BISD* 33, 196–97.

1987 Canada and the United States announced that bilateral talks (permitted by the code even while a panel was conducting an investigation) had resulted in an agreement and they thus requested that the panel not go forward with its work.[110]

Successful resolution of the softwood lumber dispute was the exception for the SCM participants. From 1980 until 1987 the dispute-settlement provisions of the SCM code were invoked in three major cases involving the United States and the EC.[111] Two of the three cases ended in deadlock. In the third case a bilateral agreement was found, but, in contrast to the lumber case, both the United States and the EC indicated in announcing the agreement that their arrangement *had not* resolved differences between the two regarding their respective rights and obligations under the code.

The first of these three disputes concerned EC subsidization of exports of wheat flour. The United States pursued bilateral consultations and committee-sponsored conciliation with the EC during the autumn of 1981 and requested a panel that December.[112] The panel's report, issued in March 1983, found that the EC had used export subsidies and had increased its share of the world market for wheat flour dramatically. However, the panel reported that it was unable to apply the key provision of the code—Article 10:1, prohibiting export subsidies on agricultural products resulting in "more than an equitable share" of world markets—for the latter concept was insufficiently clear to allow it to determine whether the EC had violated it.[113] As a result, the panel reported that it could not determine whether the EC, in the language of Article 8:3 of the code, had "nullified or impaired benefits" due the United States or had caused "serious prejudice" to its trading interests.

The panel report was catastrophic from the viewpoint of the United States and a number of other SCM signatories. The United States indicated in April 1983 that the panel's failure to apply Article 10:1 meant that "the central provisions of the Code dealing with trade in

110. See *BISD* 30, 42; SCM/M/32, 30; and SCM committee, "Minutes," June 3, 1987, GATT Doc. SCM/M/34, July 24, 1987, 20.

111. In addition to the cases discussed in the text, there were two instances in which the United States invoked but did not pursue dispute-settlement proceedings against the EC (and in one case Brazil as well); one in which the U.S. and EC roles were reversed; and one in which India complained about U.S. countervail procedures. Because there is insufficient information on these cases, they are not discussed in this book.

112. SCM/M/9, 12–15; and SCM committee, "Minutes," January 23, 1980, GATT Doc. SCM/M/Spec/1, March 6, 1980.

113. SCM committee, "Minutes," April 22, 1983, GATT Doc. SCM/M/14, June 8, 1983, 2–3, 8.

primary agricultural products were inoperative."[114] Similarly, Australia found that, in light of the EC's stated opposition to negotiations to strengthen rules on agricultural export subsidies, unqualified acceptance of the panel report "would put Signatories in a difficult situation—the Code's (and the GATT's) rules would have been found to be inoperative whilst they clearly would not be in a position, at least for the foreseeable future, to make those rules more 'operational, stringent, and effective in application' as was proposed by the Panel."[115] Finally, pointing to the sharp growth of the EC market share for wheat flour reported by the panel, the Canadian delegate argued that if one "saw the changes in market share but could nevertheless not come to the conclusion that there had been a degree of inequity, then one would despair whether the relevant provisions of the Code had any meaning."[116]

In May 1983 the United States proposed that the SCM committee, on the basis of the data in the panel report, declare the EC to be in contravention of Articles 8 and 10 of the SCM code.[117] This proposal was supported only by Australia and Chile. Most signatories—including (significantly, in light of subsequent events) the EC—argued that the committee should develop a sharper definition of the concept of "more than an equitable share."[118] (This failed effort is described in the next chapter.) The SCM committee also sought to devise a formula by which it could accept the original panel report, and the chair of the committee presented a proposed "draft conclusion" in November 1983.[119] However, these talks failed, and the panel report was suspended by the spring of 1984.[120]

A similar fate awaited the committee's second major dispute-settlement effort. In December 1981 the United States requested consultations with the EC concerning the compatibility of the latter's export subsidy program for pasta products with Article 9 of the code.[121] The EC refused consultations and instead requested a special meeting of the full SCM committee in order to obtain guidance on the

114. Ibid., 2; also see SCM/M/17, 3.
115. SCM/M/14, 8.
116. Ibid., 13.
117. SCM/M/17, 3–4.
118. See SCM/M/14, 14; SCM/M/17, 5–8; and SCM committee, "Minutes," June 9–10, 1983, GATT Doc. SCM/M/18, August 16, 1983, 17–18.
119. SCM/M/Spec/9; SCM committee, "Draft Conclusion by the Committee," GATT Doc. SCM/Spec/20, November 20, 1983; and SCM committee, "Minutes," December 14, 1981, GATT Doc. SCM/M/Spec/10, January 26, 1982, all passim.
120. SCM/M/Spec/9; SCM/M/Spec/10; SCM/Spec/20; and SCM committee, "Minutes," April 22–23, 1986, GATT Doc. SCM/M/31, June 20, 1986, 22–23.
121. See SCM/Spec/8. For comparisons of the wheat flour and pasta cases, see

meaning of Article 9. At that meeting, in early March 1982, the United States and ten other signatories criticized the EC's decision not to
accept consultations with the United States as called for by Article
12:1 of the code.[122] The committee then attempted to conciliate the
dispute but failed to do so and accepted the U.S. request for a panel in
April.[123] The pasta panel's report, submitted in May 1983, marked a
departure from GATT practice insofar as it was composed of a majority (three-panelist) and minority (one-panelist) opinion. The majority
found that the EC subsidy program contravened Article 9 of the code,
which reiterates the prohibition of Article XVI:4 of the General
Agreement on export subsidies on industrial goods. The minority
panelist dissented from this finding and accepted the basic contention
of the EC that, in signing the code, it had not believed that Article 9
would prevent it from continuing a twenty-year-old practice of subsidizing the raw material (Durum wheat) used in the manufacture of
pasta products.[124]

The United States, supported by Japan, Canada, New Zealand, and
several other signatories, proposed that the SCM committee accept
the majority report and recommend that the EC end its export subsidies on pasta.[125] The SCM chair proposed that the pasta and wheat
flour reports be combined and that the committee recommend to the
EC that it bring its subsidy programs into line with the code.[126] Both
these proposals failed to attain the support of the EC. Supported by
Spain, Switzerland, Austria, and the Nordics, the EC argued that the
division of opinion within the wheat flour panel demonstrated that
the committee needed to formulate an agreed interpretation of Article 9.[127] The committee then sought without success (see Chapter 5)

William H. Boger III, "The United States–European Community Agricultural Export
Subsidies Dispute," *Law and Policy in International Business* 16, no. 1 (1984), 173–238;
and Massimo Coccia, "Settlement of Disputes in GATT under the Subsidies Code: Two
Panel Reports on E.E.C. Export Subsidies," *Georgia Journal of International and Comparative Law* 16, no. 1 (1986), 1–44.

122. See SCM/M/Spec/2, passim.

123. See SCM committee, "Minutes," May 8, 1980, GATT Doc. SCM/M/Spec/3, June
22, 1980; SCM committee, "Minutes," October 23–24, 1980, GATT Doc. SCM/M/
Spec/4, December 11, 1980; and SCM committee, "Minutes," December 11, 1980,
GATT Doc. SCM/M/Spec/5, March 3, 1981, 5.

124. SCM/M/18, 4–6. The EC noted that the United States had entered a reserva-
tion in accepting Article XVI to the effect that the United States could provide export
subsidies to textile manufacturers using domestically produced cotton.

125. Ibid., 6–11.

126. See SCM/M/31, 22–24; also see SCM/M/Spec/9; SCM/M/Spec/10; and
SCM/Spec/20.

127. SCM/M/18, 6–8, 11–12.

to clarify the meaning of Article 9 in the same special working group already working on Article 10.

These experiences alienated the United States from the SCM code and committee. The U.S. representative placed the wheat flour report on the agenda of the April 1986 meeting of the committee, after a hiatus of two years, and indicated that he had done so "to remind this Committee of its dismal record in settling disputes brought before it."[128] Similarly, the U.S. representative observed of the pasta panel report that "the lack of progress towards resolution of this dispute was one of the reasons why the argument had been made in the United States that the GATT dispute settlement procedures were worthless or inadequate."[129]

American dissatisfaction with the code was also reflected in its response to an EC complaint about amendments in 1984 to the U.S. countervailing duty law designed to permit U.S grape growers to bring countervail claims against foreign wine producers using EC-subsidized grapes. The EC requested conciliation in January 1985, and a panel in February, to investigate whether this new U.S. law conformed with the code's definition of what elements of a national "industry" may legitimately request countervail protection against subsidized imports.[130] The panel's report, submitted in March 1986, found that the U.S. law was not in conformity with the code.[131] In April 1986 the United States reported that its wine industry legislation would expire that September and that U.S. countervail legislation would then be in full conformity with the code; however, it still would refuse to permit committee adoption of the panel report. The U.S. representative explicitly linked American blockage of the wine report to the EC's treatment of the wheat and especially the pasta panel reports, saying that "after the EC had indicated that it was ready to agree to the adoption of the report on pasta, it would be time to revisit the report on wine."[132]

Finally, the United States developed during 1985 an agricultural export subsidy—the Export Enhancement Program (EEP)—that was unambiguously aimed at punishing the EC. The three-year program

128. SCM/M/31, 23.
129. Ibid., 26.
130. See SCM committee, "Minutes," January 7, 1985, GATT Doc. SCM/M/23, February 8, 1985; and SCM committee, "Minutes," February 15, 1985, GATT Doc. SCM/M/25, April 10, 1985.
131. SCM/M/30, 20–22; and SCM committee, "United States—Definition of Industry Concerning Wine and Grape Products: Report by the Panel," GATT Doc. SCM/71, March 24, 1986.
132. SCM/M/31, 28.

involved the use of government-owned stocks of agricultural goods valued at $1.5 billion as bonuses to exporters of U.S. products. In notifying the GATT about the program in April 1986, the United States made it clear that it would use the EEP to engage in "targeting," that is, "sales will be targeted on specific market opportunities, especially those that challenge competitors which subsidize their exports."[133] The United States had thus begun to employ the very policy instrument that it had earlier sought to restrict through the SCM code.

By 1986 SCM dispute-settlement efforts had broken down. Indeed, even when the United States and the EC arrived at an arrangement outside the SCM committee, this did not lead to a mitigation of the latter's deadlock. In September 1987 the two partners reached an accord on pasta. However, this agreement did not resolve the problem of code interpretation for the United States, because, quoting from the arrangement, the U.S. representative emphasized to the SCM committee that "the provisions of this Settlement are without prejudice to the legal positions of either party regarding the consistency with GATT of the use of export subsidies or export refunds for any product processed from primary agricultural products." Therefore, according to the U.S. delegate, "the Settlement was without prejudice to the legal questions at issue in the Panel Report on pasta," and the U.S. delegate strongly rejected the EC proposal to drop the pasta panel report from the SCM committee's regular agenda.[134]

Perhaps in response to a perception that the SCM code did not discipline subsidies, national governments began in the second half of the 1980s to interpret their rights under the countervailing half of the code more liberally—an example is the U.S. wine industry legislation—which engendered an increasing number of countervail disputes. In addition to the U.S. wine industry case, in October and November 1986 the EC requested committee conciliation in a dispute with Canada arising from the latter's countervailing duties on pasta products. The two parties agreed to undertake bilateral consultations but had not reported on the result of these consultations by late 1987.[135] In addition, and in a manner similar to that of the wine industry panel discussed in the text, a panel was formed in June 1987 to investigate EC complaints concerning countervailing duties imposed by Canada on EC exports of "boneless manufacturing beef." In

133. "Subsidies: Notifications Pursuant to Article XVI:1—United States—the Export Enhancement Program," GATT Doc. L/5947/Add.5, April 18, 1986, 1.
134. SCM committee, "Minutes," October 27–28, 1987, GATT Doc. SCM/M/35, December 7, 1987, 14–15.
135. SCM/M/32, 27–30.

a report issued in October, the panel ruled against Canada: the latter reported to the SCM committee that its acceptance of the panel report would be extremely difficult.[136]

Finally, the SCM committee met in May 1987 to hear U.S. concerns about Canadian countervailing duties against American exports of grain corn. Canada had imposed the duties after it had investigated the effect on Canadian corn producers of the worldwide depression on prices and the *possible* (not actual) exportation of U.S. corn to Canada resulting from U.S. corn subsidy programs. In October 1987 the Canadian representative reported that consultations had taken place with the United States but that no agreement had been reached. He also noted that Canada might reduce the duty on U.S. corn imports. The committee agreed to reexamine the dispute if requested to do so by Canada or the United States, but neither had raised the issue by the end of 1987.[137] Thus states found it increasingly necessary by the late 1980s to find solutions outside the code in regard both to subsidies and to efforts to counter them.

SUMMARY OF CODE PERFORMANCE IN TERMS OF RULE COMPLIANCE AND RULE-BASED DISPUTE SETTLEMENT

The major rule compliance and dispute-settlement events associated with the Tokyo Round NTB codes are summarized in Table 4.4. Each event is coded in terms of whether it facilitated trade or trade-policy order (+), failed to do so (−), or had a mixed effect (o). The table also notes whether the event was characterized by U.S.-EC cooperation (Δ), discord (∇), or no clear indication of either conflict or cooperation between the two partners (□).

The table underscores the finding that the Tokyo Round NTB codes varied markedly in their success in terms of compliance with rules and in terms of their need for, and capacity to undertake, successful dispute-settlement efforts. During the 1980s the codes on customs valuation and import licensing attained high levels of rule compliance and did not witness disagreements so severe that advanced-country participants invoked these codes' respective dispute-settlement provi-

---

136. See SCM/M/32, 26–27; SCM/M/34, 21–22; SCM/M/35, 10–12; SCM committee, "Minutes," December 9, 1987, GATT Doc. SCM/M/36, January 21, 1988, passim; and SCM committee, "Minutes," February 3, 1988, GATT Doc. SCM/M/37, February 26, 1988, 1–5.

137. SCM committee, "Minutes," May 5, 1987, GATT Doc. SCM/M/33, May 26, 1987, passim; and SCM/M/35, 15–16.

Table 4.4. Summary of rule-compliance and dispute-settlement experiences associated with the Tokyo Round NTB codes, 1980–87

Basis of Assessment	Customs valuation (CV)	Import licensing (LIC)	Anti-dumping practices (ADP)	Technical barriers (TBT)	Government procurement (GPR)	Subsidies/countervailing measures (SCM)
Rule compliance: transparency	(+) Prompt submission of material to GATT (+) Increased visibility of national rules to traders	(+) Prompt submission of materials to GATT (+) Increased visibility of national rules to traders	(0) Eventual submission of materials to GATT (+) Anti-dumping action reports (+) Increased visibility of national rules to governments/traders	(0) Eventual submission of materials to GATT (0) Notification of standards to GATT but limited compliance	(+) Prompt submission of materials to GATT (0) EC (Italy, Ireland) late or incomplete submission of statistics	(+) Prompt submission of countervail materials to GATT (+) Countervail action reports (−) Incomplete EC subsidy notifications
Rule compliance: other injunctions	(+) High use of Article I valuation method	(+) Licensing system not employed as additional trade barrier Japan leather quotas	(+) Australia time limits for responses (−) U.S. 8% profit rule (0) Good overall compliance but several isolated complaints	(0) Comment periods adhered to but limited compliance	(+) Japan certification rules (−) Japan recurring purchases (+) U.S. bid-times (+) U.S. contract identification (+) EC bid-times (+) EC (France) contract identification (−) EC (Italy) contract announcements	NA (see below)

Dispute-settlement activities

Category (symbol, marker)	Items
□ None required (+)	
▷ EC–U.S. specialty steel invoice (−)	□ U.S.–India almond quota practices (0)
□ EC–Canada electrical generators (−)	
□ U.S.–Japan metal baseball bats (+)	□ EC–Spain electromedical and heating equipment (+); □ U.S.–EC/others–Japan ski equipment (+); ▷ U.S.–EC PPMs (UK poultry) (−); ▷ U.S.–EC PPMs (Animal Hormone Directive) (−)
▷ EC single-tendering (−); ▷ EC below-threshold purchases (−)	▷ U.S.–EC VAT (0); ▷ U.S.–EC (French microcomputer purchases) (−)
▷ U.S.–EC wheat flour subsidies (−)	▷ U.S.–EC pasta subsidies (0); ▷ EC–U.S. wine industry countervail (−); □ EC–Canada pasta countervail (0); □ EC–Canada manufactured beef countervail (0); □ Canada–U.S. softwood countervail (+); □ Canada–U.S. grain corn countervail (0)

Key

(+) Experience suggesting code success
(−) Experience suggesting code failure
(0) Experience suggesting mixed code effectiveness
◁ Experience characterized by U.S.–EC cooperation
▷ Experience characterized by U.S.–EC discord
□ Experience characterized neither by cooperation nor by discord between U.S. and EC

sions against one another. In stark contrast, provisions of the SCM code concerned with subsidies failed to attain high levels of compliance, often resulted in sharp disagreements between the United States (and other advanced-country signatories) and the EC as to the latter's compliance with the code's transparency obligations, and consistently failed to bring about the resolution of U.S.-EC subsidy disputes. (The pasta dispute, it will be recalled, ended in a settlement in which both parties emphasized that legal issues involved in the case had not been resolved to either's satisfaction.) Compliance with the transparency rules associated with the countervail provisions of the SCM code was better than with those relating to subsidies. However, an increasing number of unresolved disputes concerning countervailing measures developed among the advanced countries at the end of the 1980s as it became increasingly clear that international discipline over subsidies was ineffective.

The codes on anti-dumping practices, technical barriers, and government procurement attained an intermediate level of rule compliance and success in their efforts to sponsor the settlement of disputes. Provisions of these codes relating to transparency attained moderate or high levels of compliance. However, with regard to other behavioral injunctions—the notification of standards in the case of the TBT code, the employment of selective tendering only in exceptional situations in the case of the GPR code—the agreements attained only limited levels of effectiveness. Similarly, dispute-settlement efforts by the TBT and GPR committees were sometimes successful, although more frequently in the former than the latter. Very significantly, Table 4.4 highlights the finding that in both the TBT and GPR committees, it was the disputes between the United States and the EC that went unresolved or, in the case of the VAT and the GPR code, reflected a solution not grounded in code rights and obligations.

These, then, are the main rule-compliance and dispute-settlement events of the Tokyo Round NTB regime during the 1980s. The analysis of these events demonstrates that the fate of the NTB codes has been in large measure a reflection of the level of U.S.-EC cooperation or discord within the relevant committee of signatories. This dependency of the NTB regime on U.S.-EC commercial diplomacy will become even more evident in the next chapter.

CHAPTER FIVE

Rule Construction in the Tokyo Round NTB Regime, 1980–1987

The Tokyo Round NTB codes may be compared not only in terms of rule compliance and dispute settlement but also in terms of the capacity of their participants to undertake *rule construction*. Rule construction is defined here as the establishment or the revision by states of commonly held understandings of the provisions of an existing accord. Rule construction is critical to states in a cooperative endeavor because it materially affects their respective rights and obligations within such an endeavor. Moreover, if states disagree about their rights and obligations within a common endeavor, the success or failure of their efforts at rule construction may determine the level and indeed the continuation of cooperation among them.

Signatories found it necessary to pursue three types of rule construction efforts in the NTB code regime during the 1980s. First, they undertook *corrective rule construction*: the closing of loopholes or the development of agreed interpretations of provisions whose original wording might otherwise foster divergences in trade practices covered by the codes and thus induce trade conflicts. Second, they engaged in *operative rule construction*: the derivation of specific guidelines from original code language that was very general, or the resolution of problems that were left unresolved by Tokyo Round negotiators, or the extension of code disciplines after the signatories had experience with an accord. Finally, signatories pursued *restorative rule construction*: the recrafting, in the wake of complaints from or disputes among partners, of a consensus on their rights and obligations under a code.

The NTB codes provided several paths by which rule construction could be pursued. First, as noted in previous chapters, each code established a committee of signatories, and much of the work reported below was performed by them. Second, each code required an annual or biennial review, offering signatories an opportunity to raise problems as to code rules. Third, each code has provisions allowing its committee to establish subsidiary bodies to perform such tasks as rule construction.[1] Finally, two of the codes—on technical barriers and government procurement—require triennial negotiations aimed at their adjustment and expansion, providing signatories another opportunity for rule construction.[2] Thus all the code committees had rule-construction options available to them; however, the discussion below demonstrates that some of the committees were better able than others to use these options effectively during the 1980s.

CORRECTIVE RULE CONSTRUCTION

The Code on Customs Valuation

Four of the six NTB codes required corrective rule construction during the 1980s: the agreements on customs valuation, anti-dumping practices, government procurement, and subsidies and countervailing measures. One example of corrective rule construction by the Committee on Customs Valuation involved anomalies in the English, French, and Spanish translations of the CV code. In November 1981 the EC reported that the English version of Article 8:1 permitted the inclusion, for purposes of customs valuation, of services "undertaken" outside the country; this, the EC observed, could mean services "contracted for" or services actually "carried out."[3] To bring the English version of the code into line with the French and Spanish versions, the signatories adopted in March 1983 an EC-proposed interpretation specifying that services "undertaken" meant those actually "carried out."[4] In addition, the CV committee learned from its Technical Committee (discussed more fully below) in November 1983 that whereas the Spanish and French translations allowed customs authorities to

1. Citation procedures for GATT materials cited in this chapter are the same as those described in Chapter 4, footnote 2 (see p. 71). For the TBT code, see Article 13:2, in *BISD* 26, 32; for the GPR code, see Article VII:2, in *BISD* 26, 48; for the SCM code, see Article 16:2, in *BISD* 26, 75; for the ADP code, see Article 14:2, in *BISD* 26, 184. For the CV code, see below, footnote 35.

2. See Article 15:9 of the TBT code, and Article IX:6(b) of the GPR code, in *BISD* 26, 27, 53–54, respectively.

3. CV committee, "Minutes," November 4–5, 1981, GATT Doc. VAL/M/3, January 29, 1982, 15.

4. VAL/M/3, para. 73; CV committee, "Minutes," May 4–5, 1982, GATT Doc. VAL/M/4, July 19, 1982, 8–9; and CV committee, "Minutes," March 3, 1983, GATT Doc. VAL/M/6, April 19, 1983, 3–4. Also see *BISD* 30, 22.

add both research and development expenses to the value of an import under Article 8, the English version permitted inclusion only of development expenses.[5] To address this problem, the signatories (with the exception of Argentina) agreed in May 1985 that only development costs should be included in the customs value of an import.[6]

Another corrective effort by the CV committee came in response to the identification by the United States of an "unexpected result" of the CV code. In May 1982 the United States reported that, in assigning a customs value to various media carrying software (such as computer tapes), states previously adhering to the Brussels Definition of Value (BDV) system had assigned value only to the media and not to the software itself. However, the code's stress on transaction values would permit and indeed mandate valuation of both the media *and* the software, resulting in higher dutiable values for software-bearing media imports under the code than under the BDV system. The United States argued that if that interpretation were to hold, the CV code would create additional barriers to trade in software, an outcome which, according to the United States, could not have been the intent of the negotiators of the code. The United States thus proposed that the signatories exclude software from the valuation of virtually all program-bearing media.[7]

The EC provided important support for the U.S. proposal on software, reporting in May 1982 that it had begun to include software in its valuation of software-bearing media imports, but noting that "this had been an issue of considerable complexity to the customs administrations."[8] In addition, when Brazil argued in March 1983 that exempting software constituted a tariff-cutting exercise not envisioned by the code, the EC replied that the U.S. proposal "was not a tariff negotiation, but an attempt to deal with an unexpected result of the new agreement and to restore the *status quo ante*," and that "making the software element dutiable raised not only conceptual problems but also considerable practicable ones for customs administrations."[9]

The American proposal received the support of twelve signatories

5. See CV committee, "Minutes," November 10–11, 1983, GATT Doc. VAL/M/8, January 18, 1984, 13–14; and CV committee, "Minutes," April 26, 1984, GATT Doc. VAL/M/9, July 13, 1984, 7–8.
6. VAL/M/9, 7–8; CV committee, "Minutes," November 9, 1984, GATT Doc. VAL/M/11, January 24, 1985, 7–8; CV committee, "Minutes," May 9–10, 1985, GATT Doc. VAL/M/13, July 5, 1985, 8–9. Also see *BISD* 32, 177.
7. VAL/M/4, 9–11; and CV committee, "Possible Amendments to the Agreement: Communication from the United States Concerning the Valuation of Computer Software," GATT Doc. VAL/W/7, April 23, 1982, 1–2.
8. VAL/M/4, 10.
9. VAL/M/6, 5.

but was actively opposed by Brazil, Argentina, and India.[10] The EC therefore came forward in November 1983 with a compromise formula encouraging signatories to exclude software programs but allowing those states wishing to include software to do so.[11] The United States embraced the EC proposal in April 1984, and it was accepted by the CV committee in September 1984.[12] The United States and the EC both later reported that their customs officials had been instructed to exclude software from valuation of media.[13] European-American collaboration did not result in a completely uniform international practice with regard to valuation of software, but at least it helped prevent a generalized international increase in duties on software as an unintended consequence of the customs code.

The Codes on Anti-Dumping Practices and Government Procurement

The major corrective rule-construction effort undertaken by the Committee on Anti-Dumping Practices was directed toward closing a loophole opened unintentionally by Article 8:4 of the ADP code and the latter's treatment of basic-price systems. Such systems involve the specification by national authorities of base prices for a class of goods; if import prices for those goods fall below the specified prices, an anti-dumping investigation is triggered; if the investigation finds material injury, the specified prices serve as the basis for the calculation of anti-dumping duties. At the February 1981 meeting of the ADP committee, the Canadian delegate, responding to U.S. and EC criticisms offered at the previous meeting of Canada's treatment of basic-price systems in its new anti-dumping legislation, argued that Article 8:4 could be interpreted in two very different ways.[14] The first was that it simply provided guidelines by which a basic-price system could be used to calculate and collect anti-dumping duties after material injury had been determined, as required by Article 3:4 of the ADP code. However, the Canadian delegate noted that Article 8:4 could also be

10. VAL/M/6, 4–8; CV committee, "Minutes," May 10, 1983, GATT Doc. VAL/M/7, July 7, 1983, 6–12; and VAL/M/8, 15–18.

11. VAL/M/8, 17–18.

12. VAL/M/9, 8–9; CV committee, "Minutes," September 24, 1984, GATT Doc. VAL/M/10, November 5, 1984, 1–4.

13. CV committee, "Application of the Decision on the Valuation of Software—Addendum—European Communities and United States," GATT Doc. VAL/11/Add.5, August 23, 1985, 1.

14. For the U.S. and EC criticisms of Canada, see ADP committee, "Minutes," October 20–22, 1980, GATT Doc. ADP/M/3, January 7, 1981, 20–21.

interpreted as specifying circumstances in which the administration of a basic-price system could result in the application of anti-dumping duties *without* prior determination of material injury. This and other problems related to basic-price systems were voiced by the United States, the EC, Japan, and several other signatories. The U.S. delegate suggested that the committee simply delete Article 8:4, and this was supported by Canada and the EC. The ADP committee chair observed that deletion "would be extremely difficult" but suggested that the committee adjourn and undertake informal consultations.[15]

When they reconvened, the signatories had before them a "Draft Understanding on Article 8:4."[16] Its first paragraph reported that the ADP committee had examined the problem of basic-price systems. The second paragraph then specified that the exclusive intent of Article 8:4 was that such systems should serve as "a device to facilitate the calculation and collection of anti-dumping duties following a full investigation." The paragraph then noted that Article 8:4 "contained ambiguities" and that it "is not essential to the effective operation of the Agreement and shall not provide the basis for any anti-dumping investigation or for imposition and collection of anti-dumping duties." The third paragraph reported that the signatories had "reviewed special anti-dumping schemes such as trigger price mechanisms and related systems" and had found that these "give cause for concern." They therefore agreed that they "shall not, in future, be adopted by Parties." The fourth paragraph specified further that such mechanisms then in force "shall be limited to their present scope," that they "shall be temporary," and, finally, that the committee "will review annually the operation of these schemes."[17]

The February draft would have imposed new controls on basic-price systems in effect and banned their further use; however, the signatories failed to adopt it. In April the chair presented a revised draft.[18] The first two paragraphs of the original draft were retained; however, replacing the third paragraph of the February draft, which committed signatories not to adopt basic-price systems, was a new paragraph stating that such systems "can only be justified in exceptional circumstances." This meant that in "exceptional circumstances" basic-price systems *could* be used. Indeed, the third paragraph said

15. ADP committee, "Minutes," February 2–3, 1981, GATT Doc. ADP/M/4, March 19, 1981, 2–6.
16. ADP/M/4, 12.
17. Ibid.
18. ADP committee, "Minutes," April 27–28, 1981, GATT Doc. ADP/M/5, June 11, 1981, 11, 16–18.

that such schemes already in force would not be extended to "new product categories" *and* that "no new scheme shall be adopted, *unless* the conditions set out in paragraphs 4–6 to [*sic*] have been met." The conditions were that the schemes be used to monitor imports and not substitute for an anti-dumping investigation; that there be good economic cause for their adoption; and that they be notified to the ADP committee prior to implementation and be reviewed annually (paragraphs 4–6). Thus the April draft marked a retreat insofar as it legitimized basic-price systems, but at least it imposed a fence around their use.

But like the February draft, the April draft failed to gain approval by the ADP committee. It was replaced by a new draft which was presented by the chair and accepted by the committee in October 1981.[19] The October draft contained the first two paragraphs from the February and April drafts. However, the October version dropped paragraphs 3–7 of the April draft. In the new third paragraph the ADP committee indicated that special monitoring schemes "are not envisioned by Article VI of the GATT or the Agreement" and that such schemes "give cause for concern in that they could be used in a manner contrary to the spirit of the Agreement." It went on to specify that "such schemes shall not be used as a substitute for initiating and carrying out anti-dumping investigations in full conformity with all provisions of the Agreement." The revised third paragraph also indicated that because monitoring schemes "may have the effect of burdening and distorting trade," it is "advisable that the effects of such monitoring schemes on international trade continue to be examined with, *inter alia*, a view to assessing the need for strengthening international discipline in this area."

During 1981 the ADP committee finally agreed on an interpretation of Article 8:4 and basic-price systems. However, the level of discipline that would prevail over such systems deteriorated with each successive draft generated by the committee over the course of the year. The February draft would have prevented the introduction of any new basic-price system; the April draft would have provided for them but only under extremely restricted circumstances; the October final draft acknowledged that new schemes might still be employed and attached only a few conditions on their introduction. Whereas the April draft would have required prior notification and annual review of new schemes, the October draft merely suggested that "the effects"

19. ADP committee, "Minutes," October 26–30, 1981, GATT Doc. ADP/M/6, January 6, 1982, 11, 15, 18.

of such schemes would be examined by the committee without indicating how or when it would do so. Finally, although the February draft had indicated that schemes already in force should be temporary, restricted in scope, and notified to and reviewed annually by the ADP committee, the April draft dropped the review provision and the October draft dropped any explicit commitment that existing schemes be limited in time or scope.

In sum, the ADP signatories had achieved corrective rule construction, but they knew they had settled for a second- (or third-) best solution.[20] This occurred in spite of U.S.-EC consensus. For example, when the U.S. representative agreed with a Canadian statement at the February 1981 meeting that Article 8:4 should be deleted, the EC representative noted that "although the proposal of the representative of the United States to delete Article 8:4 seemed very radical it merited serious consideration."[21] Similarly, when the United States introduced the April revised draft, the EC representative interjected immediately that "he could support the revised text."[22]

In the case of the Code on Government Procurement, one problem requiring corrective action involved leasing by government agencies covered by the code. In January and April 1981 the United States argued that leasing was covered by the GPR code (a view rejected by most code members) and that leasing might be used to circumvent the code.[23] The United States thus proposed that the signatories agree to submit information on leasing and to adopt a declaration by which they would commit themselves not to use leasing to circumvent the code.[24] The signatories agreed in July to share information on leasing and did so by November.[25] In addition, seven of eleven signatories offered varying degrees of support for a U.S.-proposed draft on leasing, and one (Austria) offered no comment.[26] However, the EC ve-

20. Disappointment was expressed by the Nordics, Switzerland, the United States, the EC, Japan, Austria, India, Chile, Hungary, and Yugoslavia. See ADP/M/6, 11–15.

21. ADP/M/4, 6.

22. ADP/M/5, 11.

23. See GPR committee, "Minutes," January 15, 1981, GATT Doc. GPR/M/1, March 11, 1981, 13–15; and GPR committee, "Minutes," April 9, 1981, GATT Doc. GPR/M/2, June 5, 1981, 12–14.

24. GPR/M/1, 13–15; GPR/M/2, 12. Also see "Leasing and the Agreement on Government Procurement—Statement by the United States," GATT Doc. GPR/W/2, April 1, 1981; and "Draft Joint Declaration on Leasing—Communication from the Delegation of the United States," GATT Doc. GPR/W/3, June 25, 1981.

25. GPR committee, "Minutes," May 25–26, 1983, GATT Doc. GPR/M/8, July 27, 1983, 10; and GPR committee, "Minutes," November 3, 1983, GATT Doc. GPR/M/9, January 10, 1984, 13.

26. GPR committee, "Minutes," July 8–9, 1981, GATT Doc. GPR/M/3, September 29, 1981, 16–19.

toed a joint declaration, stating in July that while it "supported the principle that there should be no circumvention" of the code, it "would not be able to subscribe to such a declaration."[27] Japan followed in the EC's wake: its representative stated in July that "Japan's position on the proposed draft declaration was similar to that of the EC."[28] Thus, although most signatories voiced support for a declaration on leasing, this corrective effort failed in the face of strong EC opposition.

A second corrective effort by the GPR committee involved the question whether signatories should notify the committee when they began bilateral consultations concerning a dispute. The United States proposed in July 1981 that the GPR committee adopt a procedure used in the GATT since 1958, that is, to notify all such bilateral consultations. The EC representative disagreed, arguing that "he did not see the need for an equivalent procedure in the context of the Government Procurement Agreement."[29] In October the United States formally proposed that bilaterals be notified and that third parties be permitted to join them if the two original parties agreed to this. The EC accepted the second part of the U.S. proposal but rejected the first. By February 1982 most signatories supported the U.S. proposal, while Japan was the only signatory to support the EC's stand against it.[30] Ten months later the committee was still in deadlock: the chair reported that whereas there was a consensus on the inclusion of third parties in consultations, "differing views and intentions remained" as to notifications of such consultations to the committee.[31] Thus no agreed rules were established by the GPR committee on notification of bilateral consultations.[32]

The Code on Subsidies and Countervailing Measures

The NTB committee that suffered the greatest failure in the field of corrective rule construction during the 1980s was that responsible for the subsidies code. Its chair organized an informal working group

27. GPR/M/2, 13, and GPR/M/3, 17.
28. GPR/M/2, 13, and GPR/M/3, 18.
29. GPR/M/3, 22.
30. See GPR committee, "Minutes," October 13–15, 1981, GATT Doc. GPR/M/4, December 17, 1981, 13–14; and GPR committee, "Minutes," February 2–3, 1982, GATT Doc. GPR/M/5, April 19, 1982, 12–14.
31. GPR committee, "Minutes," December 16, 1982, GATT Doc. GPR/M/6, February 14, 1983, 7.
32. The United States notified its bilateral consultations with the EC regarding the latter's value-added tax. See GPR/M/4, 15.

in late 1983 to grapple with the severe crisis arising from the U.S.-EC disputes described in the previous chapter. Although the informal group concentrated its energies on restorative rule construction (its efforts in that field are discussed later in the chapter), its report—SCM/53—also attempted to undertake but failed to achieve corrective rule construction after the group discovered a major loophole in Article 9 of the SCM code.

Article 9:1 specifies that signatories "shall not grant export subsidies on products other than certain primary products," and Article 9:2 directs attention to an annexed Illustrative List containing examples of such export subsidies. Paragraph (d) of that list specifies that government deliveries of inputs are restricted export subsidies if their terms are more favorable for exporters than for local-market producers and "if (in the case of products) such terms or conditions are more favorable than those commercially available on world markets to their exporters."[33] This wording contains a loophole whereby governments could subsidize manufactured exports without violating Article 9:1 of the SCM code (or Article XVI:x of the General Agreement) by delivering primary product inputs directly to export-oriented producers and by charging world (but below-national) prices. To prevent this, SCM/53 proposed that the permissive clause "shall not be taken into consideration in any determination as to the existence of a prohibited export subsidy."[34] The problem, however, was that while the United States and several other signatories wished to accept SCM/53 and its recommendation on Paragraph (d), the EC rejected both the recommendation and the entire SCM/53 exercise.

OPERATIVE RULE CONSTRUCTION

The Codes on Customs Valuation and Import Licensing

In the case of the CV code, operative rule construction during the 1980s was performed mostly by the Technical Committee on Customs Cooperation, established by the code and mandated by it to report to the CV committee.[35] By the end of 1986, as can be noted in Appendix 1, this Technical Committee had formulated, adopted, and submitted to the CV committee some fifty-seven measures providing concrete

33. SCM committee, "Uniform Interpretation and Effective Application of the Agreement—Report by the Chairman," GATT Doc. SCM/53, November 11, 1984, 2. For the Illustrative List attached to the SCM accord, see *BISD* 26, 81.
34. SCM/53, 4.
35. See Article 18:2 and Annex II of the CV code, in *BISD* 26, 128, 146–49.

guidance on at least six articles of the CV code, and by mid-1987 the Technical Committee was finalizing an additional four instruments relating to the agreement.[36]

In October 1983, it will be recalled, the signatories to the Code on Import Licensing had decided that compliance with the transparency rules and obligations of that agreement was very satisfactory. At that time the chair observed that the Preamble to the code also mandated the "fair and equitable" administration of licensing procedures and suggested that as a first step toward operationalizing those standards the signatories might exchange information on their administration and the GATT secretariat undertake case studies.[37] However, in October 1984 the chair reported that a consensus had not been reached to conduct case studies or to move on that element of the Preamble.[38]

Although the signatories failed to make progress on the mandate to operationalize standards of fairness and equity, they did move on another standard listed in the LIC Preamble, that is, the simplification of import-licensing procedures and practices. The LIC chair noted at the October 1983 meeting that the "operational criteria" for a simplified licensing system were "defined in fairly vague language." The chair thus suggested that the committee "attempt to agree on some minimum requirements" for a simplified system as called for in the code.[39] In late 1984 the chair proposed an LIC Work Program, which produced seven guidelines for key code provisions that were adopted by the LIC committee in May 1987.[40] This success resulted in some measure from U.S.-EC cooperation. Both delegations, for example, submitted responses to LIC committee requests for information, and both submitted proposals for guidelines.[41] The United States and the EC also supported each other's proposals: for example, when the EC circulated alternative formulations in June 1985 to U.S. proposals con-

---

36. See VAL/M/3, 12; VAL/M/4, 7–8; CV committee, "Minutes," November 10–11, 1982, GATT Doc. VAL/M/5, February 10, 1983, 7; VAL/M/7, 4; VAL/M/8, 11–12; VAL/M/9, 5–6; VAL/M/11, 8–9; VAL/M/13, 7–8; and CV committee, "Minutes," November 13, 1985, GATT Doc. VAL/M/14, January 17, 1986, 4.

37. LIC committee, "Minutes," October 6, 1983, GATT Doc. LIC/M/9, November 1, 1983, 4.

38. LIC committee, "Minutes," October 4, 1984, GATT Doc. LIC/M/11, December 14, 1984, 6.

39. LIC/M/9, 4.

40. LIC/M/11, 6–7. Also see LIC committee, "Part I of Work Programme: Note by the Chairman," GATT Doc. LIC/12, June 11, 1987, 1–2; and LIC committee, "Minutes," May 19, 1987, GATT Doc. LIC/M/18, June 15, 1987, 1–2.

41. See LIC committee, "Minutes," March 13, 1985, GATT Doc. LIC/M/12, April 22, 1985, 5–6; and LIC committee, "Minutes," June 12, 1985, GATT Doc. LIC/M/13, July 24, 1985, 1–4.

cerning time periods for advanced publication of quotas, the United States "welcomed the proposals made by the European Community."[42]

The Codes on Anti-Dumping, Technical Barriers, and Government Procurement

The ADP code and Article VI of the General Agreement allow for the imposition of anti-dumping duties when dumping causes material injury to a "domestic industry." Article 4:1 of the code specifies that a domestic industry consists of domestic producers of the product (or a majority of it) or a like product with the exception of those domestic firms "related" to importers of the good or foreign producers under investigation. The term "related" is left undefined, and a footnote to the code indicates that "an understanding among Parties should be developed defining the word 'related' as used in this Code."[43] Given this mandate, the ADP committee, together with members of the SCM committee facing the same task in regard to rules on countervailing measures, established a "group of experts" in May 1980 to define the term.[44] The group of experts met during late 1980 and early 1981 and successfully developed a definition of the concept in terms of inter-firm corporate control.[45]

The Committee on Technical Barriers to Trade also undertook operative rule making during the 1980s, developing between 1981 and 1987 at least thirty measures affecting the three core articles of the TBT code (see Appendix 2). For example, the TBT committee adopted eleven measures concerning notifications of technical regulations and certification rules, as required by Articles 2:5.2 and 7:3.2 of the code, as well as a common set of criteria for the selection of technical measures that had to be notified under Article 2:5. The committee also formulated rules on the concept of a "reasonable time" during which, according to Articles 2:5.4, 2:5.5, and 7:3.4, signatories were to enjoy the opportunity to comment on notified measures, and it developed a number of rules on handling of such comments. Finally, the signatories produced nine rules on Articles 10:1 and 10:2 of the code and their obligation to establish and operate "Enquiry Points" to facilitate exchange of information among signatories on their standards and comments.

---

42. LIC/M/13, 2.
43. See *BISD* 26, 175.
44. ADP committee, "Minutes," May 5–6, 1980, GATT Doc. ADP/M/2, June 18, 1980, 2–3.
45. See ADP/M/5, 19–20, and *BISD* 28, 33–34.

Much of this success in rule operationalization reflected U.S.-EC cooperation. For example, when the United States proposed in October 1982 that the TBT committee extend the time limit for comments from six weeks to sixty days, the Nordics suggested that signatories stay with the former while urging one another to "look favorably" upon requests for extensions: this idea served as the basis for the committee's acceptance of the forty-five-day/favorable-view rule noted above.[46] At the next meeting, however, the EC offered a proposal that it said took into account "previous discussions of the proposal made by the United States."[47] It was this EC proposal—a "normal time limit" of nine weeks for comments but implementation after forty-five days if no comments or requests for extensions were received—that served as the basis of the May 1983 committee extension of the comment period to sixty days. Similarly, on the issue of the handling of comments, when the EC presented a proposal on the subject in October 1983, the U.S. representative indicated that "his delegation joined other delegations which viewed the proposal favorably," and, in introducing an alternative proposal in July 1984, the U.S. representative emphasized that there were many points of convergence between the two approaches.[48] There were still differences between the two, but in October the EC agreed to a U.S. proposal to undertake case studies and to examine the issue at an upcoming meeting of Enquiry Point officials.[49] At that time, in May 1985, the Nordics proposed a compromise set of rules, which were adopted by the TBT committee in October.[50]

In the case of the Code on Government Procurement, signatories were required by Article IX:6(b) to begin negotiations three years after the code went into effect "with a view to broadening and improv-

46. TBT committee, "Minutes," October 29, 1982, GATT Doc. TBT/M/11, January 25, 1983, 3–5.
47. See TBT committee, "Minutes," February 10, 1983, GATT Doc. TBT/M/12, March 31, 1983, 6; and TBT committee, "Minutes," May 17–18, 1983, GATT Doc. TBT/M/13, July 15, 1983, 9.
48. TBT committee, "Minutes," October 4–5, 1983, GATT Doc. TBT/M/14, November 1, 1983, 2; and TBT committee, "Minutes," July 10, 1984, GATT Doc. TBT/M/16, September 25, 1984, 4. For the EC proposal, see TBT committee, "Handling of Comments on Notifications—Proposal by the European Economic Community," GATT Doc. TBT/W/64, September 28, 1983; and for the United States, see TBT committee, "Handling of Comments on Notifications—Proposal by the United States," GATT Doc. TBT/W/71, June 21, 1984.
49. TBT committee, "Minutes," October 16–17, 1984, GATT Doc. TBT/M/17, December 17, 1984, 4–5.
50. TBT committee, "Minutes," May 6–10, 1985, GATT Doc. TBT/M/19, August 1, 1985, 8–10, 14–15.

ing this Agreement" and to "explore the possibilities of expanding the coverage of this Agreement to include service contracts."[51] Preparations for the IX:6(b) negotiations commenced in December 1982 and came to a conclusion in November 1986.[52]

Many of the signatories' efforts in the portion of the IX:6(b) talks dealing with improvements were directed toward complaints about the administration of the code, and these efforts are reported in the next section. However, on one issue not directed to complaints about the code—that is, the reduction of the threshold—the United States and the EC were barely able to agree on a very modest extension of the code. The United States proposed in October 1982 that the signatories collect information on the number of new contracts that would be opened to international competition if the threshold were reduced, and in February 1984 the United States said it hoped that the IX:6(b) talks would result in a reduction of the threshold.[53] The EC resisted this U.S. initiative. For example, when the United States offered in May 1983 to restrict its data-collection proposal to contracts above SDR 100,000, the EC representative said that "his delegation attached lower priority to this question than to any other within the information-gathering programme."[54] The committee did not collect information on the threshold, and although the latter was eventually reduced by SDR 20,000 in the negotiations, this was done on a two-year experimental basis and was accepted by the EC only with reluctance.[55]

The EC's reticence to extend the GPR code was much more evident in the other two elements of the Article IX:6(b) negotiations, that is, the inclusion of additional government purchasing entities and the inclusion of service contracts within the jurisdiction of the code. To begin negotiations on the former, the signatories agreed in December 1982 to submit lists of their government entities not covered by the code over which they had "direct or substantial control."[56] They then

51. See *BISD* 26, 53–54.
52. For an overview of the negotiations, see *BISD* 30, 36; *BISD* 31, 243–46; *BISD* 32, 147–50; and *BISD* 33, 188–91 and 193–94.
53. See GPR committee, "Proposal for a Work Programme—Communication from the United States," GATT Doc. GPR/Spec/19, November 22, 1982, 2; and GPR committee, "Article IX.6.b Negotiations—Proposals by the Delegation of the United States to Improve the Code," GATT Doc. GPR/W/53, February 10, 1984, 2.
54. GPR/M/8, 10.
55. See GPR committee, "Minutes," June 19, 1985, GATT Doc. GPR/M/18, August 23, 1985, 2, and GPR committee, "Minutes," December 12, 1985, GATT Doc. GPR/M/20, February 17, 1986, 2.
56. GPR committee, "Minutes," December 15, 1982, GATT Doc. GPR/M/Spec/2, February 14, 1983, 6.

decided in February 1983 to submit data on the total value of purchases made by these entities above SDR 150,000, and agreed in November 1983 that signatories should initiate bargaining through submission by April 1984 of "request lists," that is, notifications of which of their partners' entities were of interest to them.[57]

By late 1983 nine of the twelve signatories had submitted their lists of entities not covered by the codes and six had reported the value of total purchases made by these entities. However, the EC failed to submit either type of notification.[58] The EC reported at the end of 1983 that it "hoped to be in a position to present lists and other information in the near future," but it reported a year later that it would not be able to do so.[59] Although the EC indicated that "sufficient opportunities for extension of the Agreement existed in other areas of government," the EC did not follow through with a concrete proposal in this regard.[60] The EC (and Japanese) decision not to submit entity lists gutted the broadening element of the negotiations. Only the United States, Canada, and Sweden proceeded to the next phase, the submission of request lists.[61] By the close of the negotiations in November 1986, the signatories were able to agree only "to continue work on broadening."[62]

Absence of success also characterized the third and final element of the Article IX:6(b) negotiations, that is, extending the GPR code to include services. In December 1982 the signatories agreed to submit information on the services they procured, and in February 1983 they decided to submit information on the value of such contracts.[63] In April 1984 the signatories also accepted the idea of contributing information for a study of their procurement of insurance and architectural services, and they agreed in February 1985 to begin a third study (on management consulting) and to permit interested signatories to undertake a fourth (on freight forwarding).[64] By the end of the

57. GPR committee, "Minutes," February 24, 1983, GATT Doc. GPR/M/7, April 22, 1983, 6; and GPR/M/9, 8.

58. Japan and Austria also failed to submit this information: see GPR/M/9, 11.

59. GPR/M/9, 11; and GPR committee, "Minutes," November 14–15, 1984, GATT Doc. GPR/M/14, January 30, 1985, 4.

60. See GPR/M/14, 3; also see GPR committee, "Minutes," September 19, 1984, GATT Doc. GPR/M/13, November 12, 1984, 4.

61. Others might have submitted request lists if the EC and Japan had submitted their entity lists. In April 1984 the Nordics reported that "their own preparations were underway, constrained by the fact that some of the major Parties had not yet submitted the necessary information on their non-covered entities." See GPR committee, "Minutes," April 11–12, 1984, GATT Doc. GPR/M/11, June 6, 1984, 10.

62. BISD 33, 189.

63. GPR/M/Spec/2, 7, and GPR/M/7, 7.

IX:6(b) negotiations, however, no progress had been achieved in bringing services under the code: after four years of talks, the signatories agreed only "to work toward coverage of service contracts under the Agreement" and to establish a "work programme" toward that end.[65]

A very substantial gulf was evident between the United States and the EC in these discussions on services. The United States pressed for extensive data collection by the GPR committee and promptly supplied information on its purchases; the EC, in contrast, delayed its submission of information on the types of service contracts procured by EC governments and failed to submit information on their value.[66] The United States urged the GPR committee to take on many studies of different service industries and submitted contributions to all four studies undertaken by the committee. In contrast, the EC resisted U.S. proposals to extend the number of studies beyond the two accepted by the committee in April 1984 and failed to submit information for the committee study on management consulting (although it did submit materials on the insurance and architectural studies).[67] Finally, to facilitate completion of the services negotiations by mid-1986 (the committee's original target date had been mid-1985), the Nordics proposed in September 1985 to establish a working group similar to that then finalizing code improvements.[68] The United States and several other code members welcomed the proposal; the EC indicated that it "was not yet in a position to decide on the establishment of a separate working group," and the proposal died.[69]

64. See GPR/M/Spec/2, 6–7; GPR/M/11, 14–15; and GPR committee, "Minutes," February 13, 1985, GATT Doc. GPR/M/15, April 22, 1985, para. 81.

65. *BISD* 33, 189.

66. On the U.S. interest in services, see GPR/Spec/19, 1; GPR/M/Spec/2, 6–7; GPR/M/9, 8; and GPR/M/18, 4. The United States, Canada, and Sweden submitted data on their types of purchases of services by February 1983, and six other signatories did so by May 1983; the EC did not until November 1984: see GPR/M/7, 6–7; GPR/M/8, 9; GPR/M/14, 3; and GPR committee, "Article IX.6.b Negotiations—List of Services Purchased by Central Governments: Communication from the Delegation of the European Communities," GATT Doc. GPR/W/60, September 26, 1984. The United States submitted data by May 1983 on the value of such purchases; the EC delegate reported in September 1985 that it had encountered problems in collecting data from member-states: see GPR/M/8, 9–10; GPR/M/9, 12; GPR/M/14, 3; and GPR committee, "Minutes," September 26, 1985, GATT Doc. GPR/M/19, November 22, 1985, 3. Discussions of services then ended in the committee: see GPR/M/20, 2–5; and GPR committee, "Minutes," February 27, 1986, GATT Doc. GPR/M/21, April 28, 1986, 1–2.

67. GPR/M/13, 3–5; GPR committee, "Minutes," June 20, 1984, GATT Doc. GPR/M/12, August 31, 1984, 4; GPR/M/18, 3; GPR/M/19, 2; and GPR/M/20, 3.

68. See GPR/M/19, 3–4.

69. The EC was alone in its unwillingness to move on the idea: see GPR/M/19, 3.

Thus, although U.S.-EC cooperation facilitated operative rule construction concerning code improvements, the reluctance of the EC to broaden the code or to bring service contracts under its jurisdiction doomed the latter two elements of the IX:6(b) negotiations.

The last effort at operative rule construction in the GPR committee was initiated by Switzerland in November 1983. Its delegate proposed that while the GATT exempts public-sector firms from many of its rules, the GPR code participants might "have a reciprocal interest in utilizing [their] influence for introducing and respecting purely commercial considerations concerning the procurement of those enterprises" under their jurisdiction. Because Article I:1 of the code specifies that the agreement covers "entities under the direct *or substantial* control of Parties," the Swiss representative argued that "it should be possible likewise to include nationalized enterprises in Annex I [listing code-covered entities] of the Agreement." As a first step, the Swiss representative "suggested that information be collected from each Party."[70]

The U.S. representative immediately endorsed the Swiss initiative, suggesting in November that the information-gathering proposal "was useful" and emphasizing in February 1984 that the United States "supported its adoption."[71] In contrast, the EC representative opposed the Swiss proposal even to collect information, arguing that, under EC law, such firms had to act as purely private agents and that "to require EC member States to impose the conditions of the Agreement on these enterprises would be seen as interference in their operations."[72] Further, when the Swiss representative introduced a proposed definition of "nationalized enterprises" that might come under the scope of Article I:1, the EC delegate said that its own firms were free of governmental supervision and therefore he "could not see how the activities of such enterprises could be handled under the Agreement."[73] The Swiss delegate tried once more to raise the issue, supported in part by Canada and again fully by the United States, at the November 1984 GPR meeting; the EC, supported by Austria and the Nordics, resisted any discussion of the matter. The Swiss representative finally acknowledged that "priority seemed now rather to be given to the [IX:6(b)] negotiations," and "he suggested to revert to the matter later, after the negotiations."[74]

70. GPR/M/9, 16, emphasis added.
71. Ibid.; and GPR committee, "Minutes," February 1–2, 1984, GATT Doc. GPR/M/10, March 28, 1984, 13.
72. GPR/M/10, 13.
73. GPR/M/11, 12–13.
74. GPR/M/14, 14.

The Code on Subsidies and Countervailing Measures

The Committee on Subsidies and Countervailing Measures established two groups of experts in May 1980 to address problems in provisions of the SCM code relating to countervailing measures not resolved by the close of the Tokyo Round in 1979.[75] The first group, in the joint effort with the ADP committee discussed above, formulated guidelines in 1981 defining the concept of "related" enterprises to be used in defining the range of domestic producers on whom the impact of foreign subsidies should be assessed.[76] The task of the second group was to develop valuation methods for subsidies so that countervailing duties applied by importing countries were not, in the language of Article 4:2, "in excess of the amount of the subsidy found to exist."[77] This group formulated two sets of guidelines on this subject, and these were accepted by the SCM committee in November 1984 and October 1985.[78] The group then proposed rules, adopted by the SCM committee in April 1985, on the amortization and depreciation of subsidies.[79] Finally, at the April meeting the group submitted draft guidelines on calculating the amount of a subsidy. The SCM chair recommended adoption of the guidelines in September; however, the U.S. delegation requested that the committee delay adoption until the April 1986 meeting.[80] At that time the United States again reported that it "was not in a position to agree to adoption."[81] By late 1986 the group's work in this area had not progressed as a result of U.S. reticence to accept new rules on countervailing measures.[82]

75. SCM committee "Minutes," May 8, 1980, GATT Doc. SCM/M/3, June 27, 1980, 12–14.

76. See *BISD* 26, 65–66. For the guidelines, see SCM committee, "Minutes," April 29, 1981, GATT Doc. SCM/M/6, June 24, 1981, 6 and Annex; and SCM committee, "Minutes," October 28–30, 1981, GATT Doc. SCM/M/9, December 22, 1981, 8–9.

77. See *BISD* 26, 61.

78. See SCM committee, "Minutes," May 10, 1984, GATT Doc. SCM/M/20, July 25, 1984, 12; SCM committee, "Minutes," November 1–2, 1984, GATT Doc. SCM/M/21, December 6, 1984, 9–10. For the "Guidelines in the Determination of Substitution Drawback Systems as Export Subsidies," see *BISD* 31, 158, 257–58. Similar rules are contained in the "Guidelines on Physical Incorporation," in *BISD* 32, 156–57.

79. See SCM committee, "Minutes," April 25, 1985, GATT Doc. SCM/M/27, July 25, 1985, 18; SCM committee, "Minutes," October 23–24, 1985, GATT Doc. SCM/M/30, January 10, 1986, 14; and, for the "Guidelines on Amortization and Depreciation," see *BISD* 32, 154–56.

80. SCM/M/30, 14.

81. SCM committee, "Minutes," April 22–23, 1986, GATT Doc. SCM/M/31, June 20, 1986, 18.

82. SCM/M/31, 18; also see *BISD* 33, 200–201.

Restorative Rule Construction

The Codes on Customs Valuation and Import Licensing

Each of the NTB committees was challenged by this most critical type of rule-making activity during the 1980s. In May 1982, for example, the EC reminded its fellow participants in the customs committee that it had argued during the Tokyo Round negotiations that interest charges on deferred payments for an imported good should not be included in the valuation of the good by customs officials. The EC noted that this question had not been resolved during the Tokyo Round and that it wished to renew discussions on the issue.[83] The EC proposed an agreed interpretation excluding interest charges from the value of imported goods; this was accepted with minor amendments by the CV committee in April 1984.[84]

EC concerns also triggered an effort at restorative rule construction in the Committee on Import Licensing. As noted in the previous chapter, the EC voiced complaints during 1984–85 about the U.S. Specialty Steel Summary Invoice (SSSI) and the latter's possible contravention of Article 1:1 of the LIC code, and requested in June 1985 that the committee clarify the terms of Article 1:1 as to what constituted an import-licensing procedure. In November 1985 the EC submitted a proposal on Article 1:1 in the context of the LIC Work Program.[85] According to the EC, its proposed interpretation would "make it clear that any administrative procedures used for the management of quantitative import restrictions should be regarded as licensing procedures which were subject to the provisions [of the code], irrespective of the specific terminology used to qualify such procedures."[86] The United States, New Zealand, and Australia declined to begin an analysis of the issue, and the EC accepted an Australian recommendation that discussion be deferred until the next formal meeting of the LIC committee.[87] At that time, in March 1986, the EC suggested another approach to defining the scope of the article, but the United States and Australia remained unpersuaded that the issue required attention; Canada and Hong Kong proposed, and the committee agreed, that the matter be discussed further in informal meetings.[88] Finally, in October 1987, as the LIC Work Program

83. VAL/M/4, 10.
84. VAL/M/9, 8–9.
85. See LIC/M/13, 3; and LIC committee, "Minutes," October 9, 1985, GATT Doc. LIC/M/14/Rev.1, November 19, 1985, 6.
86. LIC/M/14/Rev.1, 6.
87. Ibid., 16.
88. LIC committee, "Minutes," March 11, 1986, GATT Doc. LIC/M/15, May 7, 1986, 5.

was winding down, and in response to another EC statement of its concern about the problem of Article 1:1, the U.S. representative "supported a review of other areas in the Articles of the Agreement which could require clarification" and went on to say that "specifically, she noted the proposal by the EC to review Article 1:1."[89]

The Codes on Anti-Dumping, Technical Barriers, and Government Procurement

Compliance with the anti-dumping code, it will be recalled, was quite good during the 1980s; however, signatories had raised many concerns during 1981 and especially 1982. In response, the ADP committee established an ad hoc group in October of that year to develop agreed interpretations of the disputed provisions of the code.[90] In November 1983 the group submitted, and the ADP committee adopted, three sets of recommendations. The first provided thirteen rules striking a balance between transparency and confidentiality in anti-dumping investigations (both are required by the code); the second specified three rules for on-the-spot visits under Article 6:5; and the third provided an additional seven days for responses to anti-dumping questionnaires.[91] The ADP committee then adopted eight additional rules in May 1984 on the use, under Article 6:8, of the "best information available" when firms under investigation fail to provide information, and in October 1985 the committee adopted four other rules to be used by investigating authorities under Article 3:6 in determining whether dumping had caused a "threat of material injury."[92] Finally, in October 1987 the chair of the group reported that although the group "had not yet reached a consensus" on rules for price undertakings (foreseen in Article 7 of the code), "some constructive proposals had been made" at a recent meeting.[93]

Hence the ADP group formulated or made progress toward constructing rules that addressed a variety of concerns of signatories. However, several efforts by the group to undertake restorative rule

89. See LIC committee, "Minutes," October 9, 1987, GATT Doc. LIC/M/20, November 18, 1987, 3–4.

90. ADP committee, "Minutes," October 25–26, 1982, GATT Doc. ADP/M/9, December 22, 1982, 15–16.

91. ADP committee, "Minutes," November 15, 1983, GATT Doc. ADP/M/11, February 7, 1984, 12; and *BISD* 30, 24–30.

92. See *BISD* 31, 283–84; ADP committee, "Minutes," May 8, 1984, GATT Doc. ADP/M/12, July 25, 1984, 12; ADP committee, "Minutes," October 21–24, 1985, GATT Doc. ADP/M/16, January 9, 1986, 3; and *BISD* 32, 182–84.

93. ADP committee, "Minutes," October 26–27, 1988, GATT Doc. ADP/M/20, January 15, 1988, 16.

making did not succeed. For example, though the ad hoc group submitted a recommendation on input dumping to the committee in October 1985, the United States and Hong Kong declined to accept it as of October 1987.[94] In addition, the ad hoc group sought to formulate rules in 1985 and 1986 on constructed value (the U.S. rule of 8 percent assumed profit), and the problem of definition of sale (raised in the EC-Canada electrical generator dispute), but the group's chair reported in June 1987 that the group had not achieved a consensus on either issue.[95]

The TBT committee also experienced mixed success in its efforts at restorative rule construction. One area in which the committee did achieve progress was in developing a mechanism to bring about better compliance with the notification rules of the code. It will be recalled that notifications were not provided by all signatories during the 1980s and that compliance with committee-recommended comment periods was incomplete. To meet these problems, the committee adopted a decision in May 1985 requiring all signatories to submit information "on any procedures established, or other efforts made, on the national level in order to gather information on proposed technical regulations," and the committee "requested Parties who had not yet done so to provide information on the procedures followed in their respective countries to determine which draft technical regulations should be notified."[96] In addition, a Nordic-sponsored proposal adopted by the TBT committee in May 1986 required agencies responsible for notifications to exchange information on their internal procedures for selecting technical measures for notification.[97] This, in turn, was toughened by a committee decision in October 1987 that the information required of all signatories on their notification procedures "should be compiled and circulated in a document."[98]

This Nordic-led effort to increase notifications was supported by the United States and not opposed by the EC. At the May 1986 TBT committee meeting, for example, the U.S. representative argued that

94. ADP committee, "Minutes," October 26–28, 1987, GATT Doc. ADP/M/20, January 15, 1988, 16–17.
95. See ADP committee, "Minutes," April 24, 1985, GATT Doc. ADP/M/15, July 26, 1985, 14; ADP committee, "Minutes," April 23, 1986, GATT Doc. ADP/M/17, June 13, 1986, 9; and ADP committee, "Minutes," June 5, 1987, GATT Doc. ADP/M/19, August 7, 1987, 21.
96. TBT/M/19, 9.
97. TBT committee, "Minutes," May 28, 1986, GATT Doc. TBT/M/22, August 21, 1986, 2–3.
98. TBT committee, "Minutes," October 12–14, 1987, GATT Doc. TBT/M/26, February 2, 1988, 5.

the Nordic proposal "would be a constructive way of identifying the relevant problems within Parties." The EC representative expressed "doubts as to the usefulness of the Nordic proposal," suggesting "Parties could achieve the results sought by the Nordic proposal in a more direct way, if they raised complaints regarding problems of notifications by other Parties" at TBT meetings. Nonetheless, he stressed that "his authorities would supply information" on the Community's internal notification mechanisms.[99]

However, on another issue—processing and production methods (PPMs)—there was continuing European-American discord. It will be recalled that the United States, in preparation for the TBT three-year review, proposed that the committee establish a working party to formulate rules "to enable signatories to complain about PPMs under the Agreement."[100] The U.S. proposal was supported by seven signatories, and Japan indicated it would accept a committee consensus for a working party. However, the EC refused to allow formation of such a group, and no improvement was attained in the capacity of signatories to bring complaints about PPMs to the TBT committee.

Another U.S. proposal during the TBT three-year review was that, in light of the 1981 revision of the GATT inventory of non-tariff measures, the signatories place those relating to technical barriers "under the jurisdiction of the Committee."[101] This proposal was resisted by several delegations, including the EC, which noted that it "was hesitant about bringing the matter before the Committee in a general and systematic way."[102] The United States achieved only a committee agreement in May 1985 to circulate the technical barriers section of the NTM inventory, and even then the EC reiterated its expectation that "the Committee would not discuss or take action on the standards notifications in the inventory, and the circulation of the notifications would merely serve as an incentive for bilateral discussions."[103] The United States also suggested that the three-year review examine service-sector technical barriers to trade. The EC indicated that it "reserved its position" regarding the U.S. proposal, and the issue was dropped from the committee's discussions.[104]

---

99. For both the U.S. and EC statements, see TBT/M/22, 3.

100. TBT committee, "Minutes," May 26–27, 1982, GATT Doc. TBT/M/10, July 26, 1982, 5.

101. Ibid., 5, and TBT/M/11, 6.

102. TBT/M/11, 6.

103. See TBT/M/12, 3; TBT committee, "Minutes," February 26, 1985, GATT Doc. TBT/M/18, April 19, 1985, 8–9; and TBT/M/19, 8.

104. TBT/M/10, 5–6.

The key area in which the TBT committee failed to achieve restorative rule construction concerned Article 5:2 and its mandate that signatories accept one another's test results "whenever possible" in determining whether imports meet national regulations and standards.[105] In February 1985 the U.S. delegation complained that "most Parties to the Standards Code do not accept foreign-generated test data for the majority of products" and that its "exporters are finding that requirements that their product be retested in every market in which they wish to sell can be extremely expensive, time consuming, and trade-inhibiting." The United States thus proposed that "an arrangement could be established under the Standards Code whereby signatories are obligated to accept test data for particular products on a mutually agreed basis." Such an arrangement, the United States suggested, "could proceed on a sector-by-sector basis" and might include agreements to grant "type-approvals" for imports.[106]

Nine signatories—including Japan, Canada, Switzerland, and the Nordic states—"agreed that discussions in the Committee on the subject of testing and inspection would be useful."[107] The EC agreed to examine the question but warned that it would be "difficult to reach binding commitments in this area."[108] When the United States reiterated its proposal in October 1985, the EC said it "could not share the approach of the United States" since that approach "involved the creation of a comprehensive regulatory mechanism."[109] As an alternative, the EC suggested that the TBT committee "encourage the progress of work" on testing and inspection in the International Organization for Standardization (ISO), the International Electro-technical Commission (IEC), and the International Laboratories Accreditation Conference (ILAC); that it "promote the conclusion" of *bilateral* testing agreements; and that it "give an international political status" to these bilateral agreements.[110] In October 1986 the TBT signatories went only so far as to accept a Nordic proposal that their testing and inspection activities "should be based on the principles and rules" presented in ISO/IEC-prepared guides, and, taking one additional small step, the committee accepted a U.S. proposal the following June

105. See *BISD* 26, 13–14.
106. TBT committee, "Testing and Type Approval—Note by the Delegation of the United States," GATT Doc. TBT/W/79, March 6, 1985, 1–2.
107. See TBT/M/18, 7.
108. Ibid., 7.
109. See TBT committee, "Minutes," October 31–November 1, 1985, GATT Doc. TBT/M/20, February 6, 1986, 8.
110. Ibid., 9.

that signatories should report on their efforts to promote national use of these guides.[111]

Two additional problems raised by the United States also did not translate into successful restorative rule making. In October 1986 the United States submitted proposals designed to increase the transparency of bilateral standards-related agreements among signatories and, reflecting U.S. concerns raised at the second three-year TBT review, the standards-related activities of regional organizations to which signatories were members. Both these proposals were rejected by the EC.[112]

The last two instances of failure in the TBT committee to achieve restorative rule construction came in the wake of problems raised by the EC in October 1985 at the second three-year review of the code. At that time the EC proposed that the committee extend the code more forcefully to local government bodies, and in particular to require the latter to notify technical regulations and certification rules. In addition, the EC proposed that the TBT committee develop a "code of good practice" for nongovernmental bodies (NGBs) in the standards issue-area and that signatories induce NGBs within their territories to subscribe to the proposed code.[113] The United States sharply attacked both proposals in March 1986. For example, in response to the EC argument that trends toward governmental decentralization required extension of the code to local governments, the United States suggested that decentralization was under way in the EC more than elsewhere, and "did not therefore call for special action by other Parties."[114] Similarly, with regard to nongovernmental bodies, the U.S. representative stated flatly that "the private and independent status of these NGBs should be recognized" and that "in his country, there was no question of widening the control of the federal government authorities on private standards bodies."[115] Although the EC reiterated its proposal to apply the TBT code to local government

111. See TBT committee, "Minutes," October 13–14, 1986, GATT Doc. TBT/M/23, December 12, 1986, 6; and TBT committee, "Minutes," June 22, 1987, GATT Doc. TBT/M/25, September 23, 1987, 3.

112. TBT/M/23, 6–7; and TBT committee, "Minutes," March 9–10, 1987, GATT Doc. TBT/M/24, June 3, 1987, 7–8.

113. See TBT/M/20, 9. The EC first raised the issue in 1981: see TBT committee, "Minutes," June 12, 1981, GATT Doc. TBT/M/7, August 5, 1981, 13; and TBT committee, "Minutes," October 20–22, 1981, GATT Doc. TBT/M/8, January 7, 1982, 10.

114. TBT committee, "Minutes," March 6–7, 1986, GATT Doc. TBT/M/21, May 6, 1986, 9.

115. Ibid., 21.

bodies in May 1986, neither this proposal nor the one on private bodies made any headway through the end of 1987.[116]

Much of the restorative rule-making efforts of the government procurement committee was based on the mandate in Article IX:6(b) of the GPR agreement that participants would attempt to improve the agreement three years after it went into force. Discussion within the GPR committee during 1982–84 and an informal working group during 1985–86 resulted in a package of twenty-six code revisions and amendments, adopted by the GPR committee in November 1986 and summarized in Appendix 3.[117] Many of these changes sought to address signatories' complaints about the operation of the agreement. For example, it will be recalled that several signatories complained that the GPR code did not cover leasing. The GPR committee failed to close this potential loophole in 1981, but it succeeded in doing so with the November 1986 improvements package.[118] Similarly, several signatories had criticized Japan's practice of qualifying suppliers only once a year. Japan agreed in December 1982 to qualify foreign suppliers on a year-round basis but warned that this revised practice would not be "indefinite."[119] However, one element of the November 1986 package specified that "suppliers may apply for qualification at any time."

In addition, the United States and the EC had criticized each other's delivery-times and bid-deadlines as not taking into account the special difficulties of foreign suppliers and the frequent delays that often characterize the publication of contract opportunities. In response, revisions of Article V stipulated that entities covered by the code should, in their purchasing practices, take into account the impact on foreign bidders of their delivery-time requirements and of delays in contract publication. Moreover, and apparently in response to the U.S.-France computer dispute, another revision of Article V indicated that "option clauses shall not be used in a manner which circumvents the provisions of the Agreement." Finally, to begin to limit purchases made on the basis of single tendering or code derogations, which were listed in the code's Annex, one revision of Article VI would require post-award justification of the use of single tendering; another would require signatories to notify the GATT within thirty days of a contract made under a derogation; and a third would require that such purchases be included in annual GPR statistical reports.

116. TBT/M/22, 6–7.
117. See GPR/M/24, 3, 13–24; *BISD* 33, 190; and GATT, *Protocol Amending the Agreement on Government Procurement* (Geneva, 1987).
118. See Article I:1 in *BISD* 26, 34.
119. GPR/M/6, 4.

In large measure, this success in revising the GPR code was a reflection of a U.S.-EC consensus on the need to restore elements of the code. Both delegations, for example, submitted proposals with specific language to strengthen the code.[120] In addition, each delegation signaled early in the negotiations that it accepted elements of the other's proposals. In April 1984, for example, the United States expressed approval of EC (and Nordic) ideas to increase information contained in contract announcements and to require more detailed statistics submitted to the GPR committee. The EC, for its part, agreed with U.S. (and Nordic) proposals to extend bid-deadlines, to liberalize qualification requirements, and to collect information on derogations and single-tendering purchases.[121] Overall, then, the IX:6(b) negotiations achieved substantial restorative rule construction and were marked by U.S.-EC cooperation.

The Subsidies Portion of the SCM Code

The last two efforts at restorative rule construction to be examined in this chapter involved the subsidies code. As noted in Chapter 4, several code members were concerned during 1981 and 1982 that subsidy notifications were incomplete or had not been submitted at all. The United States and others suggested in April 1983 that the SCM committee revise the GATT questionnaire for subsidy notifications. In response, the SCM chair instructed the GATT secretariat to prepare a study (the result was a report, SCM/49), and in December 1984 the chair obtained committee agreement to establish a group of experts to develop "draft guidelines on notifications" based on the secretariat's study and commentaries on it offered by signatories.[122]

The group of experts, including representatives of the United States, the EC, the Nordics, Canada, Japan, and Chile, missed its first deadline—October 1985—at which time the chair said that he expected the group to complete its task by April 1986.[123] At the April

120. For U.S. proposals, see GPR/Spec/19; GPR/W/53; and GPR/M/13, 2. For the EC, see GPR committee, "Article IX.6.b Negotiations—Proposals by the European Community for Improvement of the Agreement," GATT Doc. GPR/W/54, passim; GPR/M/13, 2; and GPR/M/14, 2.

121. GPR/M/11, 7–8; also see GPR/M/10, 7.

122. See SCM committee, "Minutes," April 21, 1983, GATT Doc. SCM/M/16, July 25, 1983, 8–9; SCM committee, "Minutes," November 17, 1983, GATT Doc. SCM/M/19, February 21, 1984, 7; SCM/M/20, 8; SCM/M/21, 6; and SCM committee "Minutes," December 4–5, 1984, GATT Doc. SCM/M/24, February 14, 1985, 21–22.

123. SCM/M/27, 6; and SCM/M/30, 11.

meeting the SCM committee chair reported not that the group had completed its task, but that he had decided to disband it. The chair explained that "the group had been unable to make any progress" to improve notifications and that in fact "some suggestions made in the group even seemed to undermine the existing obligations with regard to the notification of subsidies as confirmed by various decisions by the CONTRACTING PARTIES." Hence the chair said he "had to conclude that, for the time being, it would not be useful to continue the work of this group" and that "the group could resume its work when there would be a clear political will to strengthen the rules relating to notification of subsidies."[124]

The United States supported the work of the informal group, but the EC opposed it. The United States proposed several ways to strengthen the subsidy questionnaire and notification guidelines.[125] In contrast, the EC argued in April 1983 that "it seemed that [it] would not be appropriate at the present time to try to restructure the questionnaire."[126] Moreover, the EC argued that any effort to improve the questionnaire would require taking into account the results of the group of experts on subsidy calculations *and* the GATT Committee on Trade in Agriculture.[127] Also, in reaction to the group's effort to enhance the transparency of subsidies, the EC representative said that "he was against the notion of transparency for the sake of transparency and would prefer a more workable approach where signatories need not be compelled to submit voluminous and useless notifications."[128] Given this EC opposition, the SCM committee failed to strengthen its subsidy notification rules.

A similar fate awaited the SCM committee after the wheat flour and pasta panel reports left the committee in stalemate.[129] To resolve the crisis, the chair established a group (which at first did not include either the United States or the EC).[130] Its initial proposal was that the SCM signatories recommend to the EC that it reduce subsidies for wheat flour and pasta and undertake an effort to clarify Articles 9 and 10. This proposal was submitted to the committee in November

124. See SCM/M/31, 13.
125. See SCM committee, "Notifications under Article XVI.1—Addendum," GATT Doc. SCM/49/Add.4, June 25, 1984.
126. SCM/M/16, 8.
127. SCM/49/Add.1, 2; also see SCM/M/24, 20.
128. SCM/M/24, 20; also see SCM committee, "Minutes," January 7, 1985, GATT Doc. SCM/M/23, February 8, 1985, 2.
129. For overviews, see *BISD* 32, 162–63; and *BISD* 33, 202–3.
130. SCM committee, "Minutes," June 9–10, 1983, GATT Doc. SCM/M/18, August 16, 1983, 20.

but was rejected by the EC.[131] The group, joined by the United States and, at least at the beginning of 1984, the EC, then tried to develop an agreed interpretation of Articles 8, 9, and 10; its report, SCM/53, was presented to the committee in December 1984.[132]

SCM/53 undertook first to resuscitate Articles 8 and 10 after the wheat flour case. The U.S. position in the case was that the EC had caused market displacement in violation of Article 10:2(a) and had thus caused serious prejudice to U.S. interests in violation of Article 8:4(c).[133] The United States also argued that the EC subsidies had caused serious prejudice under the terms of Article 8:3(c) of the code and Article XVI:1 of the General Agreement by creating a "permanent source of uncertainty in world flour markets."[134] The EC countered that the latter effect had no basis in the code for primary products and that primary-product cases had to be assessed exclusively under Article 10.[135] The panel, finding "a lack of clarity in the provisions of Article 8" with respect to primary products, thus searched for harm only in terms of Article 10.[136]

The panel then applied only one of three possible tests to determine whether the EC had violated Article 10. That test was market displacement, which Article 10:2(a) actually specifies is one, but not the only, definitive test of "more than an equitable share." The panel determined that market displacement of individual markets "was not evident," although it also found that "it could not rule out the possibility" that EC subsidies had reduced U.S. foreign sales.[137] Regarding

131. See SCM committee, "Minutes," November 18, 1983, GATT Doc. SCM/M/Spec/9, January 16, 1984, 1–2; and SCM committee, "Draft Conclusion by the Committee," GATT Doc. SCM/Spec/20, November 16, 1983. The present discussion relies heavily on GATT Interview no. 1, Geneva, August 12, 1986.

132. See SCM committee, "Minutes," May 10, 1984, GATT Doc. SCM/M/Spec/10, June 18, 1984, 1–2; also GATT Interview no. 1, cited above. In addition to SCM/53, see SCM committee, "Uniform Interpretation and Effective Application of the Agreement—Statement by the Chairman at the Meeting of 5 December 1984," GATT Doc. SCM/56, December 13, 1984; and SCM/M/24, 24–25.

133. SCM committee, "European Economic Community—Subsidies on Export of Wheat Flour: Report of the Panel," GATT Doc. SCM/42, March 21, 1983, 37.

134. SCM/42, 20–21.

135. Ibid., 21–22. The EC could make this argument on the grounds that a footnote to Article 8:4(c) indicates that, in regard to assessments of whether adverse effects had developed as a result of market displacement in third countries, "The problem of third country markets so far as certain primary products are concerned is dealt with exclusively under Article 10 below." (The footnote is no. 5 in *BISD* 26, 68, and is referred to by SCM/53 as footnote no. 28.)

136. Ibid., 39. The panel also noted that the United States itself had based its claim about adverse effects under Article 8:4(c) primarily on the charge that the EC had violated Article 10.

137. Ibid., 37.

the second possible test—price undercutting, noted in Article 10:3—the panel said that "there was not sufficient ground to reach a definite conclusion." Finally, with respect to the third and most general test—"more than an equitable share," stated in Article 10:1—the panel said that "it was unable to conclude" whether such a market share had been achieved by the EC in large part because of the difficulty in applying the concept itself.[138]

The wheat panel had said that Article 8 did not pertain to agriculture and that it could not apply Article 10. SCM/53 thus proposed that the signatories agree that Article 8 covers both non-primary and primary products; that its list of adverse effects is not exhaustive; that adverse effects other than market displacement may result from export subsidies on primary products; and, finally, that such adverse effects may cause "serious prejudice" to the interests of signatories.[139] These points, if accepted, would have allowed code signatories to seek the protection of Article 8 in agricultural cases and, if necessary, to bypass Article 10. SCM/53 also sought to strengthen the latter, offering guidelines making it less likely that difficulties associated with "special factors" and specification of "normal market conditions" would prevent panels from applying the test of "more than an equitable share."[140]

Regarding Article 9, SCM/53 observed that primary-product export subsidies permitted by Article 10 benefited foreign users of inputs thus subsidized, making it "economically unsound" not to provide similar support to domestic input users. Yet the impact of Article 9 would be "radically reduced," SCM/53 argued, if subsidization of the primary-product component of exported processed goods were unrestricted. As a solution, SCM/53 suggested that such subsidies be treated as a "substitution drawback" coming under paragraph (i) of the Illustrative List of Export Subsidies in Article 9. It proposed that these rebates "shall not be higher than the difference between the domestic price and the world market price" and that the committee establish mechanisms to verify compliance with that limit.[141]

Most of the signatories supported the proposals in SCM/53 to some

138. Ibid., 40.
139. SCM/53 sought to incorporate into Article 8 the logic employed in two GATT panel reports that arose from complaints about EC export subsidies for sugar and that were adopted by the GATT Council in 1979 and 1980. These two panel reports went beyond Article XVI:3 and its "more than an equitable share" test for agricultural export subsidies to include the admonition in Article XVI:1 that no subsidy should cause "serious prejudice" or the "threat of serious prejudice." See *BISD* 26, 290–319, especially 319; and *BISD* 27, 69–98, especially 95.
140. See SCM/53, 4–7.
141. Ibid., 3.

degree. In April 1986, for example, the Japanese delegate called it "a viable solution"; the Swedish delegate said that it was "a compromise formula which the Nordic countries found realistic"; the Australian delegate observed that it "was a constructive document"; the Swiss delegate said it "could lead to the resolution of present and future disputes"; and the U.S. delegate observed that "there were a number of areas in SCM/53 which deserved the very careful attention of the Committee."[142] However, the EC, supported by Austria and Spain, completely rejected SCM/53.[143] The EC had favored the formation of a working group in the midst of the wheat flour and pasta disputes, and, as noted above, had participated in the informal group during early 1984.[144] However, the EC soon withdrew from the group and argued that the GATT Committee on Trade in Agriculture had exclusive jurisdiction over all agriculture-related trade issues. SCM/53, the EC argued, "was only an informal paper which did not offer any material solution to these disputes [wheat flour and pasta] as it only suggested some areas of reflection related to interpretation issues."[145] In late 1986 the SCM chair told his colleagues that he "wondered whether there was much more the Committee could do than to report this regrettable situation to the CONTRACTING PARTIES."[146]

SUMMARY OF CODE PERFORMANCE IN TERMS OF RULE CONSTRUCTION

Rule-construction activities associated with the Tokyo Round NTB codes during the 1980s are summarized in Table 5.1. It distinguishes

142. SCM/M/30, 17–19. Positive statements about SCM/56 and the working-group effort were also offered by Canada, Chile, India, New Zealand, and Uruguay. See SCM/M/24, 24; SCM/M/27, 20; SCM/M/30, 20; and SCM/M/31, 20.

143. For Austria and Spain, see SCM/M/24, 25; and SCM/M/30, 20. Hungary also opposed the report: see SCM/M/31, 20.

144. In March 1982 the EC delegate suggested that instead of a panel for the pasta dispute, "he did not see any reason why it would not be an efficient way for the Committee to establish a working party to look into some of the points raised in greater detail and to agree what provisions would be applied," and in a written submission in April 1982 on Article 9 the EC suggested that "the Committee should establish a working group of the Code signatories to examine these questions in greater detail." See SCM committee, "Minutes," March 24, 1982, GATT Doc. SCM/M/Spec/4, April 30, 1982, 8; and SCM committee, "Interpretation of Article 9 of the Agreement—Communication from the European Communities," GATT Doc. SCM/Spec/13, April 5, 1982.

145. SCM/M/30, 17; also see SCM/M/24, 24–25; SCM/M/27, 20; and SCM/M/31, 20.

146. SCM committee, "Minutes," October 27–31 and November 13, 1986, GATT Doc. SCM/M/32, January 27, 1987, 21.

Table 5.1. Summary of rule-construction activities associated with the Tokyo Round NTB codes, 1980–87

Type of rule-construction activity	Customs valuation (CV)			Import licensing (LIC)			Anti-dumping practices (ADP)		
Corrective	□	*1* Definition of "undertaken" in Art. 8:1(b)iv	(+)		*No cases*		Δ	*3* Rules on basic price systems in Art. 8:4	(0)
	Δ	*4* Rules on software	(0)						
	Δ	*1* Rule on R&D	(+)						
Operative	□	*57* Measures on Art. 1 19 Art. 2 4 Art. 3 3 Art. 7 3 Art. 8 4 Art. 15 1 General 33 *Note*: Some measures affect more than one Article	(+)	Δ	*7* Rules on Art. 1:4, 3(e) Art. 3(c), 3(d) Art. 1:6, 3(g)	(+)	□	*1* Definition of "related" in Art. 4:1	(+)
				□	Rules on "fair and equitable" administration	(−)			
Restorative	□	*1* Rule on interest charges	(+)	Δ	Rules on scope of Art. 1:1	(0)	□	*13* Rules on transparency and confidentiality in Art. 6:3, 6:6, 8:5	(+)
							□	*3* Rules on questionnaire in Art. 6:1	(+)
							□	*8* Rules on on-spot visits in Art. 6:5	(+)
							□	*7* Rules on "best information" in Art. 6:8	(+)
							□	*4* Rules on "material injury" in Art. 3:6	(+)
							∇	Rules on "input dumping"	(−)
							□	Rules on "definition of sale"	(−)
							□	Rules on "constructed value"	(−)
							□	Rules on price undertakings	(0)

Key
(+) Experience suggesting code success
(−) Experience suggesting code failure
(0) Experience suggesting mixed code effectiveness
Δ Experience characterized by U.S.-EC cooperation
∇ Experience characterized by U.S.-EC discord
□ Experience characterized neither by cooperation nor by discord between U.S. and EC

132

Technical barriers (TBT)		Government procurement (GPR)			Subsidies and countervailing measures (SCM)	
No cases		∇	Joint declaration on leasing	(−)	∇ SCM/53 rules to close paragraph (d) loophole	(−)
		∇	Rules on notification of bilateral consultations	(−)		
11 Rules on notification in Art. 2:5.2, 7:3.2	(+)	∇	Broadening element of Art. IX:6(b) negotiations	(−)	*Countervailing measures rules (Group of Experts)*	
4 Rules on documents in Art. 2:5.3, 2:6.2, 7:3.3	(+)	∇	Services element of Art. IX:6(b) negotiations	(−)	□ *1* Definition of "related" in Art. 6:5	(+)
8 Rules on comments in Art. 2:5.4, 2:5.5, 7:3.4	(+)	∇ *1*	Rule to reduce threshold	(0)	Definition of subsidy in Article 4:2:	
9 Rules on Enquiry Points in Art. 10	(+)	∇	Rules on state-owned enterprises	(−)	□ *4* Rules on substitution	(+)
					□ *5* Rules on physical incorporation	(+)
					□ *11* Rules on amortization and depreciation	(+)
					∇ Rule on specificity	(−)
2 Rules on notification procedures	(+)		26 Code revisions in improvements element of Article IX:6(b) negotiations:		*Subsidy rules*	
Rules on PPMs in Article 14:2.5	(−)	Δ *4*	Statistical requirements	(+)	∇ Rules on notification of subsidies	(−)
Rules on inclusion of services	(−)	Δ *2*	Qualification of suppliers	(+)	*SCM/53*	
Rule on NTM jurisdiction	(−)	Δ *2*	Bid-times/delivery delays	(+)	∇ Rules on harmful effects in Art. 8	(−)
Rules on mutual acceptance of test data/lab inspection in Art. 5:2	(−)	□ *1*	Inclusion of leasing	(+)	∇ Rules on non-primary product-export subsidies in Art. 9	(−)
Rules on bilateral standards agreements	(−)	□ *1*	Rule on options	(+)	∇ Rules on primary-product export-subsidies in Art. 10	(−)
Rules on regional standards agreements	(−)	□ *16*	Other	(+)		
2 Recommendations on ISO/IEC Guides	(0)					
Rules on local govt. bodies	(−)					
Rules on private bodies	(−)					

between rules or rule-making events for which there were positive statements from signatories or at least no expression of disappointment (+); events about which there were statements by signatories suggesting disappointment (o); and, finally, instances of failed rule construction (−). The table also indicates whether the rule-construction effort by a given committee was characterized by U.S.-EC active cooperation (Δ), active disagreement (∇), or no clear evidence of either cooperation or discord between the two (□).

During the 1980s the CV committee was the most successful of the code committees in the field of rule construction. The LIC committee developed only seven measures, but it also experienced only one failure and one instance of mixed success. The TBT, ADP, and GPR committees attained an intermediate level of success in rule construction, generating substantial numbers of rules but also sustaining several failures. Finally, the SCM committee generated almost as many measures and sustained almost as many failures as the GPR committee. However, the former's performance was highly skewed: every measure it produced concerned countervailing measures, and all but one of its failures concerned the subsidies portion of the agreement. In addition, the SCM committee failed to reestablish a consensus on the latter half of the code. Thus, as with rule compliance and dispute settlement, the NTB codes and code committees varied widely in their rule-construction performance during the 1980s. We now turn our attention to the major challenge in this book—to determine whether realism or neoliberalism is better able to explain that variance in performance.

CHAPTER SIX

The Tokyo Round NTB Regime and Neoliberal Institutionalism

Chapters 4 and 5 *described* the variance in administrative effectiveness of the Tokyo Round NTB codes during the 1980s; this chapter determines whether neoliberal institutionalism can help *explain* that variance. The first section demonstrates that the immediate cause of variance in code performance was the level of U.S.-EC cooperation and discord: the former facilitated code effectiveness; the latter stymied or stunted code success. With two significant exceptions, European-American discord associated with the less successful codes usually took the form of the EC pursuing a "minimalist" interpretation of code obligations and resisting a "maximalist" interpretation put forward by the United States. Thus, to understand the Tokyo Round NTB code experience, we need to understand European-American interactions in the different NTB agreements.

The second major section seeks to account for those interactions through employment of neoliberalism's understanding of the problem of cooperation. Neoliberals would predict that if the EC were reluctant to accept U.S. interpretations of some of the codes or U.S. efforts to expand or extend them, this should have been due primarily to EC concerns about cheating. The data in the second section suggest that the EC did not believe that the codes to which it assigned less support were characterized by more cheating by its partners than the codes to which it provided greater support. That empirical finding draws neoliberal theory into serious question.

Yet neoliberal institutionalists might respond that even if the EC observed no significant actual differences in cheating across the NTB codes, it still may have perceived that some of the agreements possessed characteristics that made them more vulnerable than others to cheating. This variation in EC perceptions as to the magnitude of the *potential* for cheating problems across the codes, neoliberals might argue, could explain the EC's reticence about some of them and its support for others.

The third major section investigates this possibility. Neoliberalism identifies four conditions that it believes can affect state perceptions about the attractiveness of cheating in mixed-interest situations and thus may strongly determine the severity of cheating problems in such situations. These four conditions are the degree to which relationships of partners are iterated; the size of the membership of the joint effort; the degree to which advanced democratic states constitute the membership of the cooperative arrangement; and the capacity of the arrangement to produce individual absolute gains for partners. If neoliberals are correct about the impact of these four conditions on the *potential* problem of cheating, and if the codes varied in effectiveness and, more particularly, were characterized by divergent levels of EC acceptance of the codes, we ought to find evidence that the EC perceived differences in these four conditions across the codes. What the third section actually finds is highly problematic for neoliberal theory: although there was great variation in the level of European-American cooperation across the codes during the 1980s, there was *an absence of significant variation* during that period in the four conditions neoliberals claim can affect the propensity of states to cheat or to fear cheating.

Thus the present chapter argues that neoliberal institutionalism, together with its characterization of states as rational egoists and its focus on the problem of cheating, does not readily account for EC policies toward the NTB codes. Of course, even if the chapter does substantiate that claim, one could not then immediately conclude that neoliberal institutionalism is inferior to realist theory: the failure of the former is not itself proof of the veracity of the latter. Instead, the next chapter seeks to determine whether realist theory, together with its characterization of states as defensive positionalists and its specification of the relative-gains problem for cooperation, can in fact shed greater light than neoliberalism on the behavior of the EC and others in regard to the NTB codes during the 1980s.

The Problem: Europe, America, and the
Effectiveness of the Tokyo Round NTB Codes

What is immediately apparent about the Tokyo Round NTB codes is that they attained markedly different levels of administrative effec-

Table 6.1. Effectiveness of rule compliance and dispute settlement in the Tokyo Round NTB codes, 1980–87

Code/code committee	No. of successes (+)	No. of mixed results (0)	No. of failures (−)
Customs valuation (CV)	4	0	0
Import licensing (LIC)	4	1	1
Anti-dumping practices (ADP)	3	2	2
Technical barriers (TBT)	3	3	2
Government procurement (GPR)	6	2	5
Subsidies/countervailing measures (SCM)	3	4	3
Total	23	12	13

Source: Abstracted from Chapter 4, especially Table 4.4.

tiveness during the 1980s. The two criteria employed in Chapter 4 to assess the relative effectiveness achieved by the codes were compliance with code rules and code-guided settlement of disputes, and the forty-eight experiences of the codes pertaining to these two criteria from 1980 until 1987 are summarized in Table 6.1.

The greatest divergence in performance that can be observed in Table 6.1 is between the success of the codes on customs valuations and import licensing on the one hand and the extreme difficulties encountered by the subsidies portion of the subsidies/countervail accord on the other. The CV code attained at least four instances of successful rule compliance or dispute settlement and no notable cases of mixed results or failure; the LIC code had as many successes as the CV code, and only one case of mixed results and one of failure; and the SCM code had three instances of success and seven of mixed results and failures, almost all of which concerned the subsidies provisions of the agreement. Falling in between these two poles of effectiveness are the codes on anti-dumping, technical barriers, and government procurement: each achieved a substantial number of instances of successful rule compliance and dispute settlement, but also experienced a similar or greater number of failures or mixed results.

The same basic pattern across the codes can be observed in regard to the criterion of effectiveness used in Chapter 5, that is, the construction of rules by the different code committees. These activities of the committees during the 1980s are summarized in Table 6.2.

As with rule compliance and dispute settlement, the polar cases of successful and disappointing efforts at code-committee rule construction involved the customs valuation accord and the subsidies elements of the SCM agreement. The CV committee and its technical

Table 6.2. Effectiveness of rule construction in the Tokyo Round NTB codes, 1980–87

Code committee	Measures representing success (+)	Measures (M) or efforts (E) representing mixed results (0)	No. of failed[a] efforts (−)
Customs valuation (CV)	60	4 (M)	0
Import licensing (LIC)	7	1 (E)	1
Anti-dumping practices (ADP)	36	3 (M)	3
		1 (E)	
Technical barriers (TBT)	34	2 (M)	8
Government procurement (GPR)	26	1 (M)	5
Subsidies/countervailing measures (SCM)	21	0	6
Total	184	10 (M)	23
		2 (E)	

[a]Failed efforts frequently would have resulted in more than one rule or measure, and therefore data in column three are not comparable to those in columns one and two.

Source: Abstracted from Chapter 5, especially Table 5.1.

group generated the largest number of code-based measures of any NTB code committee and experienced no observable instances of failure. The SCM code committee produced a substantial number of countervailing-measure rules, but it also experienced many rule-construction failures concerning subsidies. The committees responsible for the technical barriers, anti-dumping, and government procurement codes each produced quite large numbers of measures; however, they also experienced many failed attempts at rule construction. Thus, as with rule compliance and dispute settlement, these code committees generally fell in between the CV and SCM committees in terms of effective rule construction during the 1980s.

On the basis, then, of the three criteria used, the CV and LIC codes were relatively effective during the 1980s, as was the countervailing-measures portion of the SCM agreement; the subsidies element of the latter code was relatively ineffective; and the TBT, ADP, and GPR codes attained an intermediate level of success. How can we account for this variance in code effectiveness? At least a large measure of the immediate explanation appears to have been the level of cooperation or discord between the United States and the EC within the particular code and code committee. This can be observed in Table 6.3, which correlates the rule-compliance and dispute-settlement performance of the codes during the 1980s with U.S.-EC interactions concerning these two measures of code effectiveness.

Table 6.3. Impact of U.S.-EC interactions on NTB code rule compliance and dispute settlement, 1980–87

Type of U.S.-EC interaction	No. of successes (+)	No. of mixed results (0)	No. of failures (−)
Cooperation or absence of discord (Δ or □)	19	9	2
Discord (∇)	4	3	11
Total	23	12	13

Key
(+) Experience suggesting code success
(−) Experience suggesting code failure
(0) Experience suggesting mixed code effectiveness
Δ Experience characterized by U.S.-EC cooperation
∇ Experience characterized by U.S.-EC discord
□ Experience characterized neither by cooperation nor by discord between United States and EC
Source: Abstracted from Chapter 4, especially Table 4.4.

As noted in the table, four instances of successful rule compliance or code-guided dispute settlement occurred despite U.S.-EC discord; the disagreements concerned the government procurement code and were resolved through bilateral contacts. Of the twelve mixed-result outcomes, three were associated with discord between the United States and the EC and nine were characterized either by cooperation or an absence of disagreement between them. These data suggest that the NTB codes could occasionally be successful even if the United States and the EC were at odds with each other, and their cooperation or an absence of conflict between them did not guarantee code success. However, Table 6.3 makes it clear that discord between the United States and the EC during the 1980s was extremely likely to result in code difficulties. As can be observed in the table, there were at least thirteen code failures concerning rule compliance or dispute settlement from 1980 until 1987, and eleven of these resulted from or were associated with U.S.-EC disagreements.

A close linkage between U.S.-EC cooperation and the level of success achieved by the different codes also holds with respect to rule-making efforts undertaken by the various NTB code committees. This connection between U.S.-EC interactions and successful rule-construction efforts is presented in Table 6.4.

Successful rule-construction activity, as indicated by the number of measures produced by a code committee, was highly correlated with active cooperation between the United States and the EC or an ab-

Table 6.4. Impact of U.S.-EC interactions on NTB code rule construction, 1980–87

Type of U.S.-EC Interaction	Measures representing success (+)	Measures (M) or efforts (E) representing mixed results (0)	Failed efforts (−)
Cooperation or absence of discord (Δ or □)	184	9 (M) 2 (E)	3
Discord (∇)	0	1 (M)	20
Total	184	10 (M) 2 (E)	23

Key
(+) Experience suggesting code success
(−) Experience suggesting code failure
(0) Experience suggesting mixed code effectiveness
Δ Experience characterized by U.S.-EC cooperation
∇ Experience characterized by U.S.-EC discord
□ Experience characterized neither by cooperation nor by discord between U.S. and EC
Source: Abstracted from Chapter 5, especially Table 5.1.

sence of discord between them. In sharp contrast, twenty of the twenty-three failed efforts by NTB code committees to construct rules were associated with observable disagreements between the United States and the EC concerning the rule-construction effort.

The NTB codes varied in effectiveness during the 1980s, and the less effective codes were marked by European-American discord: this takes us two steps toward understanding the Tokyo Round code experience. The third step is to characterize the typical form of discord between the two partners in the codes. This can be accomplished by studying Tables 6.5 and 6.6.

Table 6.5 lists each of the instances of disagreement between the United States and the EC during the 1980s concerning rule compliance and dispute settlement. As demonstrated in the table, most U.S.-EC disagreements that ended with mixed results or failure concerned the GPR agreement and the subsidies portion of the SCM code. The table also indicates that in three of fourteen cases not resulting in success, the EC raised a problem regarding U.S. actions involving the codes. In the remaining eleven cases, it was the United States that raised a problem concerning EC behavior covered by the codes. Typically, then, discord between the two GATT partners in-

Table 6.5. U.S.-EC discord and setbacks in NTB code rule compliance
and dispute settlement, 1980–87

Code	Activity	Issue	Signatory raising issue	Target signatory	Outcome
LIC	Dispute settlement	Summary Steel Invoice	EC	U.S.	Failure
ADP	Compliance	8% profit rule	EC	U.S.	Failure
TBT	Dispute settlement	Production and processing methods	U.S.	EC	Failure
TBT	Dispute settlement	Production and processing methods	U.S.	EC	Failure
GPR	Compliance	Submission of statistics	U.S.	EC	Mixed
GPR	Compliance	Contract announcements and bid-deadlines	U.S.	EC (Italy)	Failure
GPR	Compliance	Single tendering	U.S.	EC	Failure
GPR	Compliance	Below-threshold purchases	U.S.	EC	Failure
GPR	Dispute settlement	Value-added taxes	U.S.	EC	Mixed
GPR	Dispute settlement	French microcomputer purchase	U.S.	EC	Failure
SCM	Compliance	Notification of subsidies	U.S.	EC	Failure
SCM	Dispute settlement	Pasta export subsidies	U.S.	EC	Mixed
SCM	Dispute settlement	Wheat flour export subsidies	U.S.	EC	Failure
SCM	Dispute settlement	Wine industry countervailing measures	EC	U.S.	Failure

Key to Code Abbreviations
LIC = Code on Import Licensing Procedures
ADP = Code on Anti-Dumping Practices
TBT = Code on Technical Barriers to Trade
GPR = Code on Government Procurement
SCM = Code on Subsidies and Countervailing Measures
Source: Chapter 4, especially Table 4.4.

volved the United States trying to use the GPR and SCM codes to
induce changes in EC actions or policies, with the EC more often than
not resisting these American efforts.

The same characterization of U.S.-EC disagreements holds for rule
construction in the various NTB code committees during the 1980s.
Table 6.6 summarizes instances of such discord that resulted in mixed
results or failures. According to the table, a very large number of
disagreements occurred in the SCM, GPR, and especially the TBT
committees. As with rule compliance and dispute settlement, U.S.-EC

Table 6.6. U.S.-EC discord and setbacks in NTB code rule construction, 1980–87

Code	Type of rule-construction effort	Issue	Signatory initiating or supporting effort	Signatory opposing effort	Outcome
LIC	Restorative	Scope of Art. 1 : 1	EC	U.S.	Mixed
ADP	Restorative	Input dumping	EC	U.S.	Failure
TBT	Restorative	Production and process-ing methods	U.S.	EC	Failure
TBT	Restorative	Services	U.S.	EC	Failure
TBT	Restorative	Non-tariff measure juris-diction	U.S.	EC	Failure
TBT	Restorative	Mutual acceptance of test data	U.S.	EC	Failure
TBT	Restorative	Bilateral standards agreements	U.S.	EC	Failure
TBT	Restorative	Regional standards agreements	U.S.	EC	Failure
TBT	Restorative	Local government bodies	EC	U.S.	Failure
TBT	Restorative	Private bodies	EC	U.S.	Failure
GPR	Corrective	Joint declaration on leas-ing	U.S.	EC	Failure
GPR	Corrective	Notification of bilaterals	U.S.	EC	Failure
GPR	Operative	Broadening under Art. IX : 6(b)	U.S.	EC	Failure
GPR	Operative	Services under Art. IX : 6(b)	U.S.	EC	Failure
GPR	Operative	Threshold under Art. IX : 6(b)	U.S.	EC	Mixed
GPR	Operative	State-owned enterprises	U.S.	EC	Failure
SCM	Corrective	SCM/53 closure of para-graph (d) loophole	U.S.	EC	Failure
SCM	Operative	Specificity of subsidy	EC	U.S.	Failure
SCM	Corrective	Notification of subsidies	U.S.	EC	Failure
SCM	Corrective	Art. 8	U.S.	EC	Failure
SCM	Corrective	Art. 9	U.S.	EC	Failure
SCM	Corrective	Art. 10	U.S.	EC	Failure

Key to Code Abbreviations
LIC = Code on Import Licensing Procedures
ADP = Code on Anti-Dumping Practices
TBT = Code on Technical Barriers to Trade
GPR = Code on Government Procurement
SCM = Code on Subsidies and Countervailing Measures
Source: Chapter 5, especially Table 5.1.

discord over rule construction has typically pitted an aggressive United States against a resistant EC. In seventeen cases the United States supported or, much more typically, initiated a rule-construction effort within a code committee, an effort which in turn was then opposed and blocked by the EC. There were, however, five instances in which the EC initiated a rule-construction effort that was resisted by the United States. Most notably, as discussed in Chapter 5, the EC sought to extend several obligations of the technical barriers code to non-central government and private standards-making bodies, and the United States vetoed both ideas. Finally, Table 6.6 shows a relative absence of rule-making discord between the United States and the EC in regard to the ADP code, although the latter, it will be recalled from Table 6.2, attained only a mixed overall level of success in the field of rule construction. The ADP code thus presents an anomaly in need of explanation: in contrast to the other codes, its effectiveness was restricted *without* the presence of European-American discord (and, indeed, *in spite* of U.S.-EC cooperation).

In sum, differences in the level of effectiveness attained by the NTB codes during the 1980s were heavily driven by EC-U.S. cooperation and discord. Specifically, the United States and the EC found themselves in disagreements very frequently in the TBT, GPR, and the SCM committees. In addition, the typical form of U.S.-EC discord relating to the codes can be summarized as the United States complaining that the EC was not living up to its code commitments, or the United States trying to strengthen or extend rule obligations in the face of EC opposition (there were, however, very interesting exceptions in the case of the TBT committee).

The next and most important challenge is to explain *why* European-American cooperation varied across the NTB codes. With a few exceptions—most notably, the EC proposals concerning private and noncentral governmental bodies under the TBT code—the United States wanted the codes to produce a higher and more extensive level of international discipline over national policies and practices than was acceptable to the EC. The United States fundamentally pursued a "maximalist" interpretation of all the codes. The EC accepted or at least did not oppose such an interpretation of the CV, LIC, and ADP codes. However, it preferred a "minimalist" interpretation of the TBT (with, again, some important exceptions) and GPR agreements, and especially the subsidies portion of the SCM code. The challenge, then, is to account for this divergence in what the United States and the EC wanted from the different Tokyo Round NTB codes, and, more specifically, to account for the differing degrees of support given to them by the EC.

THE EC, THE NTB CODES, AND THE QUESTION OF CHEATING

Explaining the variation in the EC's acceptance of the Tokyo Round codes—and in particular variation in its acceptance of American interpretations of and initiatives affecting the codes—constitutes the key problem in understanding the differences in the effectiveness achieved by those codes during the 1980s. The major challenge of the present chapter is to determine whether neoliberal institutionalism can help account for this variation in EC support for the codes. According to neoliberal theory, cheating and the fear of cheating are the major anarchy-induced constraints on the achievement and maintenance of cooperation among states in mixed-interest international situations. Neoliberals would therefore suggest that the EC probably gave less support to those codes that it believed were characterized by a higher rate of cheating, and that it assigned greater support to those codes in which it believed cheating by partners was less pronounced.

However, the available evidence does not indicate that the EC's partners complied with the provisions of the less successful codes at a substantially lower rate than did the EC itself. For example, it will be recalled from Chapter 4 that the committee responsible for the technical barriers agreement had recommended specific time periods during which code signatories would not implement proposed technical regulations they had notified to the GATT so that their code partners would have sufficient time to offer comments on those regulations: this committee-recommended time span had been six weeks during the period from 1980 until May 1983, and sixty days thereafter. One form of cheating, then, would involve the failure to provide the time period for comments.

Table 6.7 reports the rates at which the major participants complied with the two TBT committee-recommended comment periods that were in operation during the 1980s. The table reveals that the EC and its member-states produced a much higher rate of compliance with the TBT committee's recommended comment period (then six weeks) than its partners during 1980 and 1981. However, the EC compliance rate declined while others increased, so that at the end of the period under review its compliance rate was at the low end among the major code participants. The U.S. compliance rate was below that of the EC during most of the 1980s. However, non-compliance does not appear

Table 6.7. Compliance with comment periods recommended by the Committee on Technical Barriers to Trade, advanced countries, 1980–86

Country/country group	1980			1981			1982		
	Total notifications	Notifications in compliance	Compliance rate (%)	Total notifications	Notifications in compliance	Compliance rate (%)	Total notifications	Notifications in compliance	Compliance rate (%)
EC and EC member-states	17	14	82.4	50	33	66.0	37	14	37.8
United States	47	9	19.1	91	34	37.4	25	7	28.0
The Nordics	19	5	26.3	51	9	17.6	41	21	51.2
Japan	21	1	4.8	31	6	19.4	47	10	21.3
Canada	15	4	26.7	15	3	20.0	20	7	35.0
Other advanced-country signatories	11	0	0	46	27	58.7	10	2	20.0
Total	130	33	25.4	284	112	39.4	180	61	33.9

Country/country group	1983			1984			1985			1986		
	Total notifications	Notifications in compliance	Compliance rate (%)	Total notifications	Notifications in compliance	Compliance rate (%)	Total notifications	Notifications in compliance	Compliance rate (%)	Total notifications	Notifications in compliance	Compliance rate (%)
EC and EC member-states	37	9	24.3	35	15	42.9	35	11	31.4	55	12	21.8
United States	15	3	20.0	28	9	32.1	14	3	21.4	14	7	50.0
The Nordics	38	16	42.1	55	27	49.1	48	23	47.9	38	18	47.4
Japan	92	39	42.4	34	31	91.2	31	24	77.4	30	17	56.7
Canada	26	7	26.9	20	4	20.0	38	9	23.7	24	5	20.8
Other advanced-country signatories	7	0	0	18	4	22.2	13	6	46.2	17	0	0
Total	215	74	34.4	190	90	47.4	179	76	42.5	178	59	33.1

Sources: These data are from Committee on Technical Barriers to Trade, "Fifth Annual Review of the Implementation and Operation of the Agreement: Basic Document by the Secretariat," GATT Doc. TBT/18, September 28, 1984, 9–10; "Sixth Annual Review," GATT Doc. TBT/22, October 16, 1985, 8; "Seventh Annual Review," GATT Doc. TBT/25, September 25, 1986, 9; and "Eighth Annual Review," GATT Doc. TBT/28, October 5, 1987, 9.

to have been generalized—major signatories such as Japan and the three Nordic states increased their compliance rates rapidly and matched and began to surpass that of the EC as early as 1982, and the U.S. rate improved gradually during the course of the decade.

In addition, there is strong evidence that the level of compliance of the EC's partners in the GPR code was not lower than that of the EC. One way by which signatories might have evaded code disciplines during the 1980s was to avoid awarding contracts above the code-specified threshold of SDR 150,000 (for example, by breaking a single large order into a number of smaller contracts). Comparative rates of awarding contracts above the threshold by the major advanced-country signatories for 1983 are reported in Table 6.8. It reveals that about 36 percent of all contracts awarded by code-designated entities of EC member-states were valued above the threshold and thus came under the jurisdiction of the code. This percentage was about the same as Japan's and it was lower than the percentages for Canada, Switzerland, and especially the United States. Thus the EC's rate of above-threshold contract awards was no better and sometimes sub-stantially worse than that of its major GPR code partners.

Moreover, the EC would not have had much reason during the mid-1980s to believe that its partners in the GPR code were using another and perhaps more important strategy to avoid code disci-plines, that is, the awarding of nominally code-covered contracts un-der (competition-inhibiting) single-tendering procedures. Rates at which code-covered contracts were awarded under such procedures are reported in Table 6.9. It indicates that more than half of all code-covered EC contracts were awarded under single-tendering proce-dures, that the EC had the highest rate of single tendering of all the major GPR signatories, including Japan, and that the major GPR code signatory—the United States—had a single-tendering rate more than forty percentage points below the EC.

Finally, it will be recalled from Chapter 4 that the United States and other signatories criticized the reluctance of the EC member-states to notify their national subsidies to the SCM committee. This reluctance cannot be readily attributed to a failure on the part of most of the advanced-country signatories to notify their own programs. During 1984 a major subsidy-notification effort was undertaken by the SCM committee: the results in terms of country notifications as of late 1984 to the committee are reported in Table 6.10. The table indicates that virtually all signatories other than the EC member-states and Japan notified both their agricultural and industrial subsidies, and Japan submitted at least a partial notification during 1985. In contrast, the

Table 6.8. Major-signatory contracts awarded under the Code on Government Procurement, 1983 (in millions of SDR)

Value of contracts awarded by code-covered entities	EC	United States	Japan	Canada	The Nordics	Switzerland	Austria
(A) Above SDR 150,000 threshold	3,409.3	16,663.6	1,223.0	358.4	364.4	114.5	36.6
(B) Below SDR 150,000 threshold	6,100.6	6,160.8	1,945.0	449.9	1,072.4	141.7	130.2
(C) Total value of contracts by code-covered entities	9,509.9	22,824.4	3,168.0	808.3	1,436.8	256.2	166.8
(D) Above-threshold contracts/ total (A as % of C)	35.9	73.0	38.6	44.3	25.4	44.7	21.9

Sources: All data are from national reports submitted as addendum and revisions to the GPR committee document "Statistics for 1983 Reported under Article VI.9 of the Agreement": for Sweden, GATT Doc. GPR/24 Add.2, October 2, 1984; for the United States, GATT Doc. GPR/24/Add.3/Rev. 1, February 22, 1985; for Switzerland, GATT Doc. GPR/24/Add. 4, October 15, 1984; for Canada, GATT Doc. GPR/24/Add. 5/Rev. 1, February 21, 1985; for Finland, GATT Doc. GPR/24/Add. 6, October 24, 1984; for Norway, GATT Doc. GPR/24/Add. 7, November 11, 1984; for Japan, GATT Doc. GPR/24/Add. 8, November 9, 1984; for the EC, GATT Doc. GPR/24/Add. 9, January 16, 1985; and for Austria, GATT Doc. GPR/24/Add. 10, February 10, 1985.

Table 6.9. Contracts awarded under single-tendering procedures of the Code on Government Procurement, 1983 (in millions of SDR)

Code-covered contracts	EC	United States	Japan	Canada	The Nordics	Switzerland	Austria
(A) Total value of code-covered contracts	3,409.3	16,663.6	1,223.0	358.4	364.4	114.5	36.6
(B) Value of code-covered contracts awarded under single tendering	1,831.8	1,592.3	456.2	68.1	33.8	51.6	11.7
(C) Single-tender contracts/total code-covered contracts (B as % of A)	53.7	9.6	37.3	19.0	9.3	45.1	32.0

Source: See Table 6.8.

Table 6.10. Notification of subsidies to the Committee on Subsidies and Countervailing Measures, advanced-country signatories, 1984

	Type of subsidy	
Notifying signatory	Agricultural	Industrial
Australia	X	X
Austria	X	X
Canada	X	X
Finland	X	X
Japan	0	0
New Zealand	X	X
Spain	X	X
Sweden	X	X
Switzerland	X	X
United States	X	X
EC	X	X[a]
Belgium	X[b]	X
Denmark	X	0
France	X	0
Germany, Federal Republic	X	X
Greece	X	0
Ireland	X	0
Italy	X	0
Luxembourg	X	0
Netherlands	X	0
United Kingdom	X	X

Key
X = notification submitted
0 = no notification submitted
[a]But not export credits.
[b]All EC countries except the United Kingdom notified only their agricultural subsidies coming under the EC Common Agricultural Policy (CAP). The UK notified both CAP and non-CAP agricultural subsidies.
Source: Committee on Subsidies and Countervailing Measures, "Draft Report (1984) of the Committee on Subsidies and Countervailing Measures," GATT Doc. SCM/W/80/Rev. 1, November 2, 1984, 10; and Committee on Subsidies and Countervailing Measures, "Minutes of the Meeting Held on 4–5 December," GATT Doc. SCM/M/24, February 14, 1985, 1–19.

EC as a whole submitted incomplete information on its agriculture subsidy programs, and none of its member-states, except for Britain, Germany, and Belgium, notified their national industrial subsidies.[1] This suggests that, as with the TBT and GPR codes, the EC's non-

1. Subsequent SCM committee efforts to attain greater transparency of subsidies during 1985 and 1986 resulted in no improvement in notifications by EC member-states. See Committee on Subsidies and Countervailing Measures, "Report (1986) Presented to the CONTRACTING PARTIES at Their Forty-Second Session," in GATT, *Basic Instruments and Selected Documents*, 33d Supplement (Geneva, 1986), 206.

compliance with the transparency provisions in the SCM code regarding subsidies was probably not an EC response to generalized cheating by its major partners in the code.

In sum, the main causal factor specified by neoliberal institutionalism as leading to or away from the achievement of cooperation among states—cheating—does not help us explain the variation in willingness of the EC to cooperate with its partners in the different Tokyo Round NTB codes during the 1980s. This empirical finding puts neoliberal theory in an awkward analytical position, one that is made even more difficult by the findings that follow.

Neoliberal Background Conditions for Cooperation

Variance in the EC's acceptance of the different NTB codes during the 1980s cannot be readily explained in terms of differing levels of observable cheating by its code partners. However, neoliberal institutionalists argue it is cheating *or the fear of cheating* that can impede the evolution of cooperation. Hence neoliberals might argue that the EC may have believed during the 1980s that the problem with the TBT and GPR codes, and the subsidies element of the SCM agreement, was not actual cheating but instead the relatively greater potential for cheating associated with them as compared with the other NTB codes. The EC, it might be argued from the neoliberal viewpoint, may have believed and feared (incorrectly, as matters developed) that the substance or membership of what turned out to be the less successful codes could have been marked by higher rates of cheating, and thus the EC moved preemptively and defensively toward a minimalist view of those codes.

Neoliberal institutionalism thus could still account for the EC's differentiated approach to the NTB codes if it could demonstrate that the EC may have had grounds for believing during the 1980s that cheating was *more likely* to characterize certain codes as opposed to others. Neoliberalism specifies four background conditions that can affect the likelihood that states will cheat in mixed-interest situations and thus the fears of states that they may be the victims of cheating in cooperative arrangements in such situations. If these four neoliberal-specified conditions varied across the NTB codes in a way corresponding to the differences in support given to them by the EC, this would confirm neoliberalist claims that the *fear* of cheating, as well as the actuality of such behavior, can constrain the willingness of states to work together.

Cheating is the major systemic constraint on international cooperation, according to neoliberal institutionalists. Yet cooperation may occur in spite of the anarchical context of world politics, neoliberals argue, through the capacity of international institutions to ameliorate the problem of cheating. These beneficent effects of institutions, according to neoliberal theory, are augmented and accentuated by the presence of four situational or background conditions.[2] First, and perhaps most significant from the viewpoint of neoliberal theory, states will be more attracted to faithful cooperation in mixed-interest situations if they expect to interact with their current or prospective partners in an iterated manner. Iteration, neoliberals argue, has the crucial effect of extending the time horizons of states, which in turn is the principal way to reduce the attractiveness of short-term cheating and thus to enhance the prospects for long-term cooperation among egoistic actors facing anarchy and mixed interests.[3] Robert Axelrod, for example, argues that a key way to encourage cooperation among self-interested actors in such circumstances is through "enlarging the shadow of the future"; this can be accomplished, he suggests, by making the interactions "more durable" or "more frequent."[4] For neoliberals, then, the knowledge that states may possess that they will interact repeatedly with prospective partners enables them to find conditional cooperation based on reciprocity to be a relatively low-risk (and hence acceptable) strategy in the context of international anarchy.[5]

The second condition that, according to neoliberal theory, strongly affects the prospects for successful cooperation is the size of the common endeavor. Such endeavors are easier to construct and operate, according to neoliberals, if they include a small number of states. Kenneth Oye, for example, suggests that "the prospects for cooperation diminish as the number of players increases."[6] Stating the point

2. While neoliberals specify these four conditions, they do not indicate whether all must be present or whether some are more important than others.

3. Indeed, according to neoliberals, international institutions are important in large measure because they create iterativeness and the context for non-myopic, reciprocity-based interactions. As Robert Axelrod and Robert Keohane suggest, "international regimes help to link the future with the present." See Robert Axelrod and Robert O. Keohane, "Achieving Cooperation under Anarchy: Institutions and Strategies," *World Politics* 38 (October 1985), 234; also see 250.

4. Robert Axelrod, *The Evolution of Cooperation* (New York: Basic, 1984), 129, and see 130–32.

5. See Charles Lipson, "International Cooperation in Security and Economic Affairs," *World Politics* 37 (October 1984), 5–6; also see Robert O. Keohane, *After Hegemony: Cooperation and Discord in the World Political Economy* (Princeton: Princeton University Press, 1984), 75–76.

6. Kenneth A. Oye, "Explaining Cooperation under Anarchy: Hypotheses and Strategies," *World Politics* 38 (October 1985), 18; also see 19–22.

even more optimistically, Robert Keohane argues that "contemporary international relations are beset by dilemmas of collective action, but these dilemmas are rendered less intractable by the small number of states involved."[7] Similarly, Charles Lipson finds that within the international system, "A small group, or a larger one composed of overlapping small groups with extensive interactions, may be important for the establishment and diffusion of conventions, for the detection and sanction of defectors, and, in the case of truly public goods, for the formation of a viable coalition."[8]

Third, according to neoliberals, the advanced democratic states are more likely than other types of states to achieve and maintain cooperative arrangements. Keohane, it will be recalled from Chapter 1, suggests that advanced democracies undertake joint efforts in circumstances "where common interests are greatest and where the benefits of international cooperation may be easiest to realize."[9] He goes on to argue that these states find it easier to cooperate because they share a consensus as to the "proper operation" of their economies, they are enmeshed in a thick web of interdependent "nested" relationships, and they are not locked into political-military disputes with one another.[10] In addition, advanced democracies find cooperation easier to achieve because they constitute a small group; that is, "Rather than having so many actors that the contributions of each exerts no effects on the propensity of others to contribute, international political-economic bargaining among the advanced industrialized countries involves a small number of governments intensely interacting with one another and carefully monitoring each other's behavior."[11] Finally, Keohane argues that "some reflection on the problem of making agreements in world politics suggests that there are advantages

7. See Keohane, *After Hegemony*, 77. Also see Keohane and Axelrod, "Achieving Cooperation," 238, in which they suggest that one of the reasons international institutions facilitate cooperation is that they can help in "transforming N-person games into collections of two-person games" in which the cheating problem is more readily managed.

8. Lipson, "International Cooperation," 8. As a demonstration, Lipson finds in his study of bank consortia and third-world debtors that large banks prevent the otherwise quite likely defection of smaller lenders from continued participation in the original loan or the provision of new funds through a range of actions about which "*the whole point is to break down the large secondary game,* [that is, the relationship between the large and small banks] *involving hundreds of banks and considerable opportunities for free-riding, into a series of bilateral games pitting a few small holdouts against major money-center banks.*" See Lipson, "Bankers' Dilemmas: Private Cooperation in Rescheduling Sovereign Debt," *World Politics* 38 (October 1985), 220, emphasis in the original.

9. Keohane, *After Hegemony*, 7.
10. Ibid., 6–7.
11. Ibid., 77.

for the open government that cannot be duplicated by countries with more tightly closed bureaucracies."[12] That is, because their intentions and actions are more transparent and, as a result, verification of their compliance with international commitments is easier to accomplish, democratic states find it easier to reach and maintain international cooperative agreements among themselves.[13]

The fourth and final neoliberal-specified background condition affecting the attractiveness of cooperation to states is the magnitude (or, more precisely, states' perceptions about the magnitude) of absolute gains produced by joint action.[14] In general, states will be more attracted to cooperation, according to neoliberals, if they perceive that faithful adherence to cooperative commitments will result in their enjoyment of larger rather than smaller individual absolute benefits.[15] Oye, for example, suggests that, in iterated situations, "The more substantial the gains from mutual cooperation (CC-DD) and the less substantial the gains from unilateral defection (DC-DD), the greater the likelihood of cooperation."[16]

Thus, from a neoliberal viewpoint, differences in the EC's approach to the NTB codes during the 1980s could have been a reflection of its judgement that these four background conditions favored the CV, LIC, and ADP codes, as well as the countervailing-measures portion of the SCM code, and their associated committees, and disfavored the TBT, GPR, and subsidies portion of the SCM agreements and their respective committees. In fact, however, the available evidence does not suggest that variance in the four neoliberal background conditions across the NTB codes correlates with the EC's level of acceptance of the codes or their subsequent level of effectiveness.

The data pertaining to the first neoliberal-specified condition, that is, the degree to which interactions were iterated, are presented in Table 6.11. It reports the number of meetings of the committees of signatories for the various codes between 1980 and 1987. If any pattern can be discerned in Table 6.11, it is that there may have been an

---

12. Ibid., 95.

13. Ibid., 6–7.

14. On the importance of perceptions about payoffs, see Axelrod and Keohane, "Achieving Cooperation," 228–32.

15. In stressing the importance of the magnitude of payoffs from cooperation as compared to defection, neoliberals build on the work of Robert Axelrod, *Conflict of Interest: A Theory of Divergent Goals Applications to Politics* (Chicago: Markham, 1970), and Robert Jervis, "Cooperation under the Security Dilemma," *World Politics* 30 (January 1978), 167–86.

16. See Oye, "Cooperation under Anarchy," 9; also see Axelrod, *Evolution of Cooperation*, 133–34; and Axelrod and Keohane, "Achieving Cooperation," 228–32.

Table 6.11. Frequency of meetings of the NTB code committees, 1980–87

Code	1980	1981	1982	1983	1984	1985	1986	1987	Total	Annual average
Customs valuation (CV)	–	3	2	3	3	4	4	2	21	3
Import licensing (LIC)	3	2	2	2	2	3	2	4	20	2.5
Anti-dumping practices (ADP)	3	3	3	2	2	3	2	2	20	2.5
Technical barriers (TBT)	5	3	3	3	3	3	3	3	26	3.3
Government procurement (GPR)	–	4	2	3	5	6	4	5	29	4.1
Subsidies/countervailing measures (SCM)	5	5	3	6	4	7	2	4	36	4.5

Sources: GATT, *Basic Instruments and Selected Documents*, Twenty-Seventh to Thirty-Third Supplements (Geneva, 1981–87), and minutes of NTB code committees for 1980–87.

inverse relationship between code effectiveness and frequency of interactions among code signatories in the form of code committee meetings. That is, the codes with the highest total and average number of
regular meetings—government procurement and subsidies/counter-
vailing measures—achieved a mixed or low level of support, whereas
the more successful codes—customs valuation and import licensing—
had relatively fewer such interactions.[17]

The second neoliberal-specified condition is the size of the cooperative arrangements: data bearing on this condition in the case of the
NTB codes during the 1980s are reported in Table 6.12. As the table
indicates, the two more successful codes (customs valuation and import licensing), and the code that attained a mixed level of effectiveness
but which nevertheless enjoyed substantial EC support (anti-dumping),
had an average of twenty-three, twenty-four, and twenty-one signatories, respectively, during the period under review. These average membership levels were very close to that of the code with the lowest level of
effectiveness and the lowest level of EC support (subsidies and countervailing measures), which had an average membership of twenty-two
states during 1980–87. In addition, one of the agreements that was
characterized by substantial European-American discord and which
attained only a mixed level of effectiveness—the government procurement code—had the smallest membership (twelve signatories) of all the
NTB accords. Finally, the TBT code had both a mixed level of performance and a relatively large membership. However, the average of
thirty-six signatories for the TBT code during 1980–87 is inflated
because in this case the EC members were signatories as both individuals and as the Community; when this inflation of the membership
count is taken into account, the size of the membership of the TBT
code during the 1980s was very similar to that of the more successful
codes. Thus, there was very little variation in the number of signatories
across the six NTB codes during the 1980s, and what variance can be
observed does not appear to correlate with the differences in their
effectiveness or with the variance in EC support assigned to them.

An absence of variance also characterizes the third neoliberal-
specified independent variable, the level of participation of advanced
democratic states in the various codes. This can be observed in Table
6.13, which reports the 1987 composition of the membership of the

17. It should be emphasized that Table 6.11 reports only what the code committees
considered to be "regularly" scheduled meetings, that is, those meetings not scheduled
to undertake dispute settlement or to review statistical submissions of signatories (as
characterized both the government procurement and subsidies codes). Inclusion of
these meetings would have accentuated the finding that code committees with the
highest frequency of interaction also had the lowest level of effectiveness.

Table 6.12. Number of signatories associated with the NTB codes, 1980–87

Code	1980	1981	1982	1983	1984	1985	1986	1987	Annual average
Customs valuation (CV)	–	18	19	20	24	25	25	26	23
Import licensing (LIC)	19	22	23	23	24	24	26	27	24
Anti-dumping practices (ADP)	17	19	21	21	22	22	22	24	21
Technical barriers (TBT)	29 (20)[a]	32 (22)	35 (25)	37 (27)	37 (27)	38 (28)	38 (26)	39 (27)	36 (25)
Government procurement (GPR)	–	11	11	12	12	12	12	12	12
Subsidies/countervailing measures (SCM)	17	19	21	21	21	26	24	24	22

[a]The numbers in parentheses count the EC and EC member-states as a single code member of the TBT code, as was the practice in the other five codes. In the case of the TBT code, both the EC and the individual member-states signed the accord, thus inflating the signatory-counts for that code.
Sources: GATT, Basic Instruments and Selected Documents, Twenty-Seventh to Thirty-Third Supplements (Geneva, 1981–87), and NTB code committee minutes for 1987.

Table 6.13. Composition of committees for NTB codes, 1987

Country/country group	Customs valuation (CV)	Import licensing (LIC)	Anti-dumping (ADP)	Technical barriers (TBT)	Government procurement (GPR)	Subsidies/countervailing measures (SCM)
Advanced/industrialized democracies						
Australia	X	X	X	0	0	X
Austria	X	X	X	X	X	X
Canada	X	X	X	X	X	X
EC	X	X	X	X	X	X
Finland	X	X	X	X	X	X
Japan	X	X	X	X	X	X
New Zealand	X	X	X	X	0	X
Norway	X	X	X	X	X	X
Sweden	X	X	X	X	X	X
Switzerland	X	X	X	X	X	X
United States	X	X	X	X	X	X
Advanced industrialized democracies/total code members (%)	42.3	40.1	45.8	37.0 of 27 or 56.4 of 39	75	45.8
Developing countries						
Argentina	X	X	0	X	0	0
Brazil	X	0	X	X	0	X
Chile	0	X	0	X	0	X
Egypt	0	X	X	X	0	X
Hong Kong	X	X	X	X	X	X
India	X	X	X	X	0	X
Israel	0	0	0	0	X	X
Korea	X	0	X	X	0	X
Mexico	X	X	X	X	0	0
Pakistan	0	X	X	X	0	X
Philippines	0	X	0	X	0	X
Singapore	0	X	X	X	X	0
South Africa	X	X	0	0	0	0
Turkey	X	0	0	0	0	X
Yugoslavia	X	X	X	X	0	X
Other	Botswana Lesotho Malawi	Nigeria		Rwanda Tunisia	0	Indonesia Uruguay
Developing countries/total code members (%)	46.2	44.4	37.5	51.2 of 27 or 35.9 of 39	25.0	54.2
Socialist-bloc states						
Czechoslovakia	X	X	X	X	0	0
Hungary	X	X	X	X	0	0
Poland	0	X	X	0	0	0
Romania	X	X	X	X	0	0
Socialist-bloc states/total code members (%)	11.5	14.8	16.7	11.1 of 27 or 7.7 of 39	0	0

Key
X = code member as of late 1987
0 = not a code member as of late 1987
Source: GATT, *Basic Instruments and Selected Documents*, Thirty-Third Supplement (Geneva, 1987); also code committee minutes for 1987.

different codes according to whether the signatory was an advanced industrialized democracy, a developing country, or a socialist-bloc state. The table indicates that the code having the highest rate of advanced-country participation during the 1980s—the GPR code— was not a highly effective agreement but instead attained only a mixed level of success. It was also a code to which the EC gave only limited support and in which U.S.-EC conflicts were frequent. At the same time, the least successful code and the code most problematic for the EC—the SCM agreement—had advanced-democratic states as members in almost exactly the same proportion as was true of the CV, LIC, and ADP codes, the codes to which the EC gave substantial support. Finally, the TBT code, with its mixed level of effectiveness, had a relatively lower advanced-country composition rate than the (more effective) CV and LIC codes, in accord with neoliberal predictions. However, and confounding what would probably be the neoliberal expectation, the advanced-country participation rate in the TBT code was also lower than in the (much less effective) SCM code.

Attention may now be directed to the fourth condition neoliberals claim may affect cheating and the prospects for cooperation—the production of absolute gains. In turning to this question in the context of the NTB codes, we must note that the extent and economic consequences of non-tariff barriers in the international trading system are still largely undocumented.[18] Moreover, the economic effects of the different Tokyo Round NTB codes are difficult to estimate and thus to compare. This is because, as the two economists who made the most comprehensive effort to estimate the trade consequences of the Tokyo Round reported in 1984, except for the code on government procurement, "the NTB codes that were negotiated do not lend themselves to quantification."[19] To date, neither the GATT nor national

18. For a recent discussion of the problem of data on non-tariff barriers, see Data Development for International Research, "DDIR—Update," vol. 2, no. 3, Reports on the DDIR International Political Economy Data Conferences (Champaign, Ill: Merriam Laboratory for Analytic Political Research, April 1988), 1, 10. For efforts to estimate the level of protection (from both tariffs and non-tariff barriers) in the developed countries, see Bela Balassa and Carol Balassa, "Industrial Protection in the Developed Countries," *World Economy* 7 (June 1984), 179–86; Edward J. Ray and Howard P. Marvel, "The Pattern of Protection in the Industrialized World," *Review of Economics and Statistics* 66 (August 1984), 452–58; Ann D. Morgan, "Protectionism and European Trade in Manufactures," *National Institute Economic Review*, no. 109 (August 1984), 45–84; and J. Michael Finger and Sam Laird, "Protection in Developed and Developing Countries— an Overview," *Journal of World Trade Law* 21 (December 1987), 9–24.

19. See Alan V. Deardorff and Robert M. Stern, "The Effects of the Tokyo Round on the Structure of Protection," in Robert E. Baldwin and Anne O. Krueger, eds., *The Structure and Evolution of Recent U.S. Trade Policy* (Chicago: University of Chicago Press

governments have publicly reported estimates of the trade-creating effects of the codes (either for individual signatories or for code members as a group) or have provided data that could serve as a firm foundation for the construction of such estimates. Hence much of the discussion that follows must be considered tentative and only a first step toward understanding the commercial impact of the NTB agreements.

The available evidence suggests that, in accord with neoliberal expectations, the EC could have had strong reason to believe that the codes it did support or at least did not oppose during the 1980s were providing it with absolute gains. Hard data are unavailable on the absolute gains attained by the EC and other partners through participation in the import licensing code. However, it will be recalled that the LIC signatories frequently reported their satisfaction with the protection afforded by the agreement, and there is no evidence that the EC did not concur in this assessment of the code.

In contrast to the scarcity of information on the effects of the LIC code for the EC, there is strong evidence that the EC enjoyed substantial benefits through its participation in the customs valuations code. For example, a June 1985 study by the Customs Coordination Council (CCC), on the effects of the CV code on national revenues and protection afforded to national industries, found that although the EC had not undertaken a specific study of the impact of the code, it had estimated "that while there was some shrinkage in the overall taxable base, it was not of particular significance to the revenue" afforded the EC by import charges.[20] In contrast, adherence to the code by other signatories (especially Australia and Canada) had resulted, according to the council, in revisions in customs-valuation practices that were equivalent to a unilateral reduction in tariff rates. Australia, for example, reported to the council that CV code participation had the effect of lowering its overall tariff rates by two percentage points.[21]

---

for the National Bureau of Economic Research, 1984), 368. Similarly, a study issued by the Brookings Institution in 1978 on the likely effects of the Tokyo Round negotiations developed an estimate of the trade-liberalizing effects of the then-proposed code on government procurement but also noted that "for the remaining nontariff barriers, we have no quantitative estimates of prospective effects of liberalization." See William R. Cline, Noboru Kawanabe, T. O. M. Kronsjo, and Thomas Williams, *Trade Negotiations in the Tokyo Round: A Quantitative Assessment* (Washington, D.C.: Brookings Institution, 1978), 195.

20. See Customs Coordination Council, Valuation Directorate, *Customs Valuation: Economic Considerations* Doc. 32.574 (Brussels, 1985), 8.

21. Ibid., 7.

Thus in some measure the effective reduction in tariff-rate structures by Australia and Canada may have provided EC producers some increment of additional export opportunities, although to date the exact magnitudes of such an increase in export opportunities cannot be readily estimated.

Similar observations can be made about the EC and the Code on Anti-Dumping Practices. The data in Table 6.14 suggest that, in very broad terms, the EC enjoyed substantial absolute gains by virtue of its adherence to the code during the 1980s. In five of seven years since the ADP code went into force, more anti-dumping actions were initiated by signatories against the EC than the latter initiated against its fellow code participants. Adherence to the code requires that signatories follow procedures and employ standards of evidence in such a way that their anti-dumping activities do not unfairly penalize exporters. Table 6.14 thus suggests that the ADP code provided the EC absolute gains, for in exchange for agreeing to offer this code-mandated protection to foreign exporters, the EC received comparable protection *in substantially more cases.*

In very broad terms (lack of data on the levels of trade affected by the anti-dumping actions gives reason for caution), EC producers were able to enjoy a greater amount of procedural protection as a result of the existence of the ADP code than the EC was obliged to provide to foreign producers as a result of its acceptance of the code. The same favorable balance of absolute benefits appears also to have characterized the countervail portion of the Code on Subsidies and Countervailing measures. This is demonstrated by the data in Table 6.15 on the number of actions initiated by and against EC member-states during 1981–86. As with anti-dumping actions, markedly more countervail actions were initiated against the EC during the 1980s by SCM signatories than the EC began against its fellow code members; this favorable exchange was especially pronounced with regard to the United States. Thus the EC enjoyed the protection of the SCM code— including, most significantly in relation to the United States, the material-injury criterion—much more frequently during the 1980s than it had to accord such code-based protection to its partners.

Given these findings, the support or absence of resistance by the EC to the CV, LIC, and ADP codes, as well as the countervailing-measures portion of the SCM accord, would not be surprising to neoliberals. After all, they emphasize that the provision of absolute gains increases the attractiveness of cooperation. Yet, as the paragraphs that follow demonstrate, and in contradiction to neoliberal expectations, the codes for which the EC preferred a minimalist interpretation of its obliga-

Table 6.14. EC balance of initiated anti-dumping actions, 1980–86

Anti-dumping actions	1980–81	1981–82	1982–83	1983–84	1984–85	1985–86	Total
(A) Initiated by ADP sig- natories against EC	19	69	47	41	24	41	241
(B) Initiated by EC against ADP signatories	22	36	26	33	34	23	174
(C) Balance (A − B)	−3	33	21	8	−10	18	67

Sources: Committee on Anti-Dumping Practices, *Annual Report to the CONTRACTING PARTIES*, various years, in GATT, *Basic Instruments and Selected Documents* (Geneva).

Table 6.15. EC balance of initiated countervailing measures, 1980–86

Countervailing measures	1981–82	1982–83	1983–84	1984–85	1985–86	Total	Special note: EC-U.S. balance
(A) Initiated against EC	52	14	6	6	9	87	62
(B) Initiated by EC	2	3	2	1	0	8	0
(C) Balance (A − B)	50	11	4	5	9	79	62

Sources: Committee on Subsidies and Countervailing Measures, *Annual Report to the CONTRACTING PARTIES*, various years, in GATT, *Basic Instruments and Selected Documents* (Geneva).

tions *also* were providing it with substantial absolute gains during the 1980s.

First, it must be acknowledged that it is difficult to quantify absolute benefits enjoyed by the EC from its participation in the subsidies portion of the SCM accord. However, it may also be noted that the subsidy-notification exercises discussed above provided the EC with a wealth of information about the subsidies programs of its partners. Acquisition of this information by the EC would assist it in undertaking countervailing measures or in bringing complaints to the SCM committee if it believed that these notified programs contravened the SCM code or otherwise harmed EC trading interests. Hence, while precise quantitative estimates are difficult to develop, it is likely that the EC could have concluded that the transparency provisions of the subsidies portion of the SCM code was providing it with some positive benefits during the 1980s.

Hard data on EC absolute gains are more readily developed with regard to the other two codes around which there was substantial European-American discord, that is, the agreements on technical barriers and government procurement. For example, Table 6.16 reports the total number of notifications made to the TBT committee during 1980–86, the number of notifications made to the committee by the EC and its member-states, and the difference between the two. What might be called the EC's balance of notifications was highly favorable throughout the 1980s, suggesting that the EC was gaining substantially more information in absolute terms about new trade-impacting technical measures of its code partners than it had provided to those partners during the same period.

The EC's achievement of absolute gains in the TBT committee can also be measured in terms of requests for information that, under

Table 6.16. Notifications made to the Committee on Technical Barriers to Trade, showing EC absolute gains, 1980–86

Notifications	1980	1981	1982	1983	1984	1985	1986	Total
(A) Total	130	295	201	255	223	196	215	1,515
(B) Non-EC	113	245	164	203	188	161	160	1,281
(C) EC	17	50	37	52	35	35	55	234
(D) Balance (B − C)	96	195	127	151	153	126	105	1,047

Source: Committee on Technical Barriers to Trade, "Eighth Annual Review of the Implementation and Operation of the Agreement: Background Document by the Secretariat," GATT Doc. TBT/28, October 5, 1987, 7.

Article 10, signatories could present to one another about the measures they had notified to the TBT committee. Responses to these enquiries were almost always provided and thus could serve as a valuable source of information on technical measures under review by one's TBT partners. Data collected by the GATT secretariat on enquiries made by various TBT signatories are complete only for 1983 and 1984, and these are presented in Table 6.17. According to the GATT data, the EC received and answered about one hundred Article-10 enquiries from its TBT partners during 1983 and 1984. In return, it received answers to about six hundred enquiries it had presented to its TBT partners during that same two-year period. Thus, as with notifications, the balance of Article 10-generated information appears strongly to have favored the EC during the 1980s, again suggesting that the latter would perceive that it was attaining large absolute gains from the code.

The EC also appears to have had strong grounds during the 1980s to perceive that it was enjoying substantial absolute gains from the operation of the Code on Government Procurement. Statistical submissions on code-related purchasing activity by signatories are the most complete for 1983. During that year EC member-states awarded code-covered contracts (that is, those whose value exceeded the national-currency equivalent of SDR 150,000 or $169,000 and were

Table 6.17. EC balance of Article-10 enquiries under the Committee on Technical Barriers to Trade, 1983–84

	No. of Article-10 enquiries	
Type of enquiry	1983	1984
(A) EC/EC member-state enquiries to major TBT code signatories[a]	374	235
(B) Major TBT code signatory[a] enquiries to EC/EC member-states	44	65
(C) Balance (A − B)	330	170

[a]The United States, Japan, the Nordics, and Canada.

Sources: Committee on Technical Barriers to Trade, "Sixth Annual Review of the Implementation and Operation of the Agreement: Basic Document by the Secretariat," GATT Doc. TBT/22, October 16, 1985, 11–26; also see the Supplement, GATT Doc. TBT/22/Suppl. 1, January 24, 1986, 5–13, and Corrections, TBT/22/Corr. 1, January 23, 1986, 2–4.

by code-covered entities) totaling SDR 3.4 billion.[22] In exchange for opening these contracts to bidders under code-governed procurement procedures, the EC received access to code-regulated contracts awarded by its major code partners valued at almost SDR 19.0 billion.[23]

These figures suggest the potential favorable balance of GPR code-provided market access enjoyed by the EC. Table 6.18 tries to offer a rough sense of the actual absolute gains enjoyed by the EC by reporting the value of GPR code-covered contracts awarded during 1983 by the EC's major code partners to EC suppliers, the contracts awarded to suppliers from these GPR states by the EC, and the difference between the two. The table indicates that EC producers attained vastly more code-covered contracts—in the neighborhood of SDR 1.1 billion—than the EC awarded to suppliers from its major code partners, again suggesting that the EC was enjoying very substantial absolute trading gains from the operation of the GPR agreement.

THE FAILURE OF NEOLIBERAL THEORY

In accord with neoliberal institutionalist expectations, the EC supported the NTB codes—on customs valuation and anti-dumping—from which it was able to enjoy absolute gains. However, in contrast to neoliberal predictions, the EC often blocked a strong interpretation of the technical barriers and government procurement agreements (again, with important exceptions regarding the TBT accord), codes from which it was also attaining substantial absolute benefits. Neoliberals argue that cheating is the main systemic-level barrier to the achievement of cooperation by states under anarchy. However, it is difficult to sustain the thesis that the EC pursued a minimalist approach regarding the agreements on technical barriers and government procurement, and the subsidies portion of the subsidies/countervail code, because it believed there was more cheating by its major partners in those codes than in the codes on customs valuation, import licensing, and anti-dumping, and the countervail portion of the SCM accord.

22. The $169,000 dollar-equivalent of SDR 150,000 is based on an exchange rate of $1.126 = SDR 1, which is derived from GATT figures presented on the threshold during 1983 expressed in national currencies of code signatories. See Committee on Government Procurement, "Third Annual Review of the Implementation and Operation of the Agreement: Background Document by the Secretariat," GATT Doc. GPR/18, January 9, 1984, 5.
23. For sources, see Table 6.8.

Table 6.18. EC balance of contracts covered by the Code on Government Procurement, 1983 (in millions of SDR)

Code-covered contracts	United States	Japan	Canada	The Nordics	Switzerland	Austria	Total
(A) Value of contracts awarded to EC member-states	1,012.7	16.0	12.6	39.9	26.0	11.3	1,118.5
(B) Value of contracts awarded by EC member-states	4.0	0.5	None reported	None reported	0.3	None reported	4.8
(C) Balance (A − B)	1,008.7	15.5	12.6	39.9	25.7	11.3	1,113.7

Sources: See Table 6.8.

In addition, neoliberals suggest that four conditions may promote cooperation among states in mixed-interest international situations: iterated interactions, small numbers of participants, heavy representation by advanced democratic states, and the production by the joint effort of large individual absolute gains. Neoliberals could argue that, from the viewpoint of the EC, these conditions favored the customs valuation, import licensing, and anti-dumping codes, and the countervail portion of the subsidies agreement, and disfavored the technical barriers and government procurement codes, as well as the subsidies portion of the SCM accord. However, these four neoliberal-specified conditions do not appear to have varied across the NTB codes in a manner that corresponds to the variance in effectiveness that was in fact achieved by the codes during the 1980s or in a way that correlates with the variation in the level of support the EC ascribed to the different agreements.

Thus neoliberalism's specification of the cheating problem and its identification of four background conditions affecting the propensity of states to cheat fail to explain the EC's resistance to what developed into the less successful codes, the EC's resulting conflicts with the United States concerning those codes, and therefore the inevitable restrictions operating on their effectiveness during the 1980s. Differences in European-American cooperation across the codes and associated differences in their effectiveness remain unsolved empirical puzzles if we restrict our analysis to neoliberal-specified variables. Neoliberal institutionalism may provide us with a theory of *one* necessary condition for cooperation—the control of cheating. However, the NTB code experience and U.S.-EC interactions within that experience suggest that we need to go beyond the problem of cheating and locate some other condition whose variation also affects the level and quality of cooperation achieved by states. For that reason, it is time to see whether realist international theory can shed additional light on the problem of Europe, the United States, and the Tokyo Round NTB codes.

CHAPTER SEVEN

The Tokyo Round NTB Regime
and Realist International Theory

Although neoliberal institutionalism is unable to explain the variation in EC support for the different Tokyo Round NTB codes during
the 1980s, this failure, as previously noted, does not by itself prove
that realism provides a superior theory of cooperation among nations.
That question is taken up here, as I seek to determine whether realism can help us understand EC preferences and behavior regarding
the NTB codes, and therefore the variance in effectiveness achieved
by those agreements during the 1980s. Realism, viewing states as defensive positionalists, would expect EC policy toward the NTB regime
to reflect the EC's judgments about relative achievements of mutually
positive gains produced by the different codes. The discussion below
finds that the EC supported those accords yielding it a favorable share
of mutually positive gains. Most important, the discussion also demonstrates that the EC restricted its support for accords it believed
would produce gaps in benefits favoring code partners, especially the
United States.

To make this case, the first major section demonstrates that the
codes the EC strongly supported—again, the customs valuation and
anti-dumping agreements, and the countervailing measures portion
of the subsidies accord—provided it with highly favorable relative
gains. This is a necessary first step in demonstrating the usefulness of
realist theory. That is, if the EC had enjoyed favorable relative gains
from the CV and ADP codes, and the countervail rules in the SCM
accord, but nevertheless obstructed their operation, or if it had supported them in the face of unfavorable relative achievements of gains,
then realist-specified variables and the realist logic of the problem of
cooperation would be clearly unhelpful in understanding the NTB

code experience. The evidence presented in the first section makes it clear that, in fact, neither type of disconfirming evidence associated with these codes and code elements can be observed during the 1980s.

However, the most that may be inferred from observations of EC support for those codes and code elements is that they do not disprove realist theory. This is due to the fact that these agreements, by providing favorable relative gains to the EC, must have also provided it with some level of absolute gains as well. Hence both neoliberals and realists could claim that they can explain the EC's support for these NTB codes or code elements. EC support for these codes and code elements keeps realism in competition with neoliberalism, but it does not provide for a definitive test of the comparative efficacy of the two approaches. Similarly, the second major section argues that the EC's resistance to the United State in the subsidies half of the accord on subsidies and countervailing measures was driven partly by concerns about gaps in gains and partly, in regard to agricultural export subsidies, by a well-grounded fear that any gains achieved by the United States would come at the direct loss of the EC. Here, too, both realism and neoliberalism could claim to be able to account for EC behavior, and therefore we cannot judge between the two approaches by focusing on the subsidies portion of the SCM accord.

However, when we come to the agreements on technical barriers and government procurement, realism finally finds an opportunity to demonstrate its power over neoliberalism. It will be recalled that the EC member-states unambiguously enjoyed substantial absolute gains from these two NTB accords during the 1980s, but the EC often found itself in conflict with the United States over their implementation and development and this restricted their effectiveness. The third major section demonstrates that at the root of the EC's approach to these two accords was a defensively oriented concern that these two agreements provided the United States relatively greater *potential* new export opportunities than could be enjoyed by EC producers. It was this defensively positional concern about gaps in otherwise positive gains, the section argues, that directly accounts for EC reticence to support the two codes and, in the case of the TBT arrangement, to try to alter its balance of rights and obligations. Moreover, in regard to both agreements, it is possible to demonstrate that the EC's policy was not driven by an interest in maximizing its absolute potential trading gains; on the contrary, the EC sometimes actually gave up opportunities for absolute gains while attempting to minimize gaps in gains favoring the United States. Hence a realist-informed focus on defensive state positionalism and the problem of relative gains helps account for aspects of EC behavior regarding the NTB codes during the 1980s that would be unintelligible if one were to rely solely on neo-liberal institutionalism.

The last major section argues that the EC and its member-states were not the only code participants to display concerns about relative gains arising from the NTB regime. It suggests that the major setback experienced by the anti-dumping code committee—its failure to develop strong rules for basic-price systems under Article 8:4 of the anti-dumping code—occurred because several code participants believed that such rules would generate positive gains for all but would leave the United States and the EC relatively better off than they. Instead of accepting that distribution of gains, these signatories caused the ADP committee to formulate rules that were much weaker than those thought to be feasible and desirable from an absolute-gains viewpoint. The only virtue, in fact, of the rules that were formulated was that they did not institutionalize a gap in gains favoring the United States and the EC.

THE NTB CODES AND FAVORABLE ACHIEVEMENTS OF GAINS BY THE EC

Throughout the 1980s the EC strongly supported the codes on customs valuation and anti-dumping, as well as the rules on counter-vailing measures contained in the subsidies agreement. If this occurred despite unfavorable relative achievements of gains by the EC, realist theory would be flawed. In fact there is no evidence suggesting that the EC sustained unfavorable achievements of gains from these codes; rather, it enjoyed highly favorable relative shares of the gains produced by them. For example, no evidence exists that the EC was concerned during this period about its gains—absolute or relative—from the CV code. At the May 1981 meeting of the CV committee, the EC representative observed that six months of experience with the code had "led the EC to conclude that the expectations for a practicable and fair system of customs valuation had been met." He noted further that "the new system had generally been well received by customs officials and traders alike," and that "the EC had indications that many customs officials had found that it was simpler and easier to apply than the previous system."[1]

1. See CV committee, "Minutes," May 5, 1981, GATT Doc. VAL/M/2, June 17, 1981, 2. (Citation procedures for GATT materials are described in Chapter 4, footnote 2— see p. 71.)

In addition, the limited data available on actual gains generated by the operation of the customs code, as well as those on anti-dumping and countervailing measures, suggest that the EC supported them because they provided its members with a very favorable share of joint gains.[2] With regard to the customs code, for example, the Tokyo Round negotiators set January 1, 1981, as the target date on which the CV code would go into effect. However, the United States and the EC agreed to bring the treaty into force bilaterally from July 1, 1980. According to a report of the United States International Trade Commission, it was not the United States but the EC that had pressed for this: the report notes that the two partners "agreed to implement the agreement on July 1, 1980, reflecting the EC's strong interest in abolition of the 'American Selling Price' [ASP] system of customs valuation."[3]

A second piece of evidence suggesting EC enjoyment of a favorable share of the gains from the customs code comes from the CV committee meeting in November 1981. At that time the code participants examined one another's submissions of data on their use of different code-mandated valuation methods during the first year the code had been in operation. The United States provided additional data on the frequency with which it had used different valuation methods prior to the implementation of the code. On the basis of this data, the EC representative noted that U.S. employment of computed-value methods of customs valuation—probably associated with its now-defunct ASP valuation rules—had declined sharply. The EC representative said that "he was pleased to see that in the United States the use of that method which the EC had always considered as a method of last resort had decreased from a maximum of 13 per cent under the old law to 2 per cent under the Agreement."[4] Thus, from the EC viewpoint, the United States had altered its customs-valuation practices in a manner highly favorable to the former as a result of the CV code.

Finally, the EC appears not to have been obligated to make major changes in its own customs-valuation procedures as a result of the CV

2. As in the discussion of absolute gains, here too it must be stressed that data problems make it difficult to estimate with high confidence whether the NTB codes generated gaps in gains among their participants.

3. See United States International Trade Commission, *Operation of 'he Trade Agreements Program*, Thirty-Second Report, USITC Publication 1307 (Washington, 1982), 64.

4. CV committee, "Minutes," November 4–5, 1981, GATT Doc. VAL/M/3, January 29, 1982, 11. The General Accounting Office confirmed in 1982 that the computed method was used only in 2.1 percent of all import entries into the United States during October 1981 and that the transaction value was accepted for 94.2 percent of all entries; see General Accounting Office, *New U.S. Valuation System for Imported Products Is Better and Easier to Administer*, GAO Report GGD-82-80 (Washington, 1982), 5.

code. According to an EC official active in both the negotiation and operation of the NTB accords, there had been a very wide gap in the EC's stated adherence to the Brussels Definition of Value (BDV) system of customs valuation and its actual practice, for the latter was primarily based on the use of invoices, that is, on the transaction value of the goods, the preferred manner articulated in Article I of the CV code.[5] Similarly, an EC official who had previously worked in the British customs service reported that the declared prices of imports had been used for customs purposes in that country before the implementation of the CV code.[6] Last, a West German official reported that whereas the EC used the transaction value for 95 percent of all import entries by the mid-1980s, it had done so for approximately 90 percent of all imports prior to the time the code went into effect. According to this official, EC practices had changed very little as result of the code, and it had been the United States that had been obliged to alter more of its customs-valuation policies with its termination of ASP and its use of as many as nine different valuation methods.[7] Thus, while the United States may have perceived that it had gained satisfactory benefits from the CV code because of greater ease in managing its customs-valuation system and because of greater certainty about the valuation rules of its code partners, the EC believed that it also enjoyed these gains and the additional gains arising from the termination of the American Selling Price system.

Just as the EC had good reason to be satisfied with both its absolute and relative gains from the operation of the CV code, a similar finding can be made in the case of the Code on Anti-Dumping Practices. The ADP code disciplines the way in which signatories pursue anti-dumping actions against firms exporting goods from the territory of fellow signatories. As noted in the previous chapter, it is probably fair to assume that the ADP code did not cause signatories to be more willing to initiate actions against one another during the 1980s—if anything, the opposite is more likely to have been true. Thus the relative frequency of actions initiated against a signatory's firms by its code partners during that period may be taken as a measure of the relative enjoyment by that signatory (or, more precisely, firms operating in the signatory's territory) of administrative and legal due process afforded by the code: these data are presented in Table 7.1.

5. This was especially true in Belgium, the Netherlands, and Luxembourg. Interview, EC official no. 2, Geneva, August 5, 1986.

6. Interview, EC official no. 1, Geneva, August 5, 1986.

7. Interview, Federal Republic of Germany official no. 8, telephone interview from Brussels to Bonn, July 18, 1986.

Table 7.1. Anti-dumping actions initiated among all signatories to the Code on Anti-Dumping Practices, 1980–86

Target country	1980–81			1981–82			1982–83			1983–84		
	No.	Share (%)	Rank	No.	Share (%)	Rank	No.	Share (%)	Rank	No.	Share (%)	Rank
EC/EC member-states	19	30.2	1	41	47.3	1	47	33.6	1	41	30.4	1
United States	16	25.4	2	11	8.2	4	18	12.9	3	11	8.1	6
Japan	4	6.3	6	14	6.2	6	22	15.7	2	17	12.6	3
Canada	3	4.8	7	4	2.1	7	5	3.6	7	6	4.4	7
Other industrialized democracies	8	12.7	3	11	7.5	5	18	12.9	3	33	24.4	2
Less-developed countries	7	11.1	4	33	11.6	3	12	8.6	6	12	8.9	5
Socialist-bloc countries	6	9.5	5	17	17.1	2	18	12.9	3	15	11.1	4
Total	63	100.0	–	131	100.0	–	140	100.2[a]	–	135	99.9	–

Target country	1984–85			1985–86			Total, 1980–86		
	No.	Share (%)	Rank	No.	Share (%)	Rank	No.	Share (%)	Rank
EC/EC member-states	24	16.7	3	41	31.3	1	241	31.8	1
United States	17	11.8	6	11	8.4	5	85	11.2	6
Japan	20	13.9	5	14	10.7	4	86	11.3	5
Canada	6	4.2	7	4	3.1	6	27	3.6	7
Other industrialized democracies	25	17.4	2	11	8.4	5	106	14.0	3
Less-developed countries	29	20.1	1	33	25.2	2	110	14.5	2
Socialist-bloc countries	23	16.0	4	17	13.0	3	104	13.7	4
Total	144	100.1	–	131	100.1	–	759	100.1	–

[a] Percentages do not always total 100.0 because of rounding error.
Source: GATT Committee on Anti-Dumping Practices, Annual Report to the CONTRACTING PARTIES, various years, in *Basic Instruments and Selected Documents* (Geneva).

As can be observed in the table, EC firms were the target of almost one-third of all anti-dumping actions initiated by ADP code signatories against one another during the early to mid-1980s. The EC's adherence to the ADP code thus provided its firms the legal and procedural protection afforded by the code at a very high rate as compared with the rates for other advanced countries or other groups of countries, suggesting the EC enjoyed very substantial relative gains from the agreement.

This achievement by the EC of a favorable sharing of gains from the ADP code is even more evident if we focus on the code signatories responsible for most anti-dumping actions initiated during the 1980s: the United States, Australia, Canada, and the EC itself. Table 7.2 reports the balances enjoyed during the early to mid-1980s by these major code signatories between the number of anti-dumping actions they initiated and the number of instances in which the signatory's firms were the target of ADP actions by fellow code participants. (In the previous chapter, Table 6.14 reported these data only for the EC.) Table 7.2 indicates that each of the four signatories responsible for virtually every anti-dumping action during the bulk of the 1980s was itself the target of actions by code partners; however, only the EC achieved a positive balance. Each of these partners enjoyed some measure of protection from their adherence to the ADP code; however, it was the EC that achieved the best ratio between the acceptance of code disciplines and the receipt of such protection when its own firms were at risk.

Table 7.2. Anti-dumping actions initiated among major signatories to the Code on Anti-Dumping Practices, 1980–86

Total anti-dumping actions	Signatory			
	EC member-states	United States	Australia	Canada
(A) Initiated *against* signatory by other signatory	241	85	5	27
(B) Initated *by* signatory against other signatory	174	193	193	179
(C) Balance (A − B)	67	−108	−188	−152

Sources: See Table 7.1.

The EC also enjoyed a highly favorable share of gains in regard to the countervailing-measures portion of the subsidies agreement. This can be observed in Table 7.3, which follows the same procedure used with regard to the ADP code and reports the annual frequency with which code signatories were the target of countervailing-measure actions by code partners. As with the anti-dumping code, it may be assumed that a state may find itself the target of such actions regardless of whether or not it is a code signatory; what the code provides, however, is some insurance that specific procedures and rules will be followed in the countervailing-measure action. The table indicates that the EC was the most frequent target of countervailing actions by code partners during the 1980s. If the especially large number of actions initiated during 1981–82 were excluded, the EC would still have been the target of about 20 percent of all actions and would have been surpassed only by Brazil.

The favorable balance of administrative-legal protection enjoyed by the EC by virtue of the SCM code can also be observed in Table 7.4, which reports the balance of countervailing actions initiated by and against major code signatories during the 1980s. The table indicates that the EC was required to follow code rules regarding such actions in five instances during the 1980s; in exchange, it enjoyed code-based protection of its interests in some eighty cases in which it was the target of other signatories. The United States, Chile, and Australia initiated actions under the code while rarely finding it necessary to receive similar treatment. Only Canada, which had ten actions initiated against it and began eight of its own, could be said to have offered about as much legal-administrative protection as it received under the SCM code. The EC, in contrast, attained much more protection of its interests under the code than it was required to provide, suggesting a very favorable enjoyment of relative gains.

In sum, the EC enjoyed very favorable relative gains from the customs valuation and anti-dumping codes during the 1980s, and the countervailing-measures portion of the subsidies accords, and it gave these NTB accords very strong support during that period. This experience is consistent with realism and indeed offers mild support for it. Yet neoliberalism (with its focus on absolute gains) and realism (with its emphasis on relative gains) both would have correctly predicted EC support for these accords and code elements. Both theories would also have predicted the EC's opposition to the least successful part of the NTB regime, the subsidy rules in the accord on subsidies and countervailing measures, to which we now turn our attention.

Table 7.3. Countervailing measures initiated among all signatories to the Code on Subsidies and Countervailing Measures, 1981–86

Target country	Annual No. of actions initiated against target country					Total, 1981–86	Share of Total (%)
	1981–82	1982–83	1983–84	1984–85	1985–86		
Signatories that themselves initiated actions							
EC/EC member-states	52	14	6	2	9	83	33.3
United States	0	1	0	0	0	1	0.4
Canada	1	2	0	1	6	10	4.0
Australia	0	0	1	0	0	1	0.4
Chile	0	0	0	0	1	1	0.4
Other advanced-country signatories							
Spain	7	7	8	3	0	25	10.0
New Zealand	0	2	0	6	4	12	4.8
Other	0	1	1	3	0	5	2.0
Developing-country signatories							
Brazil	33	17	16	10	5	81	32.5
South Korea	3	5	0	5	2	15	6.0
Other	1	2	2	6	4	15	6.0
Total	97	51	34	36	31	249	99.8

Sources: GATT, Basic Instruments and Selected Documents (Geneva): Thirtieth Supplement (1984), 44–45; Thirty-First Supplement (1985), 264–65; Thirty-Second Supplement (1986), 165–66; Thirty-Third Supplement (1987), 204–5.

Table 7.4. Countervailing measures initiated among major signatories
to the Code on Subsidies and Countervailing Measures, 1981–86

Total countervailing measures	EC member-states	United States	Canada	Australia	Chile
(A) Initiated *against* signatory by other signatory	83	1	10	1	1
(B) Initated *by* signatory against other signatory	5	132	8	20	83
(C) Balance (A − B)	78	−131	2	−19	−82

Sources: See Table 7.3.

The EC and the Subsidies Portion of the SCM Accord

Throughout the 1980s the EC resolutely opposed an aggressive interpretation of the subsidies rules contained in the SCM code. One of the specific code obligations to which the EC ascribed a minimalist interpretation, it will be recalled, involved the notification of subsidies. Compliance by one's partners with those rules yielded very important information about those partners' subsidy programs. At the same time, however, one's own compliance involved a risk, for notifying subsidy programs could be taken as evidence that the programs were affecting trade and might be harming the trading interests of partners. Hence the more programs that it notified, the greater the risk a signatory ran of becoming a target of partners's countervailing measures or dispute-settlement actions at the GATT/SCM code level.

Table 7.5 sheds light on the relative levels of gain and risk associated with compliance with the SCM's transparency rules, for it reports the relative significance of subsidies in the EC and its major member-states compared with the United States and other advanced countries during the 1970s and early 1980s. The table indicates that the EC made greater use of subsidies as a policy instrument during that period than did the United States (or Japan). Even in market-oriented West Germany, subsidies constituted a percentage of aggregate national economic activity more than three times greater than in the United States. If subsidies programs became transparent as a result of all code partners providing full disclosure of their subsidy programs, the EC would have gained in terms of acquiring information about its partners' subsidy programs, but it would have put itself at relatively greater risk of countervail and dispute-settlement actions than would

Table 7.5. Significance of subsidies: major signatories to the Code on Subsidies and Countervailing Measures, 1970–82 (as percent of gross domestic product)

Country/country group	1970	1975	1980	1982
EC (average of 9 member-states)	2.0	2.9	3.2	3.1
Italy	1.5	2.7	3.0	3.5
France	2.0	2.4	2.5	2.7
United Kingdom	1.7	3.5	2.3	2.0
Germany	1.7	2.0	2.0	1.8
United States	0.5	0.3	0.4	0.5
Nordics	3.3	4.5	5.1	5.3
Canada	0.9	2.3	2.4	2.1
Japan	1.1	1.5	1.5	1.4

Source: Peter Saunders and Friedrich Klau, *The Role of the Public Sector: Causes and Consequences of the Growth of Government*, Special Issue of *OECD Economic Studies*, no. 4 (Spring 1985), 69.

its partners. All would have gained from full disclosure, but the EC's partners would have gained more than the EC itself. Thus the EC balked at full notification of subsidies under the code or the GATT during the 1980s.

Relative-gains calculations appear to account for at least one area of EC resistance to the United States in the subsidies portion of the SCM agreement. However, in another code-related issue-area the EC appears not to have believed that the problem with American interpretations or initiatives was that they would lead to gaps in otherwise mutually positive gains, but instead that they constituted zero-sum situations. That issue-area, of course, concerned agriculture in general and agriculture-related export subsidies in particular. Some sense of the commitment of the EC not to allow the subsidies code to change its agricultural programs can be observed in its comments about the pasta case.[8] At the first SCM committee meeting at which the report

8. The EC recognized the larger importance of the pasta case, arguing in March 1982, for example, that the U.S. position implied that "virtually all products which have undergone any processing at all are threatened." See "Statement by the Spokesman for the Commission of the European Communities: Interpretation of Article 9," GATT Doc. SCM/Spec/12, March 11, 1982, 5–6. Such statements may have involved some measure of posturing, but they are also likely to have indicated at least to some degree the real perceptions of the representatives of code signatories. These can be highly potent in shaping political action, for, as Robert Axelrod and Robert Keohane have suggested, "Perceptions define interests." See Robert Axelrod and Robert O. Keohane, "Achieving Cooperation under Anarchy: Institutions and Strategies," *World Politics* 38 (October 1985), 229; also see 230–31.

of the pasta panel was discussed, in June 1983, the EC representative referred approvingly to the minority portion of the report and its point that "some signatories when signing the Code might have believed that they could continue their existing practices." The EC argued that changing current practices would have required specific negotiations on them; in the absence of such specific agreements, the EC had assumed in accepting Article 9 that it could continue all its subsidy programs then in effect.[9] This was vital for the EC, for, according to its spokesman, acceptance by the committee of the majority report calling for a reduction of pasta subsidies, if generalized to other industries, "would lead to a brutal change of practices existing for the past 20 years, changes which would be imposed despite the EC having negotiated in good faith and despite the fact that the EC system was well known to other Signatories."

From the EC's viewpoint, then, code-based restrictions on its export subsidies on agricultural products or on the agricultural-product component of processed goods were completely unacceptable. This EC resistance to any GATT-based constraints on its agricultural export subsidies appears to have been grounded in the actual facts surrounding agricultural trade in the 1980s. During that period both the United States and the EC (the latter through its Common Agricultural Policy, or CAP) offered roughly equivalent levels of subsidy supports to their respective farming communities, with each spending about $25 billion and more per year by the middle of the decade.[10] However, whereas the United States predominantly sought to absorb the costs of its farm support programs through domestic taxes, central elements of the CAP have been variable levies on most agricultural imports and external venting of at least a significant part of EC agricultural surpluses through the use of export subsidies. For example, the U.S. Export Enhancement Program of 1986 provided farmers agricultural stocks to be used as export bonuses worth a total of $1.5 billion over three years, while EC export subsidies totaled about $5 billion in 1984 alone.[11]

A fuller picture of the differences in relative adjustment costs be-

9. See SCM committee, "Minutes," June 9–10, 1983, GATT Doc. SCM/M/18, August 16, 1983, 4–5.

10. See Dale E. Hathaway, *Agriculture and the GATT: Rewriting the Rules*, Policy Analyses in International Economics, no. 20 (Washington, D.C.: Institute for International Economics, 1987), 76–77, 86–87.

11. See "Subsidies—Notifications Pursuant to Article XVI:1—United States: The Export Enhancement Program," GATT Doc. L/5947/Add.5, April 18, 1986, 3; and "Subsidies—Notifications Pursuant to Article XVI:1—European Communities—Addendum," GATT Doc. L/5768/Add.8, 14.

tween the EC and the United States and others if export subsidies for agriculture had been disciplined during the 1980s can be obtained from Table 7.6. It presents the estimated welfare and foreign-exchange effects that would have resulted from a *complete* dismantling of *all* agricultural support programs in operation in the advanced democratic states in the middle of that decade. Had such a radical step been taken, consumers would have achieved enormous gains in welfare through lower food prices. However, more relevant from a political viewpoint are the welfare losses that would have been experienced by producers and the losses in foreign-exchange earnings that would have been sustained by national economies. Both EC and U.S. farmers would have sustained losses, but the former's would have exceeded the latter's. The major U.S.-EC discrepancy would have occurred in regard to changes in foreign-exchange earnings: whereas U.S. exports might have expanded somewhat through liberalization, the EC's would have contracted by almost $23 billion. This contraction would have been due in part to the removal of the EC's variable levies on agricultural imports and in part to the cessation of export subsidies. In the face of that prospective foreign-exchange loss, it is not surprising that the EC (as well as Japan and the Nordics) resisted the United States vigorously on agricultural export subsidies during the 1980s.

Table 7.6. Estimated economic effects of liberalized agricultural markets, advanced countries (assuming 1985 government programs)

Country/Country group	Shifts in economic welfare (in billions of 1980 dollars)		Shift in foreign exchange earnings (in billions of 1980 dollars)
	Producers	Consumers	
EC (for 12 member-states)	−23.6	45.7	−22.8
United States	−14.6	8.5	1.0
Japan	−11.7	39.6	−14.5
European Free Trade Association (for 5 member-states)	−5.0	7.5	−2.5
Canada	−1.8	1.0	−1.1
Australia	0.6	−0.2	0.7
New Zealand	0.5	−0.2	0.6
Total advanced countries	−55.6	101.9	−38.6

Source: Adapted from Dale E. Hathaway, *Agriculture and the GATT: Rewriting the Rules*, Policy Analyses in International Economics, no. 20 (Washington, D.C.: Institute for International Economics, 1987), 97. Reprinted with permission of the Institute for International Economics.

The EC's opposition to subsidy rules in the SCM code relating to agriculture appears to have been a response not to its concern about gaps in otherwise positive gains for everyone, but instead to its fear that anything approaching a firm interpretation of the code would leave the EC worse off and its partners better off. Both realists and neoliberals would argue that in such a zero-sum situation the EC would, as indeed it did during the 1980s, reject any new international discipline on its support programs for agricultural exports.

Finally, the EC's policy regarding agricultural export subsidies eventually led to American actions during the mid-1980s suggesting that the United States had itself become concerned about relative achievements of gains generated by the SCM agreement. The United States, it will be recalled, agreed during the Tokyo Round to bring its law on countervailing measures into line with GATT guidelines in exchange for stricter international discipline over the employment of national subsidies. The United States may well have understood that the EC would benefit disproportionately from the portion of the SCM accord concerned with countervailing measures, but believed it could receive compensation for that through a favorable sharing of trade benefits resulting from the subsidy rules in the accord. However, when the goals of the United States regarding subsidies were frustrated by the EC, and when the EC did in fact achieve the lion's share of the gains generated by the countervailing-measures side of the SCM accord, the United States became sharply alienated from the agreement. On the one hand, it began to block efforts of the SCM committee relating to countervailing measures such as refusing to permit committee acceptance of the panel report on the U.S. wine industry. On the other hand, it began to develop and implement an agricultural export subsidy program of its own—the Export Enhancement Program—that was probably in contravention of the code. Thus, just as the EC focused on relative-gains problems concerning the subsidies portion of the SCM accord, so too did American behavior suggest that the United States also had limits on its willingness to accept imbalanced distributions of jointly produced benefits.

Realism and neoliberal institutionalism can both claim to have the capacity to account for the EC's acceptance of support for the customs and anti-dumping accords, the countervailing measures half of the subsidies agreement, as well as the EC's hostile attitude toward international discipline over the use of agricultural export subsidies. At the same time, on the question of the transparency of subsidies and discipline over their general employment, realism sheds light on EC preferences and behavior that had been left unilluminated by neoliberal institutionalism. At this point, realism would appear to have only a modest analytical edge over its neoliberal competitor. However, that edge widens dramatically in the following sections.

THE EC AND THE CODES ON TECHNICAL BARRIERS AND GOVERNMENT PROCUREMENT

Neoliberalism failed to account for the EC's approach to the codes on technical barriers and government procurement. If realism, in contrast, does account for its policies toward these two agreements, this would suggest that realism offers a superior theory of the problem of cooperation. The following discussion presents three interrelated lines of analysis that lead to the conclusion that realism can indeed help us understand the EC's actions toward these two accords.

The first line of analysis shows that the arguments presented by EC officials in the TBT and GPR committees revealed the EC's perception that these two codes were generating unacceptable gaps in otherwise mutually positive gains in favor of the United States. Second, it is demonstrated that the actual institutional arrangements and the changes taking place in those arrangements in the issue-areas covered by the two codes during the 1980s were of such a character that the EC had good empirical grounds to be concerned about the distributions of gains generated by the two accords. Third, and finally, strong evidence is available suggesting that the EC believed during the 1980s that it could undertake policy initiatives in the government procurement and technical standards issue-areas that could help its member-states revive their economies in the face of new competitive pressures from abroad and ensure Europe's economic independence and strength in the decades to come. As a result, technical standards and government procurement became strategic issue-areas for the EC during the 1980s, and for that reason it was sensitive to gaps in gains that might be generated by the accords covering those two issue-areas.

Arguments of the EC in the TBT and GPR Committees

One sort of evidence suggesting defensive positionalism on the part of the EC concerns the arguments it presented in explaining its approach to the TBT and GPR accords. If relative-gains concerns did lead the EC to resist the United States in those two codes, and to try to revise rules in the former, one would expect to observe EC expressions of dissatisfaction with its share of joint gains.[12] In fact EC statements in the TBT and GPR committees do indicate that the EC was seriously worried about gaps in otherwise mutually positive gains arising from those two agreements.

One important example involved the EC and the question of the mutual acceptance of test data under the technical barriers code. It will be recalled that the United States suggested during 1985 that the TBT code participants develop a new, comprehensive accord requiring signatories to accept one another's test data. The United States argued that if a comprehensive accord could not be formulated immediately, for the time being the signatories might develop agreements, including mutual laboratory-accreditation accords, on a sector-by-sector basis, as the United States and Japan were seeking to do in the telecommunications industry.[13] The EC resisted this idea and proposed in its place that the TBT committee encourage bilateral agreements between individual national-testing authorities and between individual laboratories.[14]

What is of special interest to the present discussion is the EC's rationale during the 1980s for its resistance to the U.S. approach. The EC argued throughout that decade that a serious shortcoming of the TBT agreement as originally formulated was that it applied only to central-government authorities, the type of institutional arrangement in the technical-measures field characteristic of most of the European states, and not directly to private bodies or to non-central government entities. In the view of the EC, the latter two types of institutions, though not under the jurisdiction of the code, were becoming increas-

12. EC commentary in the NTB code committees is likely to have been reflective of the perceptions of EC member-states about the codes for at least three reasons. First, most arguments made by code signatories at committee meetings are based on prepared statements developed after inter-departmental deliberations at home-capitals and then read into the code committee record. Second, code participants review committee minutes before their final versions are published and may provide amplifications or revisions if these are considered necessary. Third, comments at committee meetings by EC representatives are especially likely to reflect the sentiments of most if not all the EC member-states, for several of the latter's GATT-based representatives and their relevant officials from home-capitals are themselves often at the committee meetings.

13. The U.S. proposals were presented in "Testing and Type Approval: Note by the Delegation of the United States," GATT Doc. TBT/W/79, 1–2; "Second Three-Year Review of the Operation and Implementation of the Agreement: Proposals by the United States," GATT Doc. TBT/21, September 23, 1985, 1–2.

14. See, for example, the EC comments in TBT committee, "Minutes," February 26, 1985, GATT Doc. TBT/M/18, April 19, 1985, 7; and "Testing and Inspection: Statement by the Delegation of the European Economic Community," GATT Doc. TBT/W/91, March 20, 1986.

ingly more important in the standards issue-area in the United States. The EC argued that, as a result, if new obligations were constructed in the field of testing, this would generate *relatively* greater obligations for unitary states than for federal states. To avoid such an imbalanced generation of new obligations, the EC recommended a strictly bilateral approach (which could generate agreements between private, non-central government, or central-government laboratories). As the EC representative suggested in October 1985, "The conclusion of these agreements at the level of laboratories would overcome the problem of distinguishing between the status of private laboratories and of those on central government authorities." In contrast, the U.S. approach, according to the EC, "would bring to the surface the lack of symmetry in the obligations of Parties."[15]

The EC also gave evidence of relative-gains concerns when it opposed a Nordic proposal to encourage the mutual acceptance of test data and the mutual accreditation of testing laboratories and certification institutions.[16] The EC noted in October 1986 that the proposal "failed to define the status of the competent national bodies that would administer" the accreditation process. This was a problem because "if the obligations and rights in this area were limited solely to bodies that were dependent on public entities [as in EC member-states], the proposed recommendation would not apply to those Parties [such as, in the EC view, the United States] that were in the process of deregulating gradually." The EC thus emphasized that "the European Community, for its part, could only support a recommendation that covered both public and private bodies."[17]

The same concern about relative obligations was again expressed by the EC in February 1987 when it resisted a U.S. proposal calling on signatories to report on their implementation of a 1986 committee recommendation to use guides on testing, inspection, and certification formulated by the International Organization for Standardization (ISO) and the International Electro-technical Commission (IEC).[18] The EC representative argued that the EC's own preferred approach—bilateral agreements between laboratories—was designed "with a view to safeguarding the balance of obligations between different Parties." The U.S. representative reiterated that sectoral agree-

15. TBT committee, "Minutes," GATT Doc. TBT/M/20, February 6, 1986, 9.
16. For TBT committee discussion of the Nordic proposal, see TBT committee, "Minutes," October 12–14, 1986, GATT Doc. TBT/M/23, December 12, 1986, 4–5.
17. Ibid., 5.
18. See the U.S. proposal in TBT committee, "Minutes," March 9–10, 1987, GATT Doc. TBT/M/24, June 3, 1987, 5.

ments might be a useful strategy, to which the EC spokesman replied that "the sector-by-sector approach implied that Parties would have to identify not only the product areas where they had an interest in concluding mutual recognition agreements but also the sectors in which they had the authority to impose such agreements on individual operators [that is, laboratories and test bodies]." The EC representative, reflecting the core concern of the EC, then asked "to what extent international agreements on mutual acceptance of test data concluded by the United States government would be binding on entities operating in the standards field in the United States."[19]

Relative-gains concerns also manifested themselves in the EC's opposition to the U.S. proposal in October 1986 to require signatories to notify their bilateral standards-related agreements and activities to the TBT committee.[20] The EC argued in March 1987 that the issue of transparency of such agreements and activities was related "to the problem of coexistence of public and private bodies in the standards field." The EC representative went on to explain that "parties were not always informed about bilateral standards-related agreements concluded between private bodies operating in their respective territories," and therefore the representative suggested that "he doubted that the recommendation proposed by the United States would be useful in obtaining information on a large number of agreements concluded at the private level."[21]

Finally, relative-gains concerns induced not just the EC's opposition to U.S. rule-making efforts in the TBT committee, but also its own major initiative in the committee. The EC proposed in March 1985 that the code be extended to non-central governmental agencies and to private standards bodies. The EC argued that the proposal was necessary because "there is, in the Community's view, a need to correct the present imbalance in obligations under the TBT Agreement between, on the one hand, Parties in which administration (including responsibility for the establishment of technical regulations) is highly centralized and, on the other hand, Parties in which the central government has only limited responsibilities in the standards area." The EC went on to observe that "the activity of private standards organiza-

19. Ibid., 6. It should be noted that the U.S. representative emphasized at the meeting, as at other discussions, that the U.S. government could make commitments on behalf of the national government, states of the union, and "private entities." However, this was not fully reassuring to the EC, and certain U.S. statements, reported in the text, could have given the EC pause.

20. The U.S. proposal is noted and discussed in TBT/M/24, 7–8.

21. TBT/M/24, 7.

tions is becoming increasingly important, as a number of governments are reducing their direct involvement in the formulation of technical regulations," and that "it therefore seems appropriate that Parties effectively carry out their responsibility to ensure similar levels of transparency in the private and public sector[s]."[22]

In the first major committee discussion of the two proposals, in March 1986, the EC did not argue that the technical barriers code imposed no obligations on signatories whose non-central governmental bodies were active in the standards field. Instead, it stressed that the code had generated an imbalance in obligations, suggesting that "under the existing provisions of the Agreement, Parties with centralized governments undertook far more commitments than those with decentralized administrative systems." Moreover, the EC argued that "this imbalance had increased with the recent trend towards decentralization" and that this required more formal and explicit extension of code obligations to non-governmental standards entities.[23] Similarly, the EC representative argued that "there was an increasing trend by central government authorities in some Parties to entrust non-governmental bodies (NGBs) with standards-related activities" and suggested that "any negative implications of this trend for the objectives of the Agreement could be checked by drawing up a code of good practice" for NGBs.[24] Hence in the initiatives it opposed as well as those it undertook, the EC operated in the TBT committee on the basis of a concern that relative obligations of the code and thus of its resulting trade-creating effects favored the federal system of the United States and disfavored many of the EC's more centralized member-states.

Similar concerns about relative gains and burdens were at the root of the EC's major dispute with the United States concerning the government procurement code. It will be recalled that between 1981 and 1987 the EC and the United States disagreed over the former's exclusion of value-added taxes (VAT) from its estimations of government contracts when determining whether such contracts came under the code. The United States argued that such taxes ought to be included; the EC maintained that they should be excluded. A panel ruled in favor of the United States in 1984 and called on the EC member-states to include value-added taxes in their contract estimations. The EC

22. See "Second Three-Year Review of the Operation and Implementation of the Agreement: Statement by the European Economic Community," GATT Doc. TBT/23, November 13,1985, 1.

23. TBT committee, "Minutes," March 6–7, 1986, GATT Doc. TBT/M/21, May 6, 1986, 9.

24. Ibid., 11.

rejected this proposal and offered instead to accept a unilateral reduction by all EC members of 6.5 percent and later 13 percent of the threshold value applied to EC contracts. The United States, noting that this solution was not in accord with the code, nevertheless accepted the EC offer in February 1987.

Throughout this period the EC emphasized that its concerns about relative gains compelled it to oppose inclusion of VAT charges in contract estimations. It argued that VAT rates differed among EC member-states, and, by consequence, members with higher rates would be more likely to surpass the threshold for a given product if VAT charges were included. As a result, according to the EC, if VAT were included, inequalities would result in terms of which partners had to open more contracts to foreign competition, and this inequality would manifest itself among all the GPR code signatories and especially among the EC members. Excluding taxes, the EC argued in April 1981, ensured that the threshold of contracts covered by the code would be the same across member-states. By contrast, the EC emphasized, "To add taxes which varied substantially from country to country would bring about a distortion in the value of the threshold, with more contracts falling above it in a country with a high level of taxation as compared to another country with a lower level."[25] Similarly, the EC argued in July 1982 that it excluded taxes in its own public procurement rules "because this was the only system which placed all enterprises in the Community on the same level and gave them equal chances."[26] In December of that year the EC again argued that "the purpose of the threshold was to establish a certain equitability between the Parties in terms of volumes of goods exchanged under the agreement." The EC emphasized that "very wide differences existed between levels of VAT in the Community" and that their inclusion would "create an inequitable situation where the threshold in terms of goods would be reduced—the more so the higher the

25. The EC representative added that "it was a matter of concern that so many Parties included the taxation element, with the result that the threshold was not the same for all Parties." The EC thus suggested that "serious consideration should therefore be given by other Parties to a solution similar to that practiced by the EC which secured neutrality of taxation." See GPR committee, "Minutes," April 9, 1981, GATT Doc. GPR/M/2, June 5, 1981, 16–17. The EC continued along this line at the next GPR meeting, at which it said that, in light of differing VAT rates across the code participants, "in order to enable the GATT Agreement to apply equitably between Signatories," it was necessary to exclude all VAT charges, for "to do otherwise would be to admit different threshold values depending on the tax level in question which would in turn affect the overall balance of the Agreement." See GPR committee, "Minutes," July 8–9, 1981, GATT Doc. GPR/M/3, June 29, 1981, 21.

26. GPR committee, "Minutes," July 6, 1982, GATT Doc. GPR/M/Spec/1, September 20, 1982, 1.

VAT—in one member State as compared to another member state of the Community and as compared to another Party to the Agreement."[27]

In addition, when the VAT panel report was issued in June 1984, the EC argued that it could not accept its recommendation that EC member-states include VAT charges since "the existence of different tax systems and practices affecting government purchasing, and particularly the application of differing tax rates both within the Community and in other countries, as well as different rules for tax exemptions, made it difficult, if not impossible, to see how the Panel's approach could lead to an equitable solution."[28] Finally, and emphasizing the point that the core relative-gains problem operated among the EC member-countries, the EC representative noted to the GPR committee in February 1987 that a common unilateral EC threshold reduction was necessary for, "in view of the lack of harmonization of indirect taxation between the EC member states, a pure and simple inclusion of VAT was not possible." The representative argued that "the only possible solution was a unilateral reduction in the threshold applicable to the Community by a unitary rate" and reported that the figure of 13 percent was "equivalent to the average effective rate of the different VAT regimes in the Community."[29]

Thus, in resisting inclusion of VAT charges in its contract estimations, the EC did not believe that their inclusion would shift all or even most of the "burden" of greater access to government markets onto the EC countries as a group or onto any one EC member-state. Instead the problem was one of unequal *relative* sharing of such a burden. This made inclusion of the VAT unacceptable, and the EC insisted on a solution to its dispute with the United States that would minimize relative differences in economic openness that EC members would need to provide to one another and to foreign suppliers.

Institutional Trends in Europe and the United States
in Government Procurement and Technical Standards

A second type of evidence suggesting that the EC was motivated by relative-gains calculations in the technical barriers and government procurement codes concerns the way in which differences in institu-

27. GPR committee, "Minutes," December 15, 1982, GATT Doc. GPR/M/Spec/2, February 14, 1983, 2.
28. See GPR committee, "Minutes," May 16, 1984, GATT Doc. GPR/M/Spec/9, June 15, 1984, 1.
29. GPR committee, "Minutes," February 2, 1987, GATT Doc. GPR/M/25, April 9, 1987, 14.

tional arrangements in the United States and the major EC countries during the 1980s would have led the EC to believe that the two agreements were biased in favor of the United States. For example, in the case of the TBT code, the evidence suggests that the evolution of standards-making activities within the United States and the EC during that period caused the agreement progressively to be biased in favor of the former over the latter. Some sense of this bias in the actual operation of the TBT code during the 1980s can be observed in Table 7.7, which reports the annual and total number of technical notifications submitted by the TBT code signatories between 1980 and 1986.

As the table indicates, the United States was the largest notifier of technical regulations during 1980 and 1981, with the EC and its member-states coming in third or fourth during those years. During this period, then, the EC's relative gains in terms of advance information about U.S. technical measures were quite favorable. However, beginning in 1982 the absolute number of U.S. notifications began to drop while EC notifications increased modestly: during 1983–86, the United States notified an average of about eighteen technical regulations, only about one-third its rate during 1980–82, while the EC notified an average of forty-four measures during the later period, up from thirty-four during the first years of the code's operation. Overall, while the EC gradually moved during the 1980s from serving as the third or fourth most significant notifier to the second most significant (and, in 1986, with the accession of Spain to the EC, the single largest notifier), the United States slipped from first to seventh place during the same period.

While the EC and its member-states provided progressively greater levels of transparency as to their technical measures to its code partners during the 1980s, the United States provided progressively lower (but still positive) levels. This trend in American technical notifications does not appear to have been the result of cheating but instead of shifts in the character of technical-standards activities in the United States. As the U.S. representative explained to the TBT committee in May 1986, "over the past six years, there has been a trend in his country to deregulate standards-related activities both at the federal and state level and at the same time to devolve responsibilities to the private sector. This could be an explanation for the relatively limited number of notifications by his country."[30] The U.S. representative appears to have been referring to a federal directive on standards

30. TBT committee, "Minutes," May 28, 1986, GATT Doc. TBT/M/22, August 21, 1986, 6.

Table 7.7. Technical notifications to the Committee on Technical Barriers to Trade, by signatory, 1980–86

Signatory	1980 No.	1980 Share (%)	1980 Rank	1981 No.	1981 Share (%)	1981 Rank	1982 No.	1982 Share (%)	1982 Rank	1983 No.	1983 Share (%)	1983 Rank	Total, 1980–86 No.	Total, 1980–86 Share (%)	Total, 1980–86 Rank
EC/EC member-states	17	13.1	4	50	16.9	3	37	18.4	3	52	20.4	2	281	18.5	3
United States	47	36.2	1	91	30.8	1	25	12.4	4	15	5.9	6	234	15.4	4
The Nordics	19	14.6	3	51	17.3	2	44	21.9	2	38	14.9	3	293	19.3	1
Japan	21	16.2	2	31	10.5	5	47	23.4	1	92	36.1	1	286	18.9	2
Canada	15	11.5	5	15	5.1	6	20	10.0	5	26	10.2	4	158	10.4	5
Other industrialized democracies	11	8.5	6	46	15.6	4	10	5.0	7	7	2.7	7	122	8.1	6
Less-developed countries	0	0	–	4	1.4	8	5	2.5	8	24	9.4	5	101	6.7	7
Socialist-bloc countries	0	0	–	7	2.4	7	13	6.5	6	1	0.4	8	37	2.4	8
Total	130	100.1[a]	–	295	100.0	–	201	100.1	–	255	100.0	–	1,515	99.7	–

Signatory	1984 No.	1984 Share (%)	1984 Rank	1985 No.	1985 Share (%)	1985 Rank	1986 No.	1986 Share (%)	1986 Rank
EC/EC member-states	35	15.7	2	35	17.9	3	55	25.6	1
United States	28	12.6	4	14	7.1	5	14	6.5	7
The Nordics	55	24.7	1	48	24.5	1	38	17.7	2
Japan	34	15.2	3	31	15.8	4	30	14.0	3
Canada	20	9.0	6	38	19.4	2	24	11.2	5
Other industrialized democracies	18	8.1	7	16	8.2	7	17	7.9	6
Less-developed countries	28	12.6	4	14	7.1	5	26	12.1	4
Socialist-bloc countries	5	2.2	8	0	0	–	11	5.1	8
Total	223	100.0	–	196	100.0	–	215	100.1	–

[a] Percentages do not always total 100.0 because of rounding error.

Source: Committee on Technical Barriers to Trade, "Eighth Annual Review of the Operation of the Implementation and Operation of the Agreement: Background Document by the Secretariat," GATT Doc. TBT/28, October 5, 1987, 7.

issued by the U.S. Office of Management and Budget in January 1980 and, in a revised form, in October 1982. According to the editors of a major American journal in the standards area, *ASTM Standardization News*, this federal directive (entitled "Federal Participation in the Development and Use of Voluntary Standards" and often cited as OMB Circular A-119) "encourages Federal agencies to use voluntary standards for procurement and regulatory purposes in lieu of developing such standards in-house."[31] Similarly, a former key U.S. official in the field of standards suggested in late 1981 that OMB A-119 "will admirably suit the objectives of the Reagan Administration" because "its principal policy objective is to remove the federal government from the standards-writing business and turn the job over to the private sector to the maximum extent possible."[32]

Indeed, OMB A-119, which originated in discussions among U.S. agencies and U.S. private groups in the standards area beginning in the mid-1970s, constituted a recognition by the federal government of a long-term shift in the relative importance of government and private standards-writing activities in the United States. Estimates of the number of technical regulations originating at the level of states and local municipalities are unavailable. However, a study for the National Bureau of Standards found that federal agencies and private-sector entities formulated approximately 75 percent and 25 percent, respectively, of the U.S. total inventory of 53,000 standards in 1964; by 1984 the federal share of a larger total inventory (over 80,000 measures) had declined to about 60 percent, whereas the private-sector share had increased to approximately 40 percent.[33]

Reflecting national trends over a longer term, U.S. policy from the late-1970s sought to rely increasingly on standards formulated in the private sector.[34] The intended effect of this U.S. policy was to reduce

31. See "OMB Circular A-119 Receives Final Approval," *ASTM Standardization News* 11 (January 1983), 28; the directive is reproduced on 28–31. For a discussion of the purposes of the directive by the then-deputy director of the Office of Product Standards in the U.S. Department of Commerce, see John C. Williams, "Standardization: The Role of the U.S. Government," *ASTM Standardization News* 9 (March 1981), 10–13.

32. See Howard I. Forman (retired deputy assistant secretary of Commerce for product standards and director, Office of Product Standards for the U.S. Department of Commerce), "Standards Setting in the United States: Yesterday, Today, and Tomorrow," *ASTM Standardization News* 9 (September 1981), 15.

33. See U.S. National Bureau of Standards, *Standards Activities of Organizations in the United States*, NBS Special Publication 681 (Gaithersburg, Md.: National Bureau of Standards, 1984), 1. Also see Robert B. Toth, "Putting the U.S. Standards System into Focus with the World," *ASTM Standardization News* 12 (December 1984), 19.

34. In addition to the essays cited above, see Robert W. Hamilton, "Nongovernmental Development of Regulatory Standards," *ASTM Standardization News* 11 (January 1983), 18–23; and William A. McAdams, "Standards and the United States," *ASTM Standardization News* 14 (December 1986), 40–43.

the relative importance of the federal government in the standards issue-area. However, because the TBT code applies only to central-government technical regulations, another (probably unintended) effect of the U.S. policy move toward private-sector standards was a reduction in the number of technical regulations that the United States was obliged to notify to the GATT under the terms of the code. From the EC's viewpoint, then, both U.S. actual notifications and U.S. policy developments provided grounds to conclude that the TBT code as formulated during the 1970s could only generate a widening gap in gains favoring the United States during the 1980s.

In addition, two related policy trends within the EC during the 1980s could only have accentuated EC concerns about the balance of gains arising from the TBT code. The first concerned the locus of authority for the establishment of standards within EC member-countries. In the United States there were at least twenty major *private* standards bodies during that period such as the American National Standards Institute (ANSI), the American Society for Testing and Materials (ASTM), and the well-known Underwriters Laboratories (UL). On the other hand, although already characterized by more centralized standards-formulating systems than the United States, European national governments sought to increase further the government-based centralization of their standards-making activities during the 1970s and 1980s. In West Germany, for example, most industrial standards had been formulated on a voluntary basis by the Deutsches Institut für Normung (DIN), but in 1975 that organization was linked more closely to the government through a contract for-mally designating it as the principal standards-setting organization in the country.[35] Similarly, in the United Kingdom the national govern-ment signed a memorandum of understanding in 1982 with the Brit-ish Standards Institute (BSI), making the latter the leading standards-making body in the country.[36] Finally, in France virtually all stan-dards are formulated by the Association Française de Normalization (AFNOR), which serves under the Ministry of Industry; the authority of this association in the field of standards setting was augmented in 1984.[37] Thus, whereas the United States was characterized by a tripar-

35. See Helmut Reihlen, "The Deutsches Institut für Normung (DIN): A National Standards Organization in Europe," *ASTM Standardization News* (December 1986), 30–32; also see Toth, "Putting the U.S. Standards System into Focus," 18.

36. See Gill Ashworth, "BSI and International Standards: Harmonization and Co-operation," *ASTM Standardization News* (December 1986), 26–28. Also see Toth, "Put-ting the U.S. Standards System into Focus," 18.

37. See Antoine Thiard, "Worldwide Standards—The Only Way: AFNOR and In-ternational Standardization," *ASTM Standardization News* (December 1986), 34–37. Also

tite standards system (state and local, private, and federal) and moved during the 1980s toward greater reliance on one of the legs of the triad not covered by the TBT code (private entities), the EC was moving toward even more centralized, government-oriented systems. Given this basic and indeed accelerating difference in institutional arrangements, and given the language of the TBT code, the EC had good reason to conclude that the latter obliged it to provide progressively greater transparency about its technical measures than was required of the United States.

The second European institutional trend—this one at the level of the EC itself—also offered the prospect that the asymmetry of the TBT code in terms of obligations might be further biased in favor of the United States, especially if the EC had accepted the U.S. proposal in October 1986 to extend TBT code obligations to regional organizations of which code signatories were members. As a key element of their effort to construct a single integrated market by 1992, the EC member-states agreed in the mid-1980s to make new efforts to reduce the trade-inhibiting effects of differences in technical standards among the EC member-states themselves.[38] One of its standards-related initiatives was to assign major new responsibilities to two European regional bodies—the European Committee for Standardization (known by its French acronym, CEN) and the European Committee for Electrotechnical Standardization (CENELEC)—to formulate technical regulations that, on the basis of different voting schemes, could be made mandatory across the EC.[39] The number of these CEN/CENELEC standards were few as of the mid-1980s, totaling less than two hundred at the end of 1986.[40] However, if the EC had accepted the October 1986

---

see Rhonda J. Crane, *The Politics of International Standards: France and the Color TV War* (Norwood, N.J.: ABLEX, 1979), 33–34.

38. For overviews of EC technical standards initiatives in the 1992 market-completion project, see Jacques Pelkmans, "The New Approach to Technical Harmonization," in Peter Robson and Pelkmans, eds., *Making the Common Market Work*, special issue of *Journal of Common Market Studies* 25 (March 1987), 249–69; and Patrick W. Cooke, "Summary of the New European Community Approach to Standards Development," report prepared for the U.S. National Bureau of Standards no. NBSIR 88–3793 (Gaithersburg, Md.: National Bureau of Standards, 1988). On the importance of standards-related efforts to the EC 1992 single-market project, see R. C. Hine, *The Political Economy of European Trade: An Introduction to the Trade Policies of the EEC* (Sussex: Wheatsheaf Books, 1985), 67–70; and Joan Pearce and John Sutton, with Roy Batchelor, *Protection and Industrial Policy in Europe* (London: Routledge, 1986), 49–50.

39. On the development of CEN and CENELEC, see Crane, *Politics of International Standards*, 31–33.

40. On these new efforts on the part of the EC in the standards issue-area, see Antoine B. Chambord, "European Standardization: A Challenge for Europeans, a

U.S. proposal on regional organizations, it would have been obliged to notify the CEN/CENELEC regulations to the GATT, thus exacerbating what, as noted above, was already a trend toward relatively more submissions by the EC than by the United States.

Finally, the situation in the United States and the EC in the product-testing field during the 1980s confirms the EC argument that the U.S. (comprehensive or sectoral) approach to that issue would lead to an imbalance in obligations favoring the latter, for the validity of the EC's analysis was basically accepted by the United States itself.[41] For example, in an address in January 1987 to the American Society of Testing and Materials, Donald S. Abelson, the American official then responsible for the TBT code, noted that while "the U.S. Government has a limited number of testing programs" such as the auto emission tests conducted by the Environmental Protection Agency and the tests of radio equipment performed by the Federal Communications Commission, "there are not many other programs that the U.S. federal government runs for testing private sector products," and in fact "U.S. data is [sic] by and large developed by either third party or manufacturers' testing facilities and not by government laboratories." In contrast, Abelson noted, "Most other nations have government run facilities."[42]

The EC thus had good reason to be concerned about relative gains in the testing issue-area, as indeed it said it was when it opposed U.S. proposals and presented an alternative approach to cooperation in that issue-area. Moreover, the case of cooperation in testing provides an opportunity to demonstrate that the EC was not acting on the basis of an alternative explanation, namely a desire to maximize *absolute* trading gains of the EC member-states. The argument suggesting an EC gains-maximization strategy might maintain that had the EC accepted the U.S. testing proposal that would have brought the limited number of U.S. governmental labs under a mutual testing accord with European governmental labs, the EC members probably would have

Chance for Everyone," *ASTM Standardization News* 12 (December 1986), 44–48. Also see Robert T. Gallagher, "Europe Finally Gets Moving on Standards Making: Turning a Collection of Smaller Markets into a Big One," *Electronics* (April 28, 1986), 48–49.

41. For a discussion of the level of international cooperation in the field of mutual acceptance of test data that obtained at the end of the 1980s, see John W. Locke, "International Laboratory Accreditation," *ASTM Standardization News* 16 (September 1988), 24–29.

42. See Donald S. Abelson (then-director of technical barriers to trade at the Office of the U.S. Trade Representative), "The Standards Code: Current Status and Future Prospects," *ASTM Standardization News* 15 (June 1987), 37.

attained with a high probability only a modest level of new trading opportunities for European exporters. This argument would suggest further that the EC approach of advocating laboratory-to-laboratory agreements might have had the potential of yielding greater absolute trading gains for EC exporters, and that it was in order to so increase its absolute gains that the EC advocated that approach to testing in the TBT committee.

However, the EC-proposed joint statement encouraging lab-to-lab agreements would not have been legally binding on private U.S. laboratories. In addition, according to a GATT study, there was only one such lab-to-lab accord that involved private U.S. laboratories and an EC member-state by the mid-1980s, and thus there was little in the way of precedents on which to build.[43] Finally, given the private, independent status of many U.S. testing laboratories, EC acceptance of the U.S. approach in the technical barriers agreement would not have precluded, and indeed it might have facilitated, EC pursuit of agreements with these U.S. private labs in conjunction with its negotiation of accords with U.S. governmental labs. Hence, while the EC's own proposed approach might have offered EC producers greater potential absolute gains, there was a much lower probability that such gains would have been attained. From the viewpoint of EC expected utility (which would need to combine both an estimate of the magnitude of expected gains and an estimate of the probability that the gains would be achieved), the U.S. and EC approaches would appear to have been equally beneficial to the EC. And, by consequence, it is difficult to see how an absolute-gains orientation would have led the EC to prefer its approach to that proposed by the United States.

Where the U.S. and EC policy approaches to testing differed dramatically, however, concerned likely gaps in gains they might have generated. Because the TBT code applies only to central governments, and not to private entities such as Underwriters Laboratories, new code-based obligations requiring central-government laboratories to work toward acceptance of foreign test results would have further opened only a few U.S. market segments (that is, those relative few covered by U.S. government laboratories). At the same time, however, such obligations would have opened a relatively larger num-

43. This was an agreement on mutual recognition of laboratory accreditation systems between the National Testing Laboratory Accreditation Scheme in the United Kingdom and the National Voluntary Accreditation Program, sponsored by the U.S. National Bureau of Standards, in the United States. See TBT committee, "Bilateral Arrangements on Testing and Inspection: Note by the Secretariat," GATT Doc. TBT/W/90, February 28, 1986, 1.

ber of foreign (that is, EC) markets, for more of the latter involve products tested by central-government laboratories. In contrast, the EC's laboratory-to-laboratory approach would have ensured that if the EC granted easier access in a particular sector to U.S. firms by accepting U.S.-originated test results, European producers would have obtained a similar new increase in access by virtue of an agreement with whatever particular laboratory (government or private) served as the testing agency for that product in the United States. Given that private U.S. laboratories would not have been compelled to enter into such accords, the EC approach was perhaps less likely to yield the EC substantial new trade gains; however, it was also definitely less likely to permit the development of gaps in gains favoring the United States. Thus EC opposition to U.S. ideas on testing, and its own proposals in the testing field, were a reflection of concerns—grounded in actual circumstances—about relative obligations and likely relative achievements of joint gains in new trading opportunities.

Relative-gains concerns also appear to have been well founded in at least two of the instances in which the EC found itself in conflict with the United States in regard to, or otherwise pursued a minimalist interpretation of, the agreement on government procurement. The first involves the EC's adamant refusal to include value-added taxes in members' estimates of the value of their government contracts for the purpose of determining whether particular contracts fell under the jurisdiction of the code. The EC argument, it will be recalled, was that VAT rates varied greatly across member-states and that different rules were used across the members-states in deciding whether a particular item or purchaser was exempt from such duties; therefore, if these taxes were included, imbalances would develop among the EC members in the level of government contracts opened to international bidding under the code. The validity of this EC perception can be verified by reference to Table 7.8, which reports the differing "standard," "reduced" (applied to necessities), and "high rate" (applied to so-called luxury goods) VAT rates applied by the EC member-states at the end of the 1980s.

The table indicates a markedly high degree of divergence in VAT rates across the EC during the 1980s: for example, whereas six members had "high rates," seven did not; the "standard" rate varied from a low of 12 percent in Luxembourg and Spain to a high of 25 percent in Ireland; and among the major EC members, the standard rate could vary by as much as 4.6 percentage points (France versus West Germany). Whether particular goods or particular government agencies were in fact liable to VAT charges could also vary widely, and the same good could sometimes be taxed at different VAT rates in different EC

Table 7.8. Value-added tax rates in the EC, 1988 (in percentages)

EC member	Reduced rate	Standard rate	High rate
Belgium	1.0 and 6.0[a]	19.0	25.0 and 33.0
Denmark	None	22.0	None
France	2.1 and 7.0	18.6	33.3
Germany	7.0	14.0	None
Greece	6.0	18.0	36.0
Ireland	2.4 and 10.0	25.0	None
Italy	2.0 and 9.0	18.0	38.0
Luxembourg	3.0 and 6.0	12.0	None
Netherlands	6.0	20.0	None
Portugal	8.0	16.0	30.0
Spain	6.0	12.0	33.0
United Kingdom	0	15.0	None

[a]Belgium applies two different "reduced" and "high" rates to different categories of goods, and France, Ireland, Italy, and Luxembourg do so for their "reduced" rates.

Sources: Commission of the European Communities, Directorate General for Economic and Social Affairs, *The Economics of 1992: An Assessment of the Potential Economic Effects of Completing the Internal Market of the European Community*, special issue of *European Economy*, no. 35 (March 1988), 61.

member-states. Tires, for example, were taxed at the high rate in Belgium but at the reduced rate in Ireland, and small aircraft were exempt from VAT taxes in Denmark but taxed at the high rate in Italy.[44] Thus, if the EC member-states had been required to include national VAT charges in their contract estimations, some members very likely would have had to expose more contracts to international bidding than others. Probably none of the major EC states were sure which might be so relatively "disadvantaged," and therefore all agreed that VAT should be excluded so that each carried an equal "burden" of market access granted to foreigner-suppliers under the code.[45]

44. See Dennis Parkinson, *Value Added Tax in the EEC* (London: Graham, 1981), 41–67, 207–14.

45. Interviews, EC Official no. 6, Brussels, July 14, 1986; EC official no. 14, Brussels, July 14,1986; Federal Republic of Germany Official no. 3, Bonn, July 25, 1986; French official no. 1, Geneva, August 6, 1986; French officials nos. 3 and 4, Paris, June 26, 1986; French official no. 6, Paris, June 27, 1986; French official no. 8, Paris, June 27, 1986; United Kingdom official No. 3, London, July 8, 1986; United Kingdom official no. 7, London, June 30, 1986; United Kingdom official no. 15, London, July 4, 1986. On the political efforts by the EC during the 1960s and 1970s to bring about a harmonization of VAT rates, see Donald J. Puchala, *Fiscal Harmonization in the European Communities: National Politics and International Cooperation* (London: Frances Pinter, 1984). These efforts attained only limited success, and VAT harmonization is a major element of the 1992 market-completion project, discussed below.

It will be recalled that in addition to the VAT dispute, the EC, supported by the Nordics, resisted the 1983–84 Swiss proposal (which was strongly supported by the United States) to extend the GPR code to government-owned enterprises. Although the EC did not claim that relative-gains problems would arise from inclusion of public enterprises under the jurisdiction of the code (it simply refused to entertain the proposal), the differences between the EC member-states on the one hand and the United States and Switzerland on the other would have made such concerns highly plausible. The optimal basis for measurement of the relative amounts of new contracts that would have been opened to international competition had the Swiss proposal on government enterprises been accepted would be the value of purchases made by these entities; unfortunately, as a recent study by the Organization for Economic Cooperation and Development (OECD) reported, "There is no direct information on output values or GDP [gross domestic product] contributions of public enterprises."[46] However, as a rough estimate of the relative importance of public enterprises in the major GPR code signatories, Table 7.9 reports figures from the OECD study on the contribution of government enterprise to the total gross capital formation and total national employment of those countries during the 1970s.[47]

The figures in the table highlight the relatively larger role played by public-sector firms in the EC and the Nordic countries as compared with the United States. Had the Swiss proposal been accepted, the EC and Nordic states would have had to accept greater policy changes regarding the procurement practices of public enterprises and their capacity to support local industry than would have been required of their American partners, and they might well have had to offer a much larger relative increment of new bidding opportunities (normalizing for economic size) to foreign suppliers than would have been required of the United States. This unfavorable balance of new trading opportunities would also have been true for the EC in regard to Switzerland. Data on the latter that are fully comparable to those in Table 7.9 are unavailable, but a recent OECD country survey on Switzerland reported that whereas the expenditures of Swiss public

46. See Peter Saunders and Friedrich Klau, *The Role of the Public Sector: Causes and Consequences of the Growth of Government*, special issue of *OECD Economic Studies*, no. 4 (Spring 1985), 76.
47. In addition to the 1985 Saunders and Klau study, see Leila Pathirane and Derek W. Blades, "Defining and Measuring the Public Sector: Some International Comparisons," *The Review of Income and Wealth*, series 28 (September 1982), 261–89.

Table 7.9. Significance of public enterprises, major signatories to the Code on Government Procurement, 1970s

Country	Public enterprise investments as average annual % of gross domestic product		Public enterprise investments as average annual % of gross capital formation		Public enterprise employment as average annual % of total employment	
	1970–74	1975–79	1970–74	1975–79	1970–74	1975–79
Major EC Countries						
United Kingdom	3.1	3.5	15.5	18.3	7.9	8.2
Italy	3.9	3.3	16.9	15.5	5.6	6.4
Germany	3.5	2.7	13.7	12.6	7.8	7.9
France	1.9	2.5	7.3	10.8	4.5[a]	4.4[a]
Other Major Signatories						
United States	0.7	0.9	3.7	4.7	1.6	1.6
Japan	3.7	3.8	3.7	3.8	NA	NA
Canada	2.5	3.7	10.9	15.7	4.4	4.5
Sweden	4.1	3.5	17.6	16.6	7.1	8.0
Norway	4.5	6.5	14.5	19.8	4.1[b]	4.2[b,c]

[a]Major enterprises only.
[b]Norway figures are for worker-years rather than number of employees.
[c]1975–77 only.

Source: Adapted from Peter Saunders and Friedrich Klau, The Role of the Public Sector: Causes and Consequences of the Growth of Government, special issue of OECD Economic Studies, no. 4 (Spring 1985), 77–78. Reprinted with permission from the Organization for Economic Cooperation and Development.

enterprises constituted 7.0 percent of Swiss gross domestic product in 1970, this declined to 5.7 percent in 1980.[48]

As with the EC and the issue of testing under the technical barriers accord, it might be argued that the EC resisted Switzerland and the United States on public-owned enterprises as a result of an interest in maximizing absolute gains. However, this interpretation is difficult to sustain. Had the EC been interested in achieving greater absolute gains from extension of the code to such enterprises than would have been possible under the Swiss approach, one would have expected the EC to have put forward a proposal of its own on public enterprises that would have indeed enhanced EC potential trading gains. However, it did not do that and instead basically refused to discuss the matter. At the same time, because the EC's code partners do in some measure also have state-owned enterprises, it is difficult to argue that the EC was in a zero-sum situation in which only its partners had an interest in extending the code to such enterprises. The problem does not appear to have been one of the partners gaining all and the EC losing all, nor of the EC holding out for a better arrangement; it was, instead, a problem of the partners almost surely gaining more from any arrangement than would the EC member-states.

Finally, there are substantial grounds for believing that the EC's general resistance to U.S. efforts to apply the GPR code vigorously and to extend the agreement to new areas reflected a genuine awareness and concern by the EC that international liberalization of government purchases would have involved greater relative burdens (and therefore lower relative benefits) for its member-states than would have been carried by other major GPR signatories. A very rough approximation of the relative change in government purchasing practices that would been required of the EC if it had sought to match the United States and other partners in terms of government purchases of foreign goods is presented in Table 7.10, which reports the distribution of contracts by major code signatories in 1983 to national and foreign suppliers from both GPR and non-GPR code signatories.[49]

48. See Organization for Economic Cooperation and Development, *OECD Economic Surveys: Switzerland, 1987/88* (Paris, 1988), 53.

49. This use of a foreign-participation rate in government purchases follows the development and employment by Bela and Carol Balassa of a "consumption ratio" of foreign-origin restricted items over the total consumption of the item as an index of protection afforded domestic producers of the item in question. See Bela Balassa and Carol Balassa, "Industrial Protection in the Developed Countries," *The World Economy* 7 (June 1984), 187–89. It should be noted that the Balassas track changes in the consumption ratio to estimate increases or decreases in protection: inadequacies of data preclude this in the case of GPR code-covered contracts.

Table 7.10. Foreign participation in government-procurement markets of major signatories to the Code on Government Procurement, 1983

Country/ country group	Value of code-covered awarded (in million SDR)				Foreign participation (percent)		
	Contracts to national suppliers	Contracts to GPR code-signatory suppliers	Contracts to non-GPR code-signatory suppliers	Total value	Contracts to GPR code-signatory suppliers/total contracts	Contracts to non-GPR code-signatory foreign suppliers/total contracts	Total foreign participation
EC	3,399.8	4.8	4.7	3,409.3	0.14	0.14	0.28
United States	14,021.8	1,299.1	1,342.8	16,663.7	7.8	8.1	15.9
Japan	1,074.3	72.8	75.0	1,222.1	6.0	6.1	12.1
Canada	332.1	25.4	0.8	358.3	7.1	0.2	7.3
The Nordics	240.8	120.9	21.5	383.2	31.6	5.6	37.2
Switzerland	59.5	47.6	7.3	114.4	41.6	6.4	48.0
Austria	24.5	11.9	0.2	36.6	32.5	0.5	33.0

Sources: All data are from national reports submitted as addendum and revisions to the GPR committee document "Statistics for 1983 Reported under Article VI.9 of the Agreement": for Sweden, GATT Doc. GPR/24/Add.2, October 2, 1984; for the United States, GATT Doc. GPR/24/Add.3/Rev. 1, February 22, 1985; for Switzerland, GATT Doc. GPR/24 Add. 4, October 15, 1984; for Canada, GATT Doc. GPR/24/Add. 5/Rev. 1, February 21, 1985; for Finland, GATT Doc. GPR/24/Add. 6, October 24, 1984; for Norway, GATT Doc. GPR/24/Add. 7, November 11, 1984; for Japan, GATT Doc. GPR/24/Add. 8, November 9, 1984; for the EC, GATT Doc. GPR/24/Add. 9, January 16, 1985; and for Austria, GATT Doc. GPR/24/Add. 10, February 10, 1985.

The table indicates that whereas the Nordics, Switzerland, and Austria each awarded one-third or more of their code-covered contracts to suppliers in fellow code-signatory countries, and the United States, Japan, and Canada awarded between 6 and 8 percent of their contracts to such foreign suppliers, less than 1 percent of all EC code-covered contracts were awarded to all foreign suppliers. Statistical reporting problems in the EC may have led to a significant underestimation of foreign penetration of member-states' governmental markets. However, even if the EC member-states awarded contracts to non-EC members at a rate comparable to the level awarded to their EC partners—that is, about 2 percent of all public supply contracts—the EC's foreign-award penetration rate would still be much lower than the rates for its GPR partners.[50] Overall, then, if the EC had accepted a vigorous implementation of GPR code obligations as formulated during the Tokyo Round, or if it had accepted an extension of the obligations of the code in the Article IX:6(b) negotiations, the EC's member-states would have had to undertake much more drastic changes in their government purchasing practices than would have been required of their major code partners. The likely result would have been a much greater enjoyment of new trading opportunities by the EC's partners than by the EC itself, an outcome unacceptable to the latter.[51]

50. See Commission of the European Communities, Directorate-General for Economic and Financial Affairs, *The Economics of 1992: An Assessment of the Potential Economic Effects of Completing the Internal Market of the European Community*, special issue of *European Economy*, no. 35 (March 1988), 55.

51. A similar finding can be made through the following line of analysis. A 1978 study sponsored by the Brookings Institution on the economic effects of the Tokyo Round considered what would happen if the GPR code reduced the protection afforded by buy-national policies to government contracts by 60 percent; using figures from the mid-1960s and adjusting for inflation, the study projected that U.S. contracts awarded to foreign suppliers would increase by roughly $600 million in 1974 dollars while EC contracts awarded to foreigners would increase by about $330 million. Using the same basis for adjustment in inflation as was employed by the Brookings study (that is, inflating by the wholesale price index for U.S. industrial goods as reported by the International Monetary Fund), we can calculate that these figures in 1983 dollars would be $1.134 billion in new U.S. contracts awarded to foreigners under the GPR code and $623.8 million in new EC contracts to overseas vendors. To meet these targets, the EC member-states would have needed to award about 16 percent of all their code-covered contracts to foreign suppliers; for the United States to do so, it would have needed to award approximately 6 percent of its code-covered contracts to foreigners. By 1983, as noted in Table 7.10, the United States had surpassed its target; the EC was far from its own. On the original Brookings figures and analysis, see William R. Cline, Noboru Kawanabe, T. O. M. Kronsjo, and Thomas Williams, *Trade Negotiations in the Tokyo Round: A Quantitative Assessment* (Washington, D.C.: Brookings Institution, 1978), 189–94. The inflation index to express the Brookings estimates in 1983 dollars is taken from International Monetary Fund, *International Financial Statistics Yearbook: 1987* (Washington, 1987), 63.

Strategic Importance of Technical Standards and Government Procurement for the EC

We now come to the final link in the chain of analysis that demonstrates that realism's emphasis on defensive state positionalism and the relative-gains problem for cooperation can shed important light on the behavior of the EC in the Tokyo Round NTB regime. We have already seen that many of the instances of discord between the United States and the EC involving the TBT and GPR codes—discord that seriously constrained the level of success achieved by those agreements—were due to well-founded EC concerns that other GATT partners and especially the United States were in a better position to enjoy the lion's share of otherwise mutually positive gains from those accords. This section shows why such an outcome would be unacceptable to the EC. It demonstrates that the EC believed that the technical standards and government procurement issue-areas could play a vital role in refurbishing the industrial sectors of EC member-states, and, more generally, in ensuring that Europe would remain a core region of the world economy. The EC member-states, in other words, viewed the two issue-areas as having strategic implications for their future as autonomous actors in the world economy, and therefore they approached the NTB codes covering those issue-areas as defensive positionalists.

With the circulation in the public realm of such new concepts as "Europessimism" and "Eurosclerosis," there is little doubt that many in Europe believed during most of the 1980s—especially when they lagged behind the United States and Japan in recovering from the deep recession of 1981–82—that they were increasingly at risk in the international economy.[52] For example, in the 1985 White Paper that announced the EC's effort to create a single integrated market among the member-states by 1992, the EC Commission emphasized that such an effort was critical, since "Europe stands at the crossroads. We either go ahead—with resolution and determination—or we drop back into mediocrity."[53] By the mid-1980s the commission and the EC member-

52. As Robert Z. Lawrence suggests, "The early 1980s marked the nadir of European industrial performance." See Lawrence, "Trade Performance as a Constraint on European Growth," in Lawrence and Charles L. Schultz, eds., *Barriers to European Growth: A Transatlantic View* (Washington, D.C.: Brookings Institution, 1987), 303. On the problem of European economic performance during the early to mid-1980s, also see Paul R. Krugman, "Slow Growth in Europe: Conceptual Issues," in Lawrence and Schultz, eds., *Barriers to European Growth*, 48–76. On the policy debates on how to respond to the slowdown in European economic growth, see the citations in footnote 66.

53. Commission of the European Communities, *Completing the Internal Market: White Paper from the Commission to the European Council*, Com(85) 310 (Brussels, 1985), 55.

states were well aware that Europe had lost substantial ground to the United States and especially Japan. In a 1985 study of the economic effects of the 1992 project, the commission highlighted the relative decline of European manufacturing. The commission reported that the EC's share of world exports (excluding intra-EC trade) slipped by 1.4 percentage points between 1979 and 1985, while the U.S. share increased by 0.7 percent and Japan by 5.4 percent. More ominous were trends in high-technology trade: "The Community is rapidly losing ground in the case of electrical and electronic equipment, cars and other means of transport, office machinery, information technology and industrial machinery."[54] Europe was thereby becoming dependent on external sources for high-technology products, for "imports from outside the Community . . . [were] growing appreciably more quickly than intra-Community trade in such branches as office machinery and information technology, electrical and electronic equipment, machinery and transport equipment."[55]

It was in this context that technical standards and government procurement were considered by the EC to be vital elements of its 1992 integrated-market program. The EC's basic goal was to devise institutional arrangements in these two issue-areas that would contribute to the construction of a large, truly integrated European regional market. Thus strengthened, EC member-states would then be able to begin to regain some of the economic ground lost during the last quarter-century to the United States, Japan, and the newly industrializing countries. The commission's 1985 report on the economics of 1992, for example, emphasized that EC policies to liberalize government procurement and reduce technical barriers to trade *within the EC* could reverse Europe's decline as a center of world manufacturing. The EC study suggested that if *intra*-EC government procurement were liberalized, for example, this would have as longer-term effects "mergers and reorganization, the rationalization of Community production on a smaller number of sites, falls in development costs due to a reduction in the range of products to offer, and coordination of R&D [that] will favor cost reductions."[56] These developments, of

54. Commission of the European Communities, *Economics of 1992*, 28. Both Krugman and Lawrence emphasize that overall European international competitiveness—and especially that of West Germany—was good during the 1980s. They do confirm, however, that Europe had not performed well internationally in higher-technology sectors. See Krugman, "Slow Growth in Europe," 53, 55–57; and Lawrence, "Trade Performance," 365–74.
55. Ibid., 30.
56. Ibid., 56.

course, would improve the EC's competitive position and in particular its capacity to compete with Japan and the United States.[57]

Even before the 1992 program commenced in 1985, the commission had come to view a more liberalized intra-EC government procurement system as crucial to the future of Europe's technological infrastructure. For example, in a 1984 report on government contract liberalization within the EC, the commission emphasized that the "stakes are much more than mere statistics." The commission explained that "a substantial proportion of public purchases concerns sectors whose very future depends on the size of the market open to them. This applies in particular, for example, to the telecommunications industry." Moreover, the commission warned that purely national markets—perpetuated by national governmental purchasing practices—could no longer be expected to support critical industrial sectors and that "the 'cost of non-Europe' represents a direct, serious threat to essential components of the Community's industrial potential."[58]

The EC has in fact emphasized that the key objective in liberalizing government procurement practices is enhanced international competitiveness for European high-technology industries and not necessarily a reduction in the prices for the procured goods. As Christopher Wilkinson, the official in charge of EC strategy for the information technology and telecommunication industries, argued in 1984, "The principal objective of competitive public purchasing in high-technology industries should be the integration and rationalization of the domestic EC market and industry, rather than simply reducing the price of the equipment purchased in the short term." Indeed, as a proposal, Wilkinson suggested that "the degree of protection embodied in today's national discriminatory purchasing policies should be translated into an equivalent—but not greater—Community preference." Wilkinson acknowledged that, with its emphasis on non-discrimination for non-regional suppliers, "an alternative policy is embodied in the GATT public purchasing code," but he dismissed the code simply by saying that "signatories of the GATT code were optimistic."[59]

57. In addition to the observations on this point by Michel Richonnier and Wolfgang Hager, which are presented later in the section, see Jacques Pelkmans and Peter Robson, "The Aspirations of the White Paper," in Pelkmans and Robson, eds., *Making the Common Market Work*, 190. Pelkmans and Robson also give a very useful overview of the 1992 project as a whole.

58. Commission of the European Communities, *Public Supply Contracts: Conclusions and Perspectives*, Com(84) 717 (Brussels, 1984), 4.

59. Christopher Wilkinson, "Trends in Industrial Policy in the EC: Theory and

The commission has also been very explicit that enhanced international competitiveness is a core objective in its new policy initiatives regarding technical regulations. In the EC White Paper, for example, the commission argued that until technical barriers among EC member-states are removed, "Community manufacturers are forced to focus on national rather than continental markets and are unable to benefit from the economies of scale which a truly unified internal market offers." The commission then linked this lost marketing opportunity to Europe's international position, suggesting that its "failure to achieve a genuine industrial common market becomes increasingly serious since the research, development and commercialisation costs of the new technologies, in order to have a realistic prospect of being internationally competitive, require the background of a home market of continental proportions."[60] Similarly, in its report on the economic implications of the 1992 project, the commission reported that "the Community's policy approach to removing these barriers has been evolving in important ways in recent years, and there could be quite rapid and widespread progress in the legislative actions of the Community." The commission then stressed that such progress "is of strategic importance to the Community's industrial sector, since very often the technical barriers [in place] are greatest in high-tech sectors where market fragmentation is a major competitive disadvantage *vis-à-vis* producers in the United States and Japan."[61]

Another analysis during the 1980s of Europe's economic future that assigned very great importance to the government procurement and technical standards issue-areas was provided by Michel Richonnier, who served during the early 1980s as the rapporteur for the strategy group established by the French government for national economic planning. Richonnier argued that Europe faces an "unprecedented challenge," namely, "for the first time in its history, Europe is faced with an industrial revolution—that of microelectronics—which did not originate in its continent, like the steam engine or electricity, but on the shores of the Pacific, in the USA and Japan," and asked rhetorically, "Will Europe be relegated at the end of the century to the category of former industrialized countries

---

Practice," in Alexis Jacquemin, *European Industry: Public Policy and Corporate Strategy* (Oxford: Clarendon, 1984), 63.

60. Commission of the European Communities, *Completing the Internal Market*, 17–18.

61. Commission of the European Communities, *Economics of 1992*, 49.

(FICs)?"[62] Richonnier responded that in fact the European states can rebound in vital high-technology sectors such as electronics only through actions that solidify Europe *as a regional market.* Here, according to Richonnier, technical regulations and government procurement could play a key role. Richonnier argued that Europe's industrial future depends on "improving the existing environment in which European companies exist, in other words, by creating a real European market," and he went on to suggest that this could be accomplished "notably by adopting *European* standards for all new products and by gradually opening national markets so that *European* enterprises are able to tender on an equal basis for public contracts in fields not as yet covered, such as telecommunications, transport, and energy."[63]

Thus by the mid-1980s EC efforts regarding technical barriers and government procurement were viewed in Europe as directly affecting the EC's lagging technological position vis-à-vis the United States and Japan. The failure to achieve a single market, high-level European officials warned, could have very dangerous implications for Europe's future as an independent, autonomous actor in the world political economy.[64] As the French Minister of Industry, Alain Madelin, warned in early 1988 in regard to possible domination by the United States and Japan, "Europe has no choice but to become a third pole of equivalent weight. Or else, poor in raw materials, politically divided, technologically dependent, it will fast become nothing more than a subcontractor for the other two."[65]

In sum, the EC countries considered themselves economically besieged during the 1980s by a technologically stronger United States and Japan (and, it may be added, a new set of low-cost exporters—the newly industrializing countries).[66] Given this sense of vulnerability,

62. Michel Richonnier, "Europe's Decline Is Not Irreversible," *Journal of Common Market Studies* 22 (March 1984), 228.

63. Ibid., 242, emphasis added.

64. This sense of European vulnerability is described and analyzed in Miles Kahler, "The Survival of the State in European International Relations," in Charles S. Maier, ed., *Changing Boundaries of the Political: Essays on the Evolving Balance Between the State and Society, Public and Private in Europe* (Cambridge: Cambridge University Press, 1987), especially 302–14.

65. As quoted in Paul Revzin, "U.S., European Firms Prepare for 1992 Market Deadline," *Europe* (April 1988), 17.

66. For an early statement of this position, see Wolfgang Hager, "Little Europe, Wider Europe, and Western Economic Cooperation," *Journal of Common Market Studies* 21 (September 1982), 176–77. For a fuller discussion of European concerns during the 1980s about their international economic position, see Miles Kahler, "European Protec-

and given its assignment of strategic importance to technical standards and government procurement as issue-areas materially affecting Europe's capacity to compete in the international economy, the EC
was very sensitive to the distribution of joint gains produced by the
TBT and GPR agreements. These were policy arenas where Europe
hoped it could reverse losses in economic strength and autonomy
through regional-level action, and it would not yield those gains as a
result of possible distributions of gains favoring its principal economic
competitors in the NTB regime.[67] Thus Wolfgang Hager, a major
exponent of European neo-protectionism, was on firm ground in late
1987 when he observed that "the most important source of potential
future Atlantic trade conflicts is the attempt by the European Community to find a new *raison d'être*, as the champion of a joint European
technological 'nationalism,' using infant-industry protectionism, *common industrial standards*, joint R&D policies, *and, most ambitiously, common procurement approaches*."[68]

In marked contrast, there is no evidence suggesting that the United
States viewed the issue-areas covered by the customs valuation and
anti-dumping accords, and the rules on countervailing measures contained in the subsidies code, as having the same potential impact on
U.S. industrial strength and independence as the Europeans believed
was true for them in the issue-areas covered by the technical barriers
and government procurement agreements. During the 1980s
U.S. authorities did not think customs-valuation procedures, anti-
dumping practices, and rules for countervailing measures were effective policy instruments for addressing the loss of American international competitiveness, at least with regard to the Europeans. This

---

tionism in Theory and Practice," *World Politics* 37 (July 1985), 475–502. It should be
emphasized that these concerns were more acute in France than in Britain, and more so
in the latter than in West Germany: see Kahler, "Survival of the State," 312; and Pearce,
Sutton, and Batchelor, *Protection and Industrial Policy*, 56–90. However, it should also be
recalled that it is France, in spite of West Germany's greater economic resources and
heightened activism within the EC, that still plays the lead role in defining EC interests
and policies: see, for example, the discussion of former EC Commissioner Christopher
Tugendhat, *Making Sense of Europe* (New York: Columbia University Press, 1988), 84–
105.

67. Europeans recognize that elements of the 1992 project may conflict with GATT
and other international obligations: see, for an overview, Hans-Eckert Scharrer,
"Protectionism—a Necessary Price for Achieving the Internal Market?," *Intereconomics*
22 (February 1987), 9–13; and "The Shape of Europe's Trade," *Economist* (September
3, 1988), 13–14.

68. Wolfgang Hager, "Political Implications of US–EC Economic Conflicts (II):
Atlantic Trade—Problems and Prospects," *Government and Opposition* 22 (Winter 1987),
58–59, emphasis added.

does not mean that the United States was willing to accept any distribution of gains in those codes: it will be recalled that the United
States began to block countervailing-measure activities in the subsidies
code committee during the mid-1980s when it decided that the EC
was not going to accept greater discipline on its use of agricultural
export subsidies. Nor was it true that the United States always viewed
the issue-areas covered by those agreements as unimportant to American interests: outside the scope of the ADP code, the United States
did use the threat of an anti-dumping action during the late 1980s
against Japanese integrated circuit manufacturers as one way of en-
hancing U.S. access to the Japanese market for memory chips. However, at least with respect to the EC, the United States viewed its own
international political-economic position and the salience of the customs and anti-dumping codes, as well as the rules on countervailing
measures in the subsidy code, with sufficient equanimity as to be
typically more willing to accept gaps in gains in these codes favoring
the EC than the latter was willing to accept gaps in the codes covering
what it considered to be the strategic issue-areas of technical barriers
and government procurement.

The fact that realism successfully accounts for EC behavior regarding the technical barriers and government procurement codes, behavior that had escaped the grasp of neoliberalism, offers us strong
reason to believe that the former is superior to the latter. Yet there is
even more evidence in support of the realist understanding of the
problem of cooperation, as we will discover in the following section.

THE RELATIVE-GAINS PROBLEM AND THE ANTI-DUMPING CODE

We have seen that European concerns about relative gains shaped
EC interactions with the United States and others in the NTB code
committees. The major setback experienced by the anti-dumping
committee—the mixed success it achieved in developing rules on
basic price systems under Article 8:4 of the ADP code—demonstrates
that the EC was not the only actor that approached the codes with an
eye toward distributions of mutually positive gains.

Basic-price systems, it will be recalled, are an anti-dumping procedure whereby a government announces prices for a class of goods
and through which an anti-dumping investigation may be automatically triggered or anti-dumping duties may be automatically applied
if imported goods fall below the specified prices. The ADP signatories
discovered in early 1981 that Article 8:4 constituted a serious loophole

in the anti-dumping agreement insofar as it failed to set adequate limits or restrictions on the use of such systems. The committee sought to formulate an agreed interpretation to counter the problem of Article 8:4. The first draft interpretation, discussed at the February 1981 ADP committee meeting, would have had the signatories agree that Article 8:4 could not be used as a basis for anti-dumping proceedings (paragraph 2), that no such new "special" monitoring system would be installed by any signatory (paragraph 3), and that those already in effect would be restricted to their current scope and would come under annual review by the ADP committee (paragraph 4).

This February draft proposal failed, and relative-gains concerns were at the heart of this failure. The key problem for a number of signatories was that although all would gain absolutely in some measure from the February draft insofar as a loophole in the ADP code would be closed, the proposed interpretation would also result in an asymmetry in obligations favoring the United States and the EC. Those two code parties had variants of basic-price systems already in effect in the steel industry, and under the February draft these could remain in operation while other signatories would be unable to implement any such programs.[69] That eventuality led to complaints and statements of concern by other code participants.

For example, at the February meeting, the Argentine observer, referring to paragraphs 3 and 4, said "he wanted to know whether they meant that countries which were presently operating special anti-dumping schemes were given a waiver to maintain them while all other present or future Parties would not be allowed to establish such schemes."[70] The Canadian delegate sought to offer an interpretation of the two paragraphs that would prevent such an asymmetry in rights, claiming that paragraph 4 "meant to him that any system presently in force could be picked up by any Party to this Agreement so long as it did not extend its scope" and that "the understanding was that no one would extend beyond the existing special anti-dumping systems but all Parties would be free to put in place a system similar to one of those in force, if they needed to do so." The United States supported this Canadian interpretation of paragraph 4 and did so as a reflection of its understanding that relative-gains problems would otherwise develop: the U.S. representative noted that "it would be

69. For a description of these systems, see Pearce, Sutton, and Batchelor, *Protection and Industrial Policy*, 43.

70. All statements for the February meeting are from ADP committee, "Minutes," February 2–3, 1981, GATT Doc. ADP/M/4, March 19, 1981, 1–10.

very difficult to allow some countries—only because they had already had certain special anti-dumping schemes in place—to continue these practices and to deny other countries the right to do the same."

However, the Canadian-American interpretation could not be reconciled with the actual wording of paragraph 4; as the Swiss representative observed, "the Canadian interpretation did not reflect the intention of the drafters of paragraph 4." He argued that "this paragraph meant that only those systems which were presently in place were allowed to exist," and that "other parties were therefore obliged not to introduce such systems." The Swiss delegate then emphasized the absolute gains to be achieved by the draft, stating that it represented "an important step towards strengthening the discipline in the anti-dumping area." Similarly, the EC argued that the draft interpretation, while admittedly allowing the EC and the United States to continue to have basic-price systems for steel, nevertheless "subjected them to special conditions and annual reviews." Everyone would be better off from the draft: as the EC representative argued, "It was something to take home even for those countries which did not have such systems and the deal seemed to be well equilibrated on both sides," and, in any event, "it was in everybody's interest to avoid proliferation of these dangerous anti-dumping systems."

Several of the EC's partners in the committee, however, did not see matters that way. Acknowledging that the February draft would provide all parties with absolute gains in terms of better international discipline in the anti-dumping field, the observer from Australia also argued that "while it would obviously be preferable to preclude the use of basic price systems . . . the Committee seemed to favor giving its approval to systems already in place, thereby raising questions of equity in terms of both country and product/sector coverage." Further, the Australian observer argued that it was "inappropriate that what was acceptable in the case of the two existing systems would not be acceptable in the case of any other Party which might find itself, in the future, in a similar situation." Similarly, the Canadian representative argued that "it would not be possible for him to get his Government's acceptance of a text which prevented Canada from doing something which the European Communities and the United States were allowed to do."

The U.S. representative responded that although he agreed a problem of equity existed, there were absolute gains from the February draft that ought not be lost. The draft, according to the United States, contained provisions that "were progressive in both the commitment not to use basic price systems in an abusive way and not to abuse trigger price systems." The U.S. delegate then said that "it would be a great pity if the understanding fell through only because of a narrow dispute over its coverage and application." The Argentine observer responded to this last statement by saying that "he did not agree with the opinion . . . that this was a 'narrow dispute.' The matter was that the understanding should not provide for a system which would discriminate against future Parties." Finally, when the committee chair noted to the Canadian delegate that Canada already had an "antidumping monitoring system" in place which might presumably be allowed to remain in effect under paragraph 4, the Canadian representative agreed but said "the only thing which bothered him was the Canadian system was not such a complete scheme as, for example, that of the United States and that one day his Government might wish to have a system parallel to the United States' scheme."

These relative-gains concerns of Canada, Australia, and Argentina killed the February 1981 draft interpretation of Article 8:4 in spite of the fact that the proposed text would have generated stringent new disciplines on basic-price systems and thus would have provided greater legal-administrative protection to the exporters based in each country adhering to the ADP code. A similar fate would await the second (apparently U.S.-EC drafted) revised interpretation of Article 8:4, discussed at the April 1981 meeting of the ADP committee. That revised interpretation, it will be recalled, retained the first two paragraphs from the February text but, instead of banning new basic-price systems, allowed them if they met a highly restrictive set of conditions.

Some signatories argued that this marked a retreat in the effort of the committee to discipline basic-price systems. The Swiss representative, for example, argued that "while the main concept [of the February draft] was to stop proliferation of special schemes the new draft provided for certain discipline in the use of such systems without preventing their proliferation" and that "this approach could have very dangerous implications."[71] Similarly, the Indian representative complained that although "he was prepared to go along with the understanding contained in ADP/W/14," that is, the February draft, since it would ban basic-price systems, "the modifications suggested to ADP/W/14 would result in perpetuation of such schemes." In the same vein, the observer for Chile said that "at the previous meeting he had been in favour of ADP/W/14 but now, and for the same reasons as those presented by some previous speakers, he could not support the

71. All statements for the April meeting are from ADP committee, "Minutes," April 27–28, 1981, GATT Doc. ADP/M/5, June 11, 1981, 11–13.

revised text," and the representative of Sweden said that he "had a rather favorable position as regards ADP/W/14" but that "his first reaction" to the new draft "was similar to that of the representative of Switzerland."

Yet the states that had been concerned about relative obligations in February remained so in April. The Canadian representative said that he agreed with some of the remarks made by the U.S. representative in introducing the new draft, but also stated, without elaborating, that "he had some problems with the revised draft." The Australian observer then presented the case against the April draft interpretation. Stating at the outset that the new paragraphs contained in the April draft "would be unacceptable" to Australia, the observer argued that "they established a preferential treatment for existing special schemes or, conversely, the conditions for the establishment of new schemes set out in paragraphs 4–6 imposed obligations on any such scheme which were not imposed on existing schemes." As an example, the Australian observer noted that "the provision for an annual review in paragraph 6 related to new monitoring schemes only, therefore strengthening the preferential treatment for existing schemes." Speaking more generally, the observer from Australia emphasized that "his basic position on this understanding was that equitable treatment must be accorded to existing and new agreements. Thus, if a Party or a group of Parties insisted on their rights to maintain existing monitoring schemes, then all Parties must have the right to introduce similar schemes." These views were supported by the observer for Argentina, who said he "fully shared the views" of Australia and stated that the April revised draft "contained a notion of discrimination, in particular vis-à-vis countries which had not adopted such systems." The new revised draft failed to gain committee acceptance, bringing the EC representative to say that "members of the Committee should decide whether they wanted strict discipline and certain limitations or nothing."

The ADP code participants were finally able to devise an agreed interpretation at their next meeting in October. Most of the partners (including Canada) stated at that time that the final text was a distinctly second-best solution in terms of developing adequate discipline over basic-price systems, especially compared with the original February text. In contrast, Australia's observer stated that while he shared the view of his colleagues that basic-price systems ought to be brought under greater international control, he wished to reiterate his belief "that treatment should be equitable, that there be no blessing of existing systems, and that countries have no fewer rights as a result of the adoption of this understanding in relation to other countries." In this respect the Australian observer concluded that "he saw the revised [October] text as an improvement on the draft circulated at the April 1981 meeting."[72]

The October draft provided little discipline over basic-price systems, and most of the ADP participants were disappointed with their work. However, Australia, Canada, and Argentina were willing to forego the greater discipline promised by the February and April drafts rather than accept an agreed interpretation that would have generated absolute gains for all but more gains for the United States and the EC than for others. It is difficult to argue that the three states were holding out for greater absolute gains in the negotiations. Compared with the February draft interpretation, the April and October drafts provided lower levels of discipline over the U.S. and EC basic-price systems already in effect, and each successive draft offered progressively less discipline over the introduction of any systems by any signatory, including the United States and the EC. Yet rather than accept an asymmetry in gains associated with the February and April drafts, Australia, Canada, and Argentina blocked those drafts and brought the other signatories around to the extremely weak October proposal. Despite common interests and almost no danger of cheating, relative-gains concerns had restricted the achievement of effective cooperation among the ADP signatories.

REALISM AND THE PROBLEM OF INTERNATIONAL COOPERATION

A realist-based focus on defensive state positionalism and the problem of relative gains has allowed us to explain much of the variation in the EC's approach to five of the six codes constituting the Tokyo Round regime on non-tariff barriers during the 1980s.[73] This chapter demonstrated that the EC was satisfied with its absolute and relative gains from the codes on customs valuation and anti-dumping, and from the portion of the subsidies code concerned with countervailing measures, and thus gave those codes and code elements strong support. The chapter also argued that the EC had good reason to worry about relative gains arising from the subsidies code if the agreement

72. See ADP committee, "Minutes," October 26–30, 1981, GATT Doc. ADP/M/6, January 6, 1982, 15.

73. Information on national import-licensing regimes is very sparse and precludes analysis of the EC's support for the LIC code from a realist or neoliberal viewpoint.

had been allowed to promote greater transparency of subsidies programs in general, and that it would be in a zero-sum situation if the code had been permitted to create greater international restrictions on the use of agricultural export subsidies. As a result, the EC strongly opposed the subsidies portion of the SCM accord.

These EC actions could be explained by either realism or neoliberalism, although the former did a better job than the latter of explaining EC reticence about greater transparency of subsidies. Where realism demonstrated its analytical strength over neoliberalism was in its superior capacity to explain EC policies toward the codes on technical barriers and government procurement. Defensive positionalism and relative-gains concerns were not just correlated with, but instead unambiguously caused, EC decisions to oppose U.S. interpretations and initiatives on several questions connected with those two codes, and they directly induced the EC's own efforts to re-craft elements of the technical barriers agreements.

Relative-gains concerns did not always determine EC actions vis-à-vis the codes. In the case of the subsidies code, the EC's opposition was driven not by dissatisfaction with its relative gains but by a well-grounded concern that others had much to gain from greater controls and that its member-states had everything to lose. But realism and its specification of a relative-gains problem added significantly—especially when compared with the failure of neoliberalism and its focus on rational state egoism and the problem of cheating—to our understanding of the variation in the EC's acceptance of the NTB codes, in particular the accords on technical barriers and government procurement.

Finally, the EC was not the only code participant oriented toward relative-gains calculations. Canada, Australia, and Argentina displayed a tendency to focus on relative gains in the ADP committee deliberations on Article 8:4. The United States appears also to have been driven by such concerns in the mid-1980s in regard to the overall balance of benefits produced by the two sides of the SCM accord. Across the codes and code members constituting the Tokyo Round NTB regime, then, there was a causal linkage between satisfaction or unhappiness with relative achievements of otherwise mutually positive gains generated by different NTB codes (the exception, again, involves agriculture and the SCM code) and the level of support ascribed by signatories to a particular agreement. This has important implications for theory, research, and policy, to which we now turn our attention.

CHAPTER EIGHT

Realism and Cooperation among Nations

This final chapter provides a summary of the main empirical findings about the Tokyo Round NTB code experience, and it highlights
the implications that can be derived from that experience for the
theoretical debate between realism and neoliberal institutionalism. It
also demonstrates that the relative-gains problem is not unique to the
particular case of the NTB regime but instead is a more general
characteristic of efforts among states to cooperate. The chapter then
offers elements of a research program that, informed and directed by
a realist-oriented awareness of defensive state positionalism and the
relative-gains problem for cooperation, might extend our understanding of the preferences and behavior of states in the face of
anarchy and common interests. Finally, the chapter suggests that a
focus on state positionalism and the relative-gains problem may help
us develop policy recommendations that facilitate the achievement by
states of sustainable forms of international cooperation.

EMPIRICAL FINDINGS AND THEORETICAL IMPLICATIONS

A new liberal institutionalism emerged in the 1980s that sought to
outflank realism by claiming to accept its core propositions while re-
futing its pessimistic conclusions about international cooperation and
the capacity of international institutions to help states work together.
Neoliberals seemed to have a strong position: they granted what they
claimed was the realist position that cooperation among states in anarchy and in the face of common (but mixed) interests is hard to achieve
because cheating is possible and potentially profitable, but they then

argued that institutions can help reduce cheating and thereby can make cooperation feasible. Realism was thus put at risk: it would be correct but also largely irrelevant to our understanding of the problem of interstate cooperation.

This book has argued that there are two problems with the neo-liberal institutionalist challenge to realism. First, the realist analysis of international politics is logically more compelling than the neoliberal-ist. Although neoliberals claim to accept realism's understanding of the importance of anarchy, neoliberals actually present a partial and thus defective analysis of the meaning of anarchy for states and its effects on them. Both schools define international anarchy as the absence of centralized government among nations. Yet, whereas neo-liberals argue that anarchy means that states may renege on their promises to one another, realists go much beyond this to observe that states in anarchy must also fear that others may seek to destroy or enslave them. Neoliberals maintain that states are rational egoists, interested in their own well-being. Realists argue that states are actu-ally defensive positionalists, and, concerned with their security and independence, must assess their own situation in terms of others. For neoliberals, cheating or uncertainty about the faithfulness of partners is the main systemic constraint on cooperation. Realists, on the other hand, argue that anarchy generates another, equally formidable im-pediment: the fear of states that partners will gain more from com-mon action.

The second problem with the neoliberal challenge to realism is that the latter's understanding of the problem of international coopera-tion turns out to be empirically superior to that offered by neoliberal-ism. This book did not attempt to affirm such a position through an analysis of the manner in which the United States and the Soviet Union might each worry about the gains achieved by the other as they negotiate agreements to reduce or limit their strategic or conventional military forces. Neoliberalism, after all, claims to provide a better analysis than realism not of state behavior in international security affairs but in the international political economy. For that reason, the book sought to demonstrate that realism gives us more help than neoliberal institutionalism when we try to understand the achieve-ments and failures of the efforts of even close friends—the United States, the EC member-states, and the other advanced industrialized democracies—to work together in a purely economic realm, namely the control of non-tariff barriers to trade.

The advanced democracies developed a regime to regulate and reduce NTBs during the 1970s. By the mid-to-late 1980s some of the codes constituting this new regime—the agreements on customs valuation and import licensing, and the countervail rules contained in the code on subsidies and countervailing measures—had attained substantial levels of success. In contrast, the subsidy rules contained in the subsidies/countervail accord were almost completely ineffective. In between these two poles, the codes on anti-dumping practices, technical barriers, and government procurement had achieved a mixed level of success. The immediate cause of this variance for the most part was the character of interactions between the United States and the EC: if these two GATT partners agreed on their respective rights and obligations, the code in question had a good chance of success; if they clashed—as in the technical barriers or government procurement agreement and especially the subsidy code—its prospects were markedly less favorable.

The key problem, then, was to account for discord between the United States and the EC in the latter three NTB codes and associated code committees. Such conflicts were typically characterized by one of two behaviors: either the EC resisted U.S. interpretations of code obligations, or it resisted United States initiatives to revise or extend code rules. Factors specified in neoliberal institutionalism, Chapter 6 determined, did not account for these EC actions very well, especially with regard to the government procurement and technical barriers codes. Within those latter two agreements—and in comparison with the more successful codes such as the customs agreement and the countervailing measures portion of the subsidies accord, and even the anti-dumping code, where the United States and the EC rarely clashed—the EC attained substantial absolute gains, found itself chiefly among small groupings of advanced democratic partners, was involved in highly iterated interactions, and was not an apparent victim of cheating. Yet the EC resisted U.S. initiatives and interpretations of the two codes, and, in the case of the technical barriers agreement, the EC sought to bring about a significant change in its rights and obligations.

The book suggested that realism provided much more leverage than neoliberalism on the problem of understanding the EC's approach to the NTB codes. Those agreements the EC did support strongly were also the ones generating favorable sharings of jointly produced new trading opportunities or assurances of fair treatment by trading partners for the EC. In contrast, the EC faced a problem of gaps in gains in regard to the rules for enhanced transparency of subsidy programs contained in the subsidies code, for as a result of those rules all would enjoy some level of absolute gains in terms of increased information about one another's subsidies, but non-EC states would receive greater information about EC programs than the reverse. In addition, within the subsidies agreement the EC believed that it was in an even more severe zero-sum-like situation regarding agricultural export subsidies, where others' gains would be its direct losses. Given these circumstances, the EC strongly resisted a vigorous enforcement of the subsidy rules in the subsidies code.

Both neoliberalism and realism could claim that they can explain the EC's support for the more successful NTB codes such as the agreement on customs valuation and the countervailing-measure rules in the subsidies code, for the EC's enjoyment of favorable relative gains from them meant that EC member-states must have enjoyed substantial absolute gains as well. In addition, both approaches could claim to account for the EC's behavior concerning agricultural export subsidies—neither would ever expect an actor to support an agreement yielding it absolute losses. It would not be easy to choose between the two approaches solely on the basis of the experience of those agreements or code elements.

However, neoliberalism began to have difficulty, and realism began to show its comparative strength, when we came to the EC's resistance to the subsidy notification rules in the subsidies code: here the problem was not one of absolute gains or losses, but rather of gaps in otherwise mutually positive gains favoring the EC's partners. Most significant, realism showed that it could go well beyond neoliberalism's explanatory reach when it came to accounting for the resistance of the EC and its member-states to the United States in the government procurement and technical barriers codes, as well as for the EC's own efforts to revise the latter agreement. The EC states determined—and had good reasons to conclude—that those two agreements would produce absolute gains for all but would yield the United States greater gains than they themselves would enjoy. As we would expect of a group of defensive positionalists, the EC rejected such an outcome, and, consistent with realist expectations, it resisted U.S. efforts on such issues as the mutual acceptance of test data in the technical barriers agreement, or sought to change code rules, as when the EC called for the extension of the technical barriers code to private and non-central governmental standards agencies.

Realism's analytical reach also surpassed neoliberalism's in explaining the major code setback not caused by U.S.-EC discord, that is, the case of basic-price systems and Article 8:4 of the anti-dumping code. Canada, Australia, and Argentina were not afraid that the February and April 1981 draft interpretations would allow the United States and the EC to cheat their partners because they already had basic-price systems in effect. These mechanisms were intentionally highly transparent; all the code members knew that the United States and the EC had them in effect; and the United States and the EC were quite open about them and about their likely continuation under either draft interpretation.[1] Moreover, it was not the argument of the opponents of the February and April drafts that the latter would not yield all code members absolute benefits. The problem was neither cheating nor the absence of absolute benefits for all partners. What was unacceptable to the opponents was that the first two drafts would allow the United States and the EC to continue to do something foreclosed to their partners, leaving the former relatively better off than the latter.

Hence, although the issue-area (economics), the main actors (mostly advanced democracies), and the context (small groups nested within the GATT) all favored neoliberal institutionalism, it was realism that explained U.S.-EC interactions within the Tokyo Round NTB regime more successfully, and which best accounted for the variance in effectiveness achieved by the agreements constituting that regime during the 1980s. And it was realism, not neoliberalism, that was able to explain the stunted success of the Article 8:4 negotiations. Had neoliberal institutionalism been the only theory of international politics available to us, we would have been left puzzled by large and indeed the most interesting parts of the Tokyo Round NTB experience. Fortunately, realist international theory was available and able to help us understand the fate of the different NTB codes during the 1980s.

THE RELATIVE-GAINS PROBLEM AND OTHER CASES OF COOPERATION IN THE INTERNATIONAL POLITICAL ECONOMY

Neoliberals might concede that the EC and other code participants were motivated in some measure by relative-gains concerns in the Tokyo Round NTB regime, but they might argue that the latter was an anomaly and thus does not tell us that much either about states or about the debate between realism and their perspective. However, a number of other efforts by advanced democracies to cooperate in economic issue-areas were also characterized by high common inter-

1. Indeed, because they involve the announcement of price floors and thus reduce competition and serve as an example to other industries seeking protection, the problem with basic-price systems is that they are *too* visible to both governments and traders.

ests and nesting but also experienced difficulties because of relative-gains disputes. In addition, when progress toward cooperation was made, it was because the advanced countries effectively addressed relative-gains concerns of disadvantaged partners.

For example, during the Tokyo Round of 1974–79, the United States, Japan, and the EC all believed they would gain from a further reduction in industrial tariffs. The United States preferred a single, deep (50 percent), across-the-board cut in tariffs in all industrial sectors. However, the EC, facing an American tariff structure that contained some moderately high tariff peaks, believed that an across-the-board cut, while reducing all tariffs, would still leave the peaks in the U.S. tariff structure. For the Europeans, an across-the-board cut would create relatively greater new export opportunities for the United States than for the EC. The EC thus proposed that tariff reductions be greater in industries with higher duties, a proposal resisted by the United States. Both sides eventually accepted a Swiss compromise proposal that mandated deep tariff cuts across many industries but which also included somewhat deeper cuts for industries with higher initial duty rates. Neither the United States nor the EC could employ the Swiss formula to develop or evaluate a precise estimate of the effect of the Swiss formula on relative export gains. However, each knew that it had narrowed the range of possible gaps in trade gains that might advantage the other. By thus helping to resolve U.S. and especially EC concerns not about absolute but about relative gains in export opportunities, the Swiss compromise tariff formula facilitated successful completion of a major round of trade-liberalization talks in the GATT.[2]

Of course, it could be argued that the advanced countries are concerned about gaps in mutually positive gains only when they interact in the GATT. However, such problems have in fact inhibited their achievement of cooperation in non-GATT economic contexts. For example, as Barbara Haskel demonstrates, relative-gains problems also hampered the development of a Scandinavian free-trade arrangement during the 1940s, the 1950s, and much of the 1960s. Haskel reports that in approaching the idea of a customs union at the end of the 1940s, "Norway's position was that there had to be a 'balance' of benefits among the countries" and that this was due to a

---

2. See John Whalley, *Trade Liberalization among Major Trading Areas* (Cambridge: MIT Press, 1985), 145–49; and Gilbert R. Winham, *International Trade and the Tokyo Round Negotiation* (Princeton: Princeton University Press, 1986), 17–18, 160–63, 200–205.

desire on the part of Norway "to prevent what it feared might be an improperly skewed distribution of benefits or losses."[3] Norway, according to Haskel, was particularly concerned that Sweden would enjoy the lion's share of the new trade opportunities created by such an arrangement. It was only when Norway developed confidence during the 1950s and 1960s in its ability to hold its own against Sweden in trade, and when it received offers of side-payments from Sweden (see discussion in the next section), that it could accept a proposed Nordic commercial arrangement—Nordek—during 1968–70. (The proposal for Nordek was vetoed by Finland in March 1970 in the face of its concerns about Soviet disapproval.)[4]

Moreover, advanced industrial states are concerned about gaps in gains in political-economic matters other than international trade. In the monetary field, for example, Loukas Tsoukalis and others have shown that Italy, Britain, Ireland, and France determined during the early 1970s that their participation in a joint float with West Germany and several smaller European states—the Economic and Monetary Union (EMU) of 1972–76—may have been yielding all partners absolute gains in terms of protection against monetary instability originating in the United States, but it was also resulting in the imposition of greater burdens on them than on Germany. As a result, the four dissatisfied states exited from the EMU.[5] The European Monetary System (EMS), which was founded in 1978 as the successor to the failed EMU, and which has brought France, Italy, and Ireland (but, to date, not Britain) back into a joint float with Germany and its Deutsche-mark partners, was designed with the specific intent to address relative-gains concerns of weaker participants through differential treatment of weaker partners and outright side-payments to them. The EMS doubled the financial resources available under the EMU to support weaker members' exchange rates, assigned Italy a much greater range of variation for its exchange rate (6 percent as opposed to 2.5 percent for the other seven partners), provided Italy

3. Barbara G. Haskel, "Disparities, Strategies, and Opportunity Costs: The Example of Scandinavian Economic Market Negotiations," *International Studies Quarterly* 18 (1974), 15–16.

4. See Haskel, "Disparities," and Haskel, *The Scandinavian Option: Opportunities and Opportunity Costs in Postwar Scandinavian Foreign Policies* (Oslo: Universitetsforlaget, 1976), 124–27.

5. See Loukas Tsoukalis, *The Politics and Economics of European Monetary Integration* (London: Allen & Unwin, 1977), 129–36, 157; D. C. Kruse, *Monetary Integration in Western Europe: EMU, EMS, and Beyond* (London: Butterworths, 1980), 111–71; and Peter Coffey, *The European Monetary System: Past, Present, and Future* (Dordrecht: Martinus Nijhoff, 1984), 13, 123–24.

and Ireland about $1 billion in subsidies, and allowed for the adjustment of currency rates more easily than had been true in the EMU. In addition, a core new element of the EMS (its indicator of divergence among members' exchange rates) is constituted in such a way as to impose a somewhat greater obligation on Germany that it as well as the deficit countries in the EMS have a responsibility to adjust economic policies to promote stability in EMS exchange rates.[6]

Finally, relative-gains calculations have not been unique to advanced democratic states but instead have been a major impediment to economic cooperation among developing countries as well.[7] This can be observed in the difficulties states in Latin America, Central America, and East Africa have encountered as they have sought to construct regional economic integration arrangements.[8] For example, founded in 1960, the Latin American Free Trade Association (LAFTA) faltered within ten years: in December 1969 member-states in the association publicly acknowledged that they would not reach their goal of regional free trade.[9] Absolute-gains or cheating problems do not appear to have been the main sources of LAFTA's decay. Instead, as Edward Milensky reports, LAFTA members that identified themselves as possessing "insufficient markets" (Colombia, Chile,

6. See Coffey, *European Monetary System*, 21–26, 126–27; Hugo M. Kaufman, "The European Monetary System and National Policy Constraints," *Comparative Social Research* 5 (1982), 107–28; Jocelyn Statler, "EMS: Cul-de-Sac or Signpost on the Road to EMU?" in Michael Hodges and William Wallace, eds., *Economic Divergence in the European Community* (London: Allen & Unwin, 1981), 113–25; Jacques Ypersele and Jean-Claude Koene, *The European Monetary System: Origins, Operation, and Outlook* (Brussels: Commission of the European Communities, 1984), 47–63; George Zis, "The European Monetary System, 1979–1984: An Assessment," *Journal of Common Market Studies* 23 (1984), 58; and Paul Taylor, *The Limits of European Integration* (New York: Columbia University Press, 1983), 170–87.

7. The literature on regional integration among developing countries strongly emphasizes the problem of relative gains. See, for example, Lynn K. Mytelka, "The Salience of Gains in Third-World Integrative Systems," *World Politics* 25 (January 1973), 236–46; W. Andrew Axline, "Underdevelopment, Dependence, and Integration: The Politics of Regionalism in the Third World," *International Organization* 31 (Winter 1977), 83–105; and Constantine V. Vaitsos, "Crisis in Regional Economic Cooperation (Integration) among Developing Countries: A Survey," *World Development* 6 (June 1978), 747–50.

8. The following draws on my "International Anarchy and the Embedded Rationality of States: Realist and Neoliberal Theories and the Problem of Regional Economic Cooperation," delivered at the annual meeting of the American Political Science Association, Atlanta, Georgia, August 31–September 3, 1989.

9. On LAFTA, see Edward S. Milensky, *The Politics of Regional Organization in Latin America* (New York: Praeger, 1973), 17–36, 61–101; and Milensky, "Latin America's Multilateral Diplomacy: Integration, Disintegration, and Interdependence," *International Affairs* 53 (January 1977), 77–78; also see James D. Cochrane and John W. Sloan, "LAFTA and the CACM: A Comparative Analysis of Integration in Latin America," *Journal of Developing Areas* 8 (October 1973), 13–23.

Peru, and Venezuela) or as "relatively least developed" vis-à-vis the other members (Ecuador, Paraguay, Uruguay, and Bolivia) complained that the three stronger states in the group (Argentina, Brazil, and Mexico) were garnering the bulk of new trade opportunities created by the arrangement.[10] According to James Cochrane and John Sloan, "this fact, plus the inability of the entire membership to agree on some formula to ensure an equitable distribution of the benefits of economic integration, brought LAFTA to the point of crisis in the late 1960s."[11]

Similarly, the Central American Common Market (CACM), also founded in 1960, already "was on the verge of collapse" in 1969 when it was effectively terminated by the outbreak of war between El Salvador and Honduras.[12] Disputes about relative achievements of otherwise mutually positive new trading opportunities contributed to this demise of the arrangement. Specifically, studies by Stuart Fagan and Miguel Wionczek emphasize that Honduras and Nicaragua concluded in the course of the 1960s that Costa Rica, El Salvador, and Guatemala were enjoying a disproportionate share of the gains generated by their common market agreement.[13] As a result, according to Wionczek, beginning in 1966, "the unequal distribution of benefits accruing from integration became the key issue [within CACM] and Honduras and Nicaragua began to press for special concessions."[14]

The same problem of relative-gains appears to have hobbled the Andean Pact, founded by six states in the wake of the collapse of LAFTA. By 1980 one member (Chile) left the pact; another (Bolivia) threatened to do so; and several contravened or delayed implementation of important pact decisions.[15] After describing the disputes that

10. Milensky, *Politics of Regional Organization*, 75–78.
11. Cochrane and Sloan, "LAFTA and CACM," 19.
12. Stuart Fagan, *Central American Economic Integration: The Politics of Unequal Benefits* (Berkeley, Calif.: Institute of International Studies, 1970), 1; also see Milensky, "Multilateral Diplomacy," 82–83; and Cochrane and Sloan, "LAFTA and CACM," 117–23.
13. See Fagan, *Politics of Unequal Benefits*, 16–18; and Miguel Wionczek, "The Rise and Decline of Latin American Integration," *Journal of Common Market Studies* 9 (September 1970), 55–56.
14. Wionczek, "Latin American Integration," 59.
15. See Kevin J. Middlebrook, "Regional Organizations and Andean Economic Integration, 1969–1975," *Journal of Common Market Studies* 17 (September 1978), 78; Rafael Vargas-Hildalgo, "The Crisis of the Andean Pact: Lessons for Integration among Developing Countries," *Journal of Common Market Studies* 17 (March 1979), 219–20; Lynn Krieger Mytelka, *Regional Development in a Global Economy: The Multinational Corporation, Technology, and Andean Integration* (New Haven: Yale University Press, 1979), 39–61; and David E. Hojman, "The Andean Pact: Failure of a Model of Economic Integration," *Journal of Common Market Studies* 20 (December 1981), 146–47.

incapacitated the pact, William Avery reports that "although a variety of factors can be identified as contributing to this state of affairs, most are related to the common problem of the distribution of benefits."[16] These concerns about relative achievements of trade gains were centered on Ecuador and especially Bolivia. According to Kevin Middlebrook, for example, Bolivia argued "that it has not received its 'fair' share of benefits and since 1970 has balked regarding its required annual contribution" to the pact.[17] Similarly, Avery reports that when the pact was formed, each member "perceived its opportunities to derive benefits from the market to be more or less proportionate to the opportunities of the other members." However, "*after* the structure for distributing benefits was in place and a record of performance had been established," then "equity assumed its greatest empirical importance," and "the record to date has caused particular dissatisfaction to Bolivia."[18] The same focus on relative outcomes in the Andean Pact is adopted by Alicia Puyana de Palacios. A pact study in 1979, she reports, emphasized the perception of Ecuador and Bolivia that Colombia, Peru, and Venezuela were achieving relatively greater gains from the regional arrangement than they, and Puyana de Palacios observes that "the negative effect of concentration on Ecuador, and especially on Bolivia, continues to be plainly manifest, which has led to new frictions between these two countries and the other three."[19]

Finally, composed of Kenya, Tanzania, and Uganda, the East African Community (EAC) was begun in 1967 and for a time was considered to be "one of the best examples of cooperation among developing countries."[20] However, in February 1977 Tanzania closed its border with Kenya, and in June the EAC collapsed when the partners failed to agree on a budget for the organization; by the end of the next year Uganda and Tanzania were at war with one another.[21] As in

16. William P. Avery, "The Politics of Crisis and Cooperation in the Andean Group," *Journal of Developing Areas* 17 (January 1983), 155.
17. Middlebrook, "Andean Economic Integration," 78.
18. Avery, "Crisis and Cooperation in the Andean Group," 161.
19. Alicia Puyana de Palacios, *Economic Integration among Unequal Partners: The Case of the Andean Group* (New York: Pergamon, 1982), 275–76.
20. Domenico Mazzeo, "The Experience of the East African Community: Implications for the Theory and Practice of Regional Cooperation in Africa," in Mazzeo, ed., *African Regional Organizations* (Cambridge: Cambridge University Press, 1984), 151. On East African regional cooperation prior to the EAC, see Joseph S. Nye, Jr., *Pan-Africanism and East African Integration* (Cambridge: Harvard University Press, 1965); and Arthur Hazlewood, *Economic Integration: The East African Experience* (London: Heinemann, 1975).
21. On the decline of the EAC, see Arthur Hazlewood, "The End of the East

the previous cases, relative-gains disputes were a major corrosive force operating on the EAC. Domenico Mazzeo, for example, argues that "the survival of regional cooperation in East Africa was constantly threatened by the perceived uneven distribution of benefits among member states," and he observes further that "regional cooperation in East Africa would have survived if the question of the maldistribution of benefits had been solved satisfactorily."[22] According to Thomas Cox, by the mid-1970s Tanzania had become "more convinced than ever that the Community needed to pay greater attention to the 'distributive' function and less to trade liberalization."[23] This was not accomplished to Tanzania's satisfaction, and in February 1977 it closed its borders to Kenya in retaliation for the latter's grounding of the EAC's jointly managed airline.[24] It was this border action by Tanzania that set off the budgetary crisis and the collapse of the EAC later in the year. Both developed and developing countries, this brief overview suggests, possess a propensity to experience relative-gains concerns, although what surely divides them is the greater capacity of developed states to construct institutions that sometimes address these concerns effectively.

In sum, differences in U.S.-EC cooperation in regard to the Tokyo Round NTB codes, and thus variance in code success achieved during the 1980s, are more readily and more fully explained by realism and its focus on defensive state positionalism and the relative-gains problem than by neoliberal institutionalism and its focus on rational state egoism and the problem of cheating. Realism also accounts more effectively than neoliberalism for a major NTB regime experience unrelated to U.S.-EC interactions: the negotiations over basic-price systems and Article 8:4 of the anti-dumping agreement. Interstate interactions within the GATT not related to the NTB codes, and efforts by both developed and developing states to cooperate not within the GATT but rather at the regional level in the monetary and

African Community: What Are the Lessons for Regional Integration Schemes," *Journal of Common Market Studies* 18 (September 1979), 40–58; and Allen L. Springer, "Community Chronology," in Christian P. Potholm and Richard A. Fredland, *Integration and Disintegration in East Africa* (Lanham, Md.: University Press of America, 1980), 28–29.

22. Mazzeo, "The East African Community," 152; also see Hazlewood, "End of the East African Community," 44–54.

23. Thomas S. Cox, "Northern Actors in a South-South Setting: External Aid and East African Integration," *Journal of Common Market Studies* 21 (March 1983), 292.

24. Reginald Herbold Green, "The East African Community: Death, Funeral, Inheritance," in Colin Legum, ed., *Africa Contemporary Record, 1977–1978* (New York: Holmes & Meier, 1979), A125–33.

trade fields, have also been characterized and affected by defensive state positionalism and the relative-gains problem for cooperation, and thus have also displayed behavioral characteristics in keeping with realist expectations. All this leads to the conclusion that realism remains the most effective starting point for the analysis of world politics in general and for the problem of international cooperation in particular.[25]

A RESEARCH PROGRAM FOR INTERNATIONAL COOPERATION

This book has suggested that realism offers a more complete and compelling understanding of the problem of cooperation than does neoliberal institutionalism. However, additional empirical tests of the two theories can and should be undertaken. For example, a core neoliberal proposition is that in the face of anarchy and mixed-interests, a longer time-horizon (or a more powerful "shadow of the future") facilitates the achievement of cooperation. Realism would offer a very different argument. If states are oriented toward the long term, they will be more likely to believe that joint gains produced in the present can and will be converted into power resources both within the arrangement and across issue-areas. Therefore they will be acutely sensitive to relative achievements of gains and will bargain very hard to ensure that the arrangement will not produce gaps in benefits favoring partners, possibly leading to the cooperative arrangement failing to ever get under way. From a realist viewpoint, then, and in strong opposition to neoliberal theory, an extended state time-perspective might make cooperation more difficult, and not easier, to achieve.

A second, related pair of competing hypotheses that may be derived from realism and neoliberalism concerns their respective expectations as to the durability of arrangements states prefer when they engage in joint action. Neoliberal theory argues that cheating is less likely to occur in a mixed-interest situation that is iterated; hence it suggests that "the most direct way to encourage cooperation is to make the relationship more durable."[26] If two states that are inter-

25. For example, Kenneth Waltz argues that states fear they may become dependent on their partners: see Waltz, *Theory of International Politics* (Reading, Mass.: Addison-Wesley, 1979), 106–7.
26. See Robert Axelrod, *The Evolution of Cooperation* (New York: Basic, 1984), 129; and Axelrod and Robert O. Keohane, "Achieving Cooperation under Anarchy: Strategies and Institutions," *World Politics* 38 (October 1985), 234, in which they argue that

ested in cooperation could choose between two arrangements that offered comparable absolute gains but that differed in their expected durability—one arrangement might, for example, have higher exit costs than the other—neoliberalism would expect the states to prefer the former over the latter, for each state could then be more confident that the other would remain in the arrangement. Realism generates a markedly different hypothesis. If two states are worried or uncertain about relative achievements of gains, each will prefer a less durable cooperative arrangement, for each will want to be more readily able to exit from the arrangement in the event that gaps in gains favor the other.

Another pair of competing hypotheses concerns the number of partners states prefer in a cooperative arrangement. Advocates of neoliberalism find that a small number of participants facilitates verification of compliance and sanctioning of cheaters. Hence they would predict that states with a choice would tend to prefer a smaller number of partners. Realism would offer a very different hypothesis. A state may believe that it might do better than some partners in a proposed arrangement but not as well as others. If it is uncertain about which partners would do relatively better, the state will prefer more partners, for larger numbers would enhance the likelihood that relative gains advantaging (what turn out to be) better-positioned partners could be offset by more favorable sharings arising from interactions with (as matters develop) weaker partners.

A fourth and final pair of competing empirical statements derived from realism and neoliberalism concerns the effects of linkages of issues on the prospects for international cooperation. Proponents of neoliberalism find that tightly knit linkages within and across issue-areas accentuate the iterativeness of relationships among states and thus facilitate their working together.[27] Realism, again, offers a very different proposition. Assume that a state believes that two issue-areas are linked, and that it believes that one element of this linkage is that changes in relative capabilities in one domain affect relative capabilities in the other. Assume also that the state believes that relative achievements of jointly produced gains in one issue-area would advantage the partner. This state would then believe that cooperation

---

international regimes promote cooperation because they "link the future with the present."

27. See Robert O. Keohane, *After Hegemony: Cooperation and Discord in the World Political Economy* (Princeton: Princeton University Press, 1984), 91–92, 103–6; and Axelrod and Keohane, "Achieving Cooperation," 239–43.

would provide additional capabilities to the partner not only in the domain in which joint action is undertaken but also in the linked issue-area. Cooperation would therefore be unattractive to this state in direct proportion to its belief that the two issue-areas were interrelated. Thus linkages of issues may impede rather than facilitate cooperation.

These and other tests are likely to demonstrate that realism offers a fuller, richer, and more persuasive understanding of the problem of international cooperation than does neoliberal institutionalism. Yet this would certainly not mark the end of the broader challenge posed to realism by the liberal institutionalist tradition. This is because there are at least two related clusters of modern literature that are firmly rooted in such a tradition, that have attempted no compromise with realism, and that are able to present an understanding of the dynamics of and prospects for international cooperation that is both potentially compelling and markedly at odds with realist theory. The first cluster argues that international institutions embody and reinforce norms and beliefs that are held in common among states and that facilitate and guide their cooperative endeavors.[28] The second cluster suggests that international institutions help states develop, accept, and disseminate consensual theoretical and empirical knowledge that can reinforce or introduce into interstate relations norms that promote cooperation.[29] Both these groupings of scholarship challenge realism insofar as they argue that states may transcend their

28. The key works in this cluster include John Gerard Ruggie, "International Responses to Technology: Concepts and Trends," *International Organization* 29 (Summer 1975), 557–83; Ruggie, "International Regimes, Transactions, and Change: Embedded Liberalism in the Postwar Economic Order," in Stephen D. Krasner, ed., *International Regimes* (Ithaca: Cornell University Press, 1983), 195–231; Friedrich Kratochwil, "The Force of Prescriptions," *International Organization* 38 (Autumn 1984), 685–708; Ruggie and Kratochwil, "International Organization: The State of the Art on an Art of the State," *International Organization* 40 (Autumn 1986), 753–76; and Donald J. Puchala and Raymond F. Hopkins, "International Regimes: Lessons from Inductive Analysis," in Krasner, ed., *International Regimes*, 61–92.

29. Ernst Haas presented this argument in *Beyond the Nation-State: Functionalism and International Organization* (Stanford: Stanford University Press, 1964), 12–13, 47–48, 79–85; also see Haas, "Is There a Hole in the Whole? Knowledge, Technology, Interdependence and the Construction of International Regimes," *International Organization* 29 (Summer 1975), 827–76; Haas, Mary Pat Williams, and Don Babai, *Scientists and World Order: The Uses of Technical Information in International Organizations* (Berkeley: University of California Press 1977); Haas, "Why Collaborate? Issue-Linkage and International Regimes," *World Politics* 32 (April 1980), 357–405; Haas, "Words Can Hurt You; or, Who Said What to Whom about Regimes," in Krasner, ed., *International Regimes*, 23–59; and Beverly Crawford and Stefanie Lenway, "Decision Modes and International Regime Change: Western Collaboration on East-West Trade," *World Politics* 37 (April 1985), 375–402.

fears of one another as they develop new, cooperation-promoting collective cognitive understandings (at the bureaucratic-institutional level) of the international system.

However, there may be a realist response even to this most serious liberal institutionalist challenge. That is, it may be possible to argue that states, aware of their anarchical political environment, seek in their ongoing interactions to develop commonly shared norms or consensual knowledge that reflect their concerns about anarchy but nevertheless allow for cooperative endeavors. For example, one might determine through historical analysis that the norm of compensation or of the periodic review of treaties is the result of state experiences with the relative-gains problem and that they mark a way by which states have "learned" to manage that problem. In other words, realists would agree that norms may indeed evolve as a part of international history and that some may facilitate cooperation, but realists would suggest that the norms may themselves be a state response to international anarchy.

Beyond contributing to the ongoing dialogue between realists and liberals, the realist-based concepts of defensive state positionalism and the relative-gains problem for cooperation generate a number of questions about state calculations regarding opportunities to cooperate. For example, how do states estimate future gains from cooperation? What are the standards by which they compare their gains with those of their partners? Finally, can we identify variations in the sensitivity of states to gaps in gains across different cooperative arrangements, and can any such observed differences be related to the fungibility or convertibility of gains generated by the endeavors?

In addition, a focus on defensive state positionalism and the problem of relative gains may shed light on the bargaining agenda that states pursue in cooperative arrangements. For example, as they establish the terms of a cooperative endeavor, do states try to communicate to their prospective partners an inflated image of their sensitivity to gaps in gains in order to bring about institutional arrangements favoring them or in order to extract side-payments? Similarly, do states in the formative and operational phases of cooperative arrangements find it necessary first to establish and then to employ a single metric or perhaps a range of mutually acceptable metrics for the estimation of gains in order to facilitate bargaining, the exchange of concessions, and the readjustment of the terms of the arrangement and the compensation of what turn out to be disadvantaged partners? Do states in such negotiations also press for the use of a metric to measure possible joint gains that depicts their benefits from the arrangement in the least favorable light in order, again, to yield the fewest concessions and to attain the best possible treatment? Is there, in other words, a politics of sensitivity coefficients and metrics of gains that is intrinsic to cooperative endeavors among states?

Finally, if concerns about relative gains do act as a constraint on cooperation, we should undertake to identify methods by which states have been able to address them through unilateral bargaining strategies or through the mechanisms and operations of international institutions. For example, we might investigate the use by states of side-payments to mitigate the relative-gains concerns of disadvantaged partners. The provision of side-payments appears to be at the core of cooperative endeavors both within and among states.[30] Karl Deutsch and his associates, for example, determined that the capacity of advantaged regions to extend symbolic and material side-payments to disadvantaged regions was essential to national integration and amalgamation in such cases as Switzerland and Germany.[31] Similarly, when many developing countries complained during the 1960s that the international trade order generated disproportionate gains for the advanced capitalist states, the latter responded with an offer within the framework of the GATT of a special, limited program of non-reciprocal trading preferences—the Generalized System of Preferences—that essentially provided trade-gain side-payments to developing countries. In addition, according to studies by Paul Taylor and by George Zis, it was the special subsidized loans that finally led Ireland and Italy back to the European Monetary System.[32] Moreover, Barbara Haskel and Claes Wiklund have suggested in separate analyses that Norway was attracted to the proposed Nordek arrangement during 1968–70 in part because Sweden offered to provide the bulk of the funds for a Nordic development bank that would have been used in large measure to support Norwegian industrial projects.[33] Finally, as Gregory Treverton has demonstrated, West Germany has sought to ameliorate U.S. concerns about relative burden-sharing in NATO through special "offset" programs aimed at reducing U.S. foreign-exchange expenditures associated with its European commitment.[34]

30. On the general concept of side-payments, see R. Duncan Luce and Howard Raiffa, *Games and Decisions: Introduction and Critical Survey* (New York: Wiley, 1957), 168–69; and William H. Riker, *The Theory of Political Coalitions* (New Haven: Yale University Press, 1962), 34, 108–23.

31. See Karl Deutsch et al., *Political Community in the North Atlantic Area* (Princeton: Princeton University Press, 1957), 55.

32. See Taylor, *European Integration*, 182–84; and Zis, "European Monetary System," 58.

33. See Haskel, *Scandinavian Option*, 127; and Claes Wiklund, "The Zig-Zag Course of the Nordek Negotiations," *Scandinavian Political Studies* 5 (1970), 322.

34. See Gregory F. Treverton, *The "Dollar Drain" and American Forces in Germany:*

The relative-gains problem and its grounding in defensive state positionalism help us pinpoint a wide range of new research problems regarding the preferences of states as they consider opportunities to cooperate. An awareness of defensive state positionalism and of the relative-gains problem also generates important questions about the kinds of issues and problems states must resolve in order to pool their efforts in a joint endeavor. Finally, these concepts, and the realist tradition from which they arise, lead us to ask interesting questions about the strategies states may use to resolve or at least to manage their relative-gains problems and thereby achieve cooperation.

IMPLICATIONS FOR POLICY

Realist political theory helps us think about not only the problem of international conflict but also that of international cooperation. As a result, realism may help us offer guidance to states that could benefit through common action. At least one such policy insight serves as a constraint on advice derived from neoliberal theory. The latter, according to Robert Keohane, leads to the insight that states may incur serious costs in any relationship if they decline to make firm commitments to their partners in cooperative arrangements and instead seek to "keep their options open."[35] If a state does not make a clear and firm commitment to a cooperative endeavor that would be hard to break, Keohane suggests, then partners will be unsure that the state will abide by its cooperative undertakings, and this will reduce the prospects for successful joint action.

This argument is perfectly valid if the problem of cooperation centers only on the problem of cheating. However, realists would argue that defensive state positionalism requires that a balance has to be struck between rigidity and flexibility of obligations within a cooperative arrangement. States must indeed believe that their partners have made definite, clear promises and that they will not renege on them. Yet at the same time states must also believe that if unfavorable gaps in gains begin to emerge within an arrangement, or if some other unfavorable development becomes manifest such as a growing dependency on partners for some vital good, there will be opportunities for

Managing the Political Economics of the Atlantic Alliance (Athens: Ohio University Press, 1978).

35. See Keohane, *After Hegemony*, 257–59.

the terms of the arrangement to be revised, or for the disadvantaged states to be excused temporarily from their commitments, or, at the extreme, for the disadvantaged states to leave the arrangement altogether.

The actual international economic order constructed after World War II seeks to strike precisely such a balance between firmness and clarity of obligations, on the one hand, and an awareness that states may need on occasion to derogate from or to seek a revision of their cooperative undertakings, on the other. The Bretton Woods/GATT international economic system seeks to oblige participating states not to interfere with international flows of goods and money. However, it also allows for limited forms of state interventionism to mitigate external disruptions of the domestic economy. This intermediate position between free and managed commerce—what John Ruggie calls "embedded liberalism"—allows states to achieve absolute gains from freer world markets, but it also allow states to limit the economic stress a national participant would be expected to sustain as a result of temporary or longer-term changes in its relative capacity to compete internationally.[36] Temporary derogations established by the safeguard provisions in Article XIX of the GATT, or the "open season" periodic renegotiations of tariff concessions as permitted in Article XXVIII, or indeed the whole notion of periodic rounds of multilateral trade negotiations, enhance—and are designed to enhance—the confidence of states that, if necessary, they may take steps to limit national dislocations that might evolve through trade liberalization.[37] Indeed, without these elements of flexibility within the GATT system (or, for that matter, other international economic regimes), it is unlikely that states would have accepted the risks associated with the obligations that they have in fact accepted and substantially honored since the late 1940s.[38]

Flexibility of commitment and a capacity to keep options somewhat open may add in some measure to state uncertainties about the faithfulness of their partners and thus may complicate the politics of international cooperation. Yet they may also be prerequisites for states to agree to undertake common action in the first place. That is one lesson learned from realist theory. In addition, realist theory would agree—perhaps to the surprise of some neoliberals—that international institutions *do* matter for states as they attempt to cooper-

36. Ruggie, "International Regimes," 195–232.
37. See Kenneth W. Dam, *The GATT: Law and International Economic Organization* (Chicago: University of Chicago Press, 1970), 81–86, 99–107; and Winham, *Tokyo Round*, 120–23.
38. This point is emphasized in Dam, *GATT*, 99; and Winham, *Tokyo Round*, 120.

ate. Indeed realists would argue that the problem with neoliberal institutionalism is not that is stresses the importance of institutions but that it *understates* the range of functions that institutions must perform to help states work together. Realists would agree that international institutions are important because they reduce cheating; yet, realists would also argue, they must do much more than that if cooperation is to be achieved.

For example, regimes and institutions can promote cooperation insofar as states may use them to set the outer boundaries on the generation of gaps in otherwise mutually positive gains generated by joint action. That is precisely why periodic reviews and safeguard clauses are included in the GATT, as noted in the discussion above of Articles XIX and XXVIII. Through such institutionalized review and escape mechanisms, states can seek redress to problems connected with the balance of rights and obligations of relationships and thus with the balance of benefits and burdens among their participants.

Second, as discussed in the research section, international institutions can provide formalized side-payment programs by which stronger partners can compensate weaker members and thus retain the loyalty of the latter to the cooperative endeavor. Third, and finally, international institutions, by providing for periodic reviews and renegotiation efforts, provide states with an element of "voice" through which they can signal their concerns about relative gains or other possible unfavorable developments associated with their cooperative endeavors.[39] Because they know they have these voice alternatives, states are probably more willing to join such arrangements in the first place and, if problems do arise, to remain loyal to them while seeking to reconfigure the balance of benefits they produce. Thus international institutions are important, realists would conclude, but for many more and for very different reasons than are suggested by the neoliberals.

These, then, are the policy implications generated by the realist insight into the defensively positional character of states and the resulting relative-gains problem for cooperation. Fortified by an awareness and appreciation of them, we may hope to help states establish lasting, mutually beneficial cooperative relationships. If that is accomplished, the debate between realism and neoliberal institutionalism will have been truly worthwhile.

39. This notion of voice is taken from Albert O. Hirschman, *Exit, Voice, and Loyalty* (Cambridge: Harvard University Press, 1970).

Operative Rule Construction, Technical Committee on Customs Valuation, 1981–1987

1981

1. Advisory Opinion: the concept of sale (situations in which imported good deemed not to have been subject of a sale)
2. Advisory Opinion: prices and Article 1.1 (if latter's conditions are met, a price lower than prevailing market prices should be accepted)
3. Advisory Opinion: the meaning of "are distinguished" in the Interpretative Note to Article 1
4. Advisory Opinions (4): treatment of royalties in various situations
5. Explanatory Note: the time element in Article 1 and Articles 2 and 3.

1982

1. Advisory Opinion (addendum): the concept of sale and goods imported for destruction
2. Advisory Opinion: trademark royalties should not be added by virtue of Article 8.1(c) to the price paid or payable
3. Commentary: identical and similar goods and the application of Articles 2 and 3
4. Commentary: treatment of goods subject to export subsidies
5. Commentary: treatment of goods sold at dumping prices
6. Explanatory Note: commissions and brokerage
7. Explanatory Note: treatment of goods not in accordance with contract
8. Advisory Opinions (2): treatment of cash discount under the Agreement
9. Case Study: interpretation of Article 8:1(b)(iv) concerning engineering, development, artwork, etc.
10. Advisory Opinions (2): treatment of barter or compensation deals and acceptability of test values under Article 1:2(b)
11. Commentary: treatment of price review clauses
12. Advisory Opinion: treatment of credits in earlier transactions
13. Commentary (Addendum): identical and similar goods (three additional examples)
14. Report: practices concerning the treatment of interest for deferred payment

15. Report: practices concerning the treatment of computer software
16. Guidelines: designation and use of instruments in the Technical Committee
17. Commentary (Addendum): identical and similar goods (four additional examples)
18. Advisory Opinion: deduction of anti-dumping and countervailing duties
19. Study: treatment of used motor vehicles

1983

1. Commentary (Addendum): identical and similar goods (three additional examples)
2. Case Study: application of Article 8:1(d) of the Agreement (treatment of the proceeds of resale accruing to seller)
3. Commentary: treatment of goods returned for manufacturing, processing, or repair
4. Advisory Opinion: royalties and license fees
5. Advisory Opinion: treatment of cash discount (discount provided to buyer who had not made payment for the goods at the time of valuation)
6. Commentary: treatment of split shipments under Article 1
7. Commentary: treatment of storage and related expenses under Article 1
8. Advisory Opinion: treatment of fraudulent documents
9. Advisory Opinion: hierarchical order in applying Article 7
10. Advisory Opinion: use of data from foreign sources in applying Article 7
11. Advisory Opinion: application of Article 7
12. Advisory Opinion: scope of the word "insurance" under Article 8:2(c)

1984

1. Commentary: treatment of package deals
2. Advisory Opinion: treatment of inadvertent errors and of incomplete documentation
3. Commentary: treatment of costs of activities taking place in country of importation
4. Commentary: adjustments for difference in commercial level and in quantity under Article 1:2(b) and Articles 2 and 3

1985

1. Commentary: treatment of tie-in-sales
2. Advisory Opinion: meaning of the expression "sold for export to the country of importation" in Article 1
3. Case Study: restrictions and conditions in Article 1
4. Case Study: treatment of proceeds under Article 8:1(d)
5. Report: false invoicing
6. Explanatory Note: question of "relationship" under Article 15.5
7. Commentary: meaning of the term "restrictions" in Article 1:1(a)(iii)

1986

1. Advisory Opinion (Addendum): examples to illustrate Advisory Opinion on the meaning of the expression "sold for export to the country of importation" in Article 1
2. Study: treatment of rented or leased goods
3. Advisory Opinion (Addendum): examples to illustrate Advisory Opinion on the meaning of the expression "sold for export to the country of importation" in Article 1
4. Case Study: specific leasing transactions, supplementing study on the treatment of rented or leased goods
5. Advisory Opinion: treatment of quantity discounts

1987
(Instruments under review)

1. Draft Commentary: application of the CV committee decision on the valuation of carrier media-bearing software for data-processing equipment
2. Draft Advisory Opinion: meaning of the expression "the fact that the buyer and the seller are related within the meaning of Article 15 shall not in itself be grounds for regarding the transaction value as unacceptable"
3. Draft Instrument: meaning of the expression "the sale or price is subject to some condition or consideration for which a value cannot be determined with respect to the goods being valued" in Article 1:1(b)
4. Draft Instrument: conversion of currency in cases where the contract provides for a fixed rate of exchange

Sources: VAL/M/3, 12–13; VAL/M/4, 7–8; VAL/M/5, 7; VAL/M/7, 4–5; VAL/M/8, 11–12; VAL/M/9, 5; VAL/M/11, 8; VAL/M/13, 7–8; VAL/M/14, 3–4; VAL/M/17, 3–4; VAL/M/19, 4; VAL/M/20, 3–5. For method of citation, see Chapter 4, footnote 2, p. 71.

Operative Rule Construction, Committee on Technical Barriers to Trade, 1980–1987

I. Notifications of Technical Measures: Articles 2:5.2 and 7:3.2

1. June 1980	Format and contents of notifications (Rec)
2. June 1981	Format and contents of notifications (Rec)
3. June 1981	Preferred mode of delivery of notifications (telex) (Req)
4. June 1981	GATT secretariat should process/make available notifications within three days of their receipt (Req)
5. October 1981	Availability of translated documents or summaries of documents should be indicated in notification (Dec)
6. October 1981	Notification should indicate address of source of documents if source is not the Enquiry Point (Dec)
7. May 1983	Notification should be made when draft regulation or certification rule is available and when amendments are still possible (Rec)
8. July 1984	Definition of scope of measures that might have a "significant effect on trade" and thus should be notified (Rec)
9. June 1987	Intention to translate notified measure should be indicated in original notification (Ag)
10. October 1987	GATT secretariat should process/make available notifications within five days of their receipt (Rec)
11. October 1987	Definition of scope of measures that might have a "significant effect on trade" (amendment) and thus should be notified (Ag)

II. Provision of Documents: Articles 2:5.3, 2:6.2, and 7:3.3

1. October 1981	Format and content of requests for documents (Ag)
2. October 1981	Requests for documents should be processed within five working days (Ag)
3. October 1981	Summaries of documents available in official GATT language or language of requestor should be sent automatically with the original of documents requested (Dec)
4. June 1987	Notifying party, if requested, should advise party seeking documents that are not in its GATT working language of other parties who have sought document and may have translated it (Rec)

III. "Reasonable" Time for Comments and Handling of Comments: Articles 2:5.4, 2:5.5, and 7:3.4

Comment Period

1. June 1980	Six-week suggested minimum comment period, extensions "where possible" (Rec)
2. October 1981	Parties should, "as a rule," give "sympathetic consideration" for extensions "when necessary to overcome delays in obtaining documents" (Rec)
3. October 1982	Parties should "effectively" provide forty-five day comment period and "look favorably" upon requests for extensions (Ag)
4. May 1983	"Normal time limit" for comments should be sixty days with proviso that notifications may indicate that measure will go into effect after forty-five days if no comments or requests for an extension are received within that time period (Rec)

Treatment of Comments

1. October 1985	Notification to GATT of identity of government authority or agency (for example, enquiry point) responsible for handling comments
2. October 1985	Responsibilities of authority or agency so designated: —acknowledge receipt of comments —explain process by which they are to be taken into account —provide final version of measure adopted or report that no measure adopted

IV. Enquiry Points: Articles 10:1 and 10:2

1. October 1982	Regular biennial meetings of officials responsible for Enquiry Points (Ag)
2. May 1982	Common format and contents of booklets prepared by signatories on their respective Enquiry Points (Rec)
3. May 1983	Definition of "reasonable" enquiries (Rec)
4. May 1983	Contents of enquiries (Rec)
5. May 1983	Enquiry Points should provide responses to enquiries regarding signatory's participation in international and regional standardizing or certification bodies (Rec)
6. May 1985	Parties should report the annual number of enquiries received by enquiry point, their subject, and the number of requests answered (invitation)
7. October 1987	Enquiry point should, without request, acknowledge receipt of request (Rec)
8. October 1987	Parties should specify the subparagraphs of Article 10:1 or 10:2 under which they are reporting annual number of enquiries (Ag)
9. October 1987	Parties should provide Enquiry-Point telefax numbers in GATT document on Enquiry Points (Ag)

Key:

(Ag) = committee agreement

(Dec) = committee decision

(Rec)= committee recommendation

(Req) = committee request

Sources: TBT/M/3, 5, 12, TBT/M/7, 6; TBT/M/8, 3–4; TBT/M/10, 4; TBT/M/11, 4–5; TBT/M/13, 4–5; TBT/M/16, 5, 9; TBT/M/19, 9; TBT/M/20, 5, 14; TBT/M/25, 2, 7; TBT/M/26, 5–6. Also see *BISD* 27, 38; *BISD* 28, 35; *BISD* 29, 38–39; *BISD* 30, 32; *BISD* 31, 236, 239; *BISD* 32, 141, 144; *BISD* 33, 187. For method of citation, see chapter 4, footnote 2, p. 71.

Highlights of November 1986 Package of GPR Code Improvements

ARTICLE I—SCOPE AND COVERAGE OF CODE

Article I:1(a)—scope extended to leasing
Article I:1(b)—threshold lowered from SDR 150,000 to SDR 130,000
Article I:1(b)—valuation of contract should anticipate recurring purchases over twelve months and should not be done to circumvent code obligations

ARTICLE II—NATIONAL TREATMENT/MOST-FAVORED-NATION

New Article II:2—most-favored nation treatment extended to all Party-affiliated suppliers regardless of degree of foreign ownership

ARTICLE III—DEVELOPING COUNTRIES

New Article III:10—greater technical assistance (specifically, translations of documents) to developing-country signatories

ARTICLE IV—TECHNICAL SPECIFICATIONS

New Article IV:4—signatories shall not obtain advice on specifications for a procurement in which the firms have a commercial interest in a manner precluding foreign competition

ARTICLE V—TENDERING PROCEDURES

Amend Article V:2(b)—conditions imposed by signatories for participation by foreign suppliers in tendering must be related to ensuring capacity to execute contract

Amend Article V:2(b)—assessment of foreign suppliers' capacity to fulfill contracts should be on the basis of assessment of global business

Amend Article V:2(d)—suppliers may apply for qualification at any time

Amend Article V:2(f)—signatories should use a single qualification system or minimize differences in qualification procedures across covered by the code entities

New Article V:3—entities should not provide information to any potential supplier in a way precluding competition

New Article V:5 (previously Article V:4)—tender notices should include information on options and recurring purchases

New Article V:10—delivery dates should take into account "complexity of proposed procurement"

Amend Article V:11(a), (b), and (c) (previously V:10[a], [b], and [c])—bid-times extended from thirty days to forty days,

Amend Article V:11(d) (previously V:10[d])—second publications of bids need not have forty-day bid-times but must have at least twenty five-day bid-times and refer to first publication

New Article V:11(e)—purhases made in state of urgency must have at least ten-day bid-times

New Article V:11(f)—when setting final date for receipt of tenders, entitites should take publishing delays into account

Amend Article V:13 (previously V:12)—tender documentation should contain sufficient information

Amend Article V:15(h)—offsets or other conditions of procurement should be indicated in tender notice

New Article V:15(i)—"option clauses shall not be used in a manner which circumvents the provisions of the Agreement"

New Article V:15(j)—contracts should be made on the basis of criteria cited in tender notice

Article VI—Information and Review

New paragraph Article VI:1—post-award notices of contracts shall be made by code-covered entity including information on product procured, name of winning bidder, value of contract or highest and lowest bids, and, if applicable, justification for use of Article V:16 single-tendering procedures

Amend Article VI:4 (previously VI:3)—publication of winning bidder

Amend Article VI:10 (a)–(d) (previously VI:9)—greater statistics requirements, including those made on the basis of single-tender procedures (VI:10[c]) and derogations (VI:10[d])

Source: General Agreement on Tariffs and Trade, *Protocol Amending the Agreement on Government Procurement* (Geneva, 1987).

Index

Abelson, Donald S., 194
Absolute gains, 20, 35, 44
  from Anti-Dumping Practices Code,
    160, 161, 210–214
  cheating problem and, 153, 158–160,
    161–165, 167
  from Customs Valuation Code, 159–
    160
  European Community perception of,
    159–160, 163–165, 167
  from Government Procurement Code,
    164–165, 166
  from Subsidies and Countervailing
    Measures Code, 160, 162, 163
  from Technical Barriers to Trade
    Code, 163–165
  testing regulations and, 194–195
AFNOR (Association Française de Nor-
    malization), 192
Africa, relative gains problems in, 225–
    226
Agricultural subsidy dispute (U.S. vs.
    EC), 94–98, 178–180
Agriculture-related export subsidies,
    178–179
Aho, Michael, 16–17, 64–65
Almond licensing dispute (U.S. vs. In-
    dia), 85
Amended Deadlock game, 43–44
Amended Prisoner's Dilemma game,
    41–44
American National Standards Institute,
    192
American Selling Price system, 55, 171–
    172
American Society for Testing Materials,
    191–192, 194

Anarchy
  definition of, 20–21
  as force in state actions, 4
  international cooperation and, 1–26
  neoliberal view of, 2, 36, 48, 49, 50
  realist view of, 32, 37–39, 49–50
  war and, 38
Andean Pact, 224–225
Animal Hormone Directive dispute (U.S.
    vs. EC), 90–91
ANSI (American National Standards In-
    stitute), 192
Anti-Dumping Agreement of 1967, 55,
    60
Anti-Dumping Practices Code
  actions initiated under, 172, 173–174
  Article 2:4, 75
  Article 4:1, 113
  Article 6, 121
  Article 7, 121
  Article 8:4, 106–109, 209–214
  Article 14:4, 74
  basic-price systems in, 106–109, 209–
    214
  committee meeting frequency for, 154
  confidentiality in, 121
  countries represented on committees,
    155, 157, 158
  description of, 60–61
  disputes involving, 85–86, 101
  European Community and, 153, 155,
    158, 160, 161, 171, 209–214
  interpretation of, 143–144
  material injury and, 106–109
  neoliberal background conditions
    effects on, 153, 154
  on-the-spot visits in, 121

243

Anti-Dumping Practices Code (*cont.*)
  performance evaluation of, 66, 137–
    138, 141–142, 143
  questionnaire response time in, 121
  relative gains in, 172, 173–174, 209–
    214
  rule compliance in, 74–76, 100–101,
    141
  rule construction for, 106–109, 113,
    121–122, 132, 134, 138, 142, 143
  signatories associated with, 155, 156
  transparency in, 74, 121
  U.S. position on, 208–209
Argentina
  Anti-Dumping Practices Code position
    of, 210–212, 214
  corrective rule construction actions of,
    106
  as Latin American Free Trade Asso-
    ciation member, 224
Aron, Raymond, 38–39
Aronson, Jonathan, 16–17, 64–65
Association Française de Normalization,
  192
ASTM (American Society for Testing
  Materials), 191–192, 194
Atomistic action by states (rational ego-
  ism), 10, 34–36
Australia
  Anti-Dumping Practices Code and,
    74–75, 174, 210–214
  restorative rule construction actions
    of, 120, 131
  Subsidies and Countervailing Mea-
    sures Code actions initiated by, 175,
    176–177
  in wheat flour dispute, 95
Austria
  above-threshold contract awards by,
    147
  restorative rule construction actions
    of, 131
  single-tendering procedures and, 148
Avery, William, 225
Axelrod, Robert, 12–13, 29–30, 33, 36,
  38–39, 48, 151

Background conditions for cooperation,
  150–165
Baldwin, Robert, 15
Baseball bat exports dispute (U.S. vs. Ja-
  pan), 86–87
Basic-price systems in Anti-Dumping
  Practices Code, 106–109, 209–214
Beef export dispute (EC vs. Canada),
  98–99
Bid-deadlines, 126

Bolivia, 224–225
Brazil, 105–106, 224
British Standards Institute, 192
Brussels Definition of Value system, 105,
  172

CACM (Central American Common
  Market), 224
Canada
  above-threshold contract awards by,
    146, 147
  Anti-Dumping Practices Code and,
    174, 210–214
  boneless beef dispute with EC, 98–99
  comment period compliance of, 145
  corrective rule construction actions of,
    106–107, 109
  grain corn exports dispute with U.S.,
    98–99
  product dumping dispute with Italy,
    86
  restorative rule construction actions
    of, 120, 124, 127
  single-tendering procedures and, 148
  softwood exports dispute with U.S.,
    93–94
  Subsidies and Countervailing Mea-
    sures Code actions initiated by, 175–
    177
Capabilities of states, 39–40, 45
Carr, E. H., 38–39
CEN (European Committee for Standardization), 193–194
CENELEC (European Committee for
  Electrotechnical Standardization),
  193–194
Central America, relative gains problems
  in, 224
Central American Common Market, 224
Cheating problem, 10, 19
  absolute gains and, 153, 158–160,
    161–165, 167
  in advanced vs. developing countries,
    152–153, 155, 157, 158
  background conditions for, 136, 150–
    165
  common endeavor size and, 151–152,
    155, 156
  European Community position and,
    150–165
  in mixed interest situations, 151
  neoliberal view of, 34–35, 48, 135–
    136, 144–165
  realist view of, 36–37, 47
Chile
  as Andean Pact member, 224–225

Chile (*cont.*)
  Anti-Dumping Practices Code position
    of, 212
  as Latin American Free Trade Asso-
    ciation member, 223–224
  restorative rule construction actions
    of, 127
  Subsidies and Countervailing Mea-
    sures Code actions initiated by, 175–
    177
Cochrane, James, 224
Colombia, 223, 225
Comment period in TBT Code, 113–
  114
  compliance with, 144, 145, 146
  rule construction on, 239
Commission of the European Communi-
  ties, 16, 21, 203–206
Committee of Signatories, Tokyo Round,
  59, 84, 103
Committee on Trade in Agriculture, 128
Committee on Trade in Industrial Prod-
  ucts, 58–59
Common Agricultural Policy, 53, 179
Computer contract dispute (U.S. vs.
  France), 92–93
Computer software valuation, 105–106
Consultation notification in Government
  Procurement Code, 110
Consumer Product Safety Association of
  Japan, 88
Cooperation among states. *See* Interna-
  tional cooperation
Corn exports dispute (U.S. vs. Canada),
  98–99
Corrective rule construction, 103–111,
  132–133, 142
Costa Rica, 224
Countervailing measures. *See* Subsidies
  and Countervailing Measures Code
Cox, Thomas, 226
Customs Coordination Council, 159
Customs Valuation Code
  Article 8, 104–105
  Article 25, 70, 72
  Brussels Definition of Value system
    and, 105, 172
  committee meeting frequency for, 154
  countries represented on committees,
    155, 157, 158
  customs valuation practices in, 171–
    172
  description of, 59–60
  disputes involving, 84, 101, 141
  European Community position on,
    153, 158–160, 162, 171
  interest charges and, 120

interpretation of, 143–144
neoliberal background conditions
  effects on, 153
performance evaluation of, 65, 137–
  138, 141
relative gains in, 171–172
rule compliance in, 70–72, 100,
  137
rule construction for, 104–106, 111–
  112, 120, 132, 134, 137–138, 142,
  235–237
signatories associated with, 155, 156
Subsidies and Countervailing Measures Code position of, 171
translation problems with, 104–105
transparency in, 70–71
valuation methods of, 71, 72
CV code. *See* Customs Valuation Code

Dairy products, tariff accords for, 58
Deadlock game, 43–44
Defensive state positionalism, 10, 28–29,
  36–40, 45
  European Community and, 182–183
  realism-neoliberalism controversy and,
    230
Delivery-time requirements, 126
Denmark, 197
Derogation notification in Government
  Procurement Code, 126
Deutsch, Karl, 45–46, 231
Deutsches Institut für Normung, 192
Developing countries
  cheating in, 152–153, 155, 157, 158
  economic preference program for,
    231
  See also specific countries
Diebold, William, 17
Dispute settlement, 83–99, 137, 138,
  139, 141–142, 143
  almond licensing (U.S. vs. India), 85
  for Anti-Dumping Practices Code, 85–
    86, 101
  baseball bat exports (U.S. vs. Japan),
    86–87
  bilateral consultations in, 110
  boneless beef exports (EC vs. Canada),
    98–99
  computer contract (U.S. vs. France),
    92–93
  for Customs Valuation Code, 84, 101,
    141
  Export Enhancement Program (EC vs.
    U.S.), 97–98
  for Government Procurement Code,
    91–93, 101, 139–141

Dispute settlement (*cont.*)
  grain corn exports (U.S. vs. Canada), 98–99
  heating radiators (EC vs. Spain), 87
  hormones in meat (U.S. vs. EC), 90–91
  for Import Licensing Procedures Code, 84–85, 101, 141
  pasta products (U.S. vs. EC), 95–98, 178–179
  poultry processing (U.S. vs. EC), 88–90
  product dumping (Canada vs. Italy), 86
  ski equipment standards (EC, others, vs. Japan), 88
  softwood exports (Canada vs. U.S.), 93–94
  •specialty steel imports (EC vs. U.S.), 85
  for Subsidies and Countervailing Measures Code, 93–99, 101, 140–141
  for Technical Barriers to Trade Code, 86–91, 101, 141
  value added tax (U.S. vs. EC), 91–92, 186–188, 196–198
  wheat flour (U.S. vs. EC), 94–97
  wine industry (EC vs. U.S.), 97–98
Dumping of products. *See* Anti-Dumping Agreement of 1967; Anti-Dumping Practices Code

East African Community, 225–226
Eberle, William, 57
EC. *See* European Community
Economic and Monetary Union (1972–1976), 222–223
Ecuador, 225
EFTA (European Free Trade Association), 53, 56
Egoism, rational state, 10, 34–36
El Salvador, 224
"Embedded liberalism", 233
Enquiry points in TBT Code, 113–114, 240
European Committee for Electrotechnical Standardization, 193–194
European Committee for Standardization, 193–194
European Community
  above-threshold contract awards by, 146, 147
  absolute gains perceived by, 159–160, 163–165, 167
  Anti-Dumping Practices Code actions initiated by, 174

Anti-Dumping Practices Code complaints of, 75
Anti-Dumping Practices Code position of, 153, 155, 158, 160, 161, 171, 209–214
  vs. Canada (boneless beef dispute), 98–99
  cheating potential and, 150–165
  cheating problem and, 144–150
  comment period compliance of, 144, 145, 146
  Common Agricultural Policy of, 53
  corrective rule construction actions of, 104–107, 109, 111
  Customs Valuation Code and, 71, 153, 158–160, 162
  decentralization in, 125–126
  discriminatory trade practices of, 53
  economic stagnation in, 203–209
  favorable achievements of gains by, 170–177
  government contracts awarded by, 200, 201, 202
  Government Procurement Code and, 79–80, 150, 153, 158, 182–209
  vs. Japan (ski equipment standards dispute), 88
  LIC code position of, 158–160
  material-injury test and, 62–63
  meat hormones dispute with U.S., 90–91
  1992 economic program of, 203–206
  notification of subsidies by, 146, 149–150
  NTB code effectiveness and, 18–20, 136–144
  NTB code strategic importance to, 203–209
  NTB rejection by, 56
  operative rule construction actions of, 112–113, 115–118
  pasta products dispute with U.S., 95–98, 178–179 policy of, 21–22
  restorative rule construction actions of, 120–121, 123, 125–131
  single-tendering procedures and, 146, 148
  vs. Spain (heating radiators dispute), 87
  Subsidies and Countervailing Measures Code actions initiated by, 175, 176–177
  Subsidies and Countervailing Measures Code compliance of, 81–83
  Subsidies and Countervailing Measures Code position of, 150, 153, 158, 160, 171, 177–182

European Community (*cont.*)
Technical Barriers to Trade Code
position of, 150, 153, 155, 158,
163–165
technical standards/regulations notification by, 189, 190
Tokyo Round proposed by, 57
vs. U.S. (Export Enhancement Program dispute), 97–98
vs. U.S. (steel imports dispute), 85
value-added tax and, 91–92, 186–188,
196–198
wheat flour dispute with U.S., 94–97
White Paper (1985) of, 203–206
wine industry dispute with U.S., 97–
98
European Free Trade Association, 53,
56
European Monetary System, 222–223
"Europessimism," 203
"Eurosclerosis," 203
Export Enhancement Program, 97–98,
178–181

Fagan, Stuart, 224
"Federal Participation in the Development and Use of Voluntary Standards" (OMB A-119), 191
Finland, Nordek veto by, 222
Flour dispute (U.S. vs. EC), 94–97
Flour market uncertainty, 129–130
France
computer contract dispute with U.S.,
92–93
as Economic and Monetary Union
member, 222–223
Government Procurement Code compliance of, 79–80
standards formulation in, 192
Functional integration theory, 4–6, 27

Gains
balancing of, 47–48
gaps in, 41, 44–47, 195
See also Absolute gains; Relative gains
GATT. *See* General Agreement on Tariffs and Trade
"GATT Wisemen," 17–18, 64
General Agreement on Tariffs and
Trade, 8
article(s) of, 54–55
Article VI, 54, 113. *See also* Anti-Dumping Practices Code
Article VII, 54. *See also* Customs Valuation Code
Article VIII, 54

Article IX, 54
Article XI, 54
Article XVI, 54–55, 63, 81, 96, 129
Article XIX, 233–234
Article XX, 54
Article XXVIII, 233–234
commerce included in, 51
Committee on Trade in Agriculture,
128
Generalized System of Preference of,
231
involvement in Tokyo Round negotiations, 58–59
members of, 51
Ministerial Meeting of November
1982, 65
on NTB codes significance, 15–16
Protocol of Provisional Application of,
55–56
tariff rates under, 51–52
"Wisemen" report of, 17–18, 64
Germany, 192, 222–223
Gilpin, Robert, 39–40
Good practice code for nongovernmental bodies, 125–126
Government-owned enterprises, Government Procurement Code extension
to, 198, 199, 200
Government Procurement Code
above-threshold contract awards in,
146, 147
Articles I to VI, 241–242
Article IX:6(b) negotiations, 114–118,
202
comment period compliance with, 146
committee meeting frequency for, 154
consultation notification in, 110
contract awards under, 200, 201, 202
countries represented on committees,
155, 157, 158
derogation and, 126
description of, 62
disputes involving, 91–93, 101, 139–
141
European Community and, 150, 153,
158, 164–165, 166, 182–209
extension to government-owned enterprises, 198, 199, 200
improvements in (November 1986),
241–242
international institutions and, 188–
189, 196–202
leasing under, 109–110
neoliberal background conditions
effects on, 153, 154
performance evaluation of, 66–67,
137–141, 143

Government Procurement Code (*cont.*)
relative gains and, 182–183, 186–188, 196
rule compliance in, 77, 79–81, 100–101, 141
rule construction for, 109–110, 114–118, 126–127, 133, 134, 138, 140–141, 142, 143
service contracts and, 115–118
signatories associated with, 155, 156
single-tendering procedures in, 126, 146, 148
strategic importance of, 203–209
Switzerland position on, 198, 200
threshold reduction of, 115
transparency in, 77, 79
U.S. position on, 183–186, 194–196, 200, 202
value-added tax and, 91–92, 186–188, 196–198
GPR Code. *See* Government Procurement Code
Grain corn exports dispute (U.S. vs. Canada), 98–99
Grape industry subsidy dispute (EC vs. U.S.), 97–98
Great Britain, 88–90, 222–223
Guatemala, 224

Haas, Ernst, 6
Hager, Wolfgang, 208
Haggard, Stephan, 23
Haskel, Barbara, 221–222, 231
Heating radiators dispute (EC vs. Spain), 87
Honduras, 224
Hong Kong, 120, 122
Hormones in meat dispute (U.S. vs. EC), 90–91

IEC (International Electro-technical Commission), 124, 185
ILAC (International Laboratories Accreditation Conference), 124
ILO (International Labor Organization), 6–8
Import Licensing Procedures Code
Article 1:1, 120–121
committee meeting frequency for, 154
countries represented on committees, 155, 157, 158
description of, 60
disputes involving, 84–85, 101, 141
European Community position on, 158–160
interpretation of, 143–144

neoliberal background conditions effects on, 153, 154
performance evaluation of, 65–66, 137–138, 141
rule compliance in, 72–73, 100, 137
rule construction for, 112–113, 120–121, 132, 134, 138
signatories associated with, 155, 156
transparency in, 72–73
Work Program of, 120–121
India
almond licensing dispute with U.S., 85
Anti-Dumping Practices Code position of, 212
corrective rule construction actions of, 106
Institutions. *See* International institutions
Interdependence theory, 4–6, 27
Interest charges in Customs Valuation Code, 120
International Chamber of Commerce, 67
International cooperation
balancing in, 47
cheating in. *See* Cheating problem
conditional, 31, 33
definition of, 22
economic, 12
in 1970s, 8–9
NTB codes effectiveness and, 18–20
research program for, 227–232
rules in, 23
standards of behavior in, 23
systemic-level analysis of, 20–25
International Electro-technical Commission, 124, 185
International Energy Agency, 8
International institutions, 234
Government Procurement Code and, 188–189, 196–202
neoliberalism and, 9, 31, 33
realism-neoliberalism controversy and, 229
rules in, 23
Technical Barriers to Trade Code and, 188–189, 190, 191–196
International Laboratories Accreditation Conference, 124
International Labor Organization, 6–8
International Monetary Fund, 8
International Organization for Standardization, 124, 185
International regime, 22–23, 33
Ireland, 196–197, 222–223
ISO (International Organization for Standardization), 124, 185

Italy
　as Economic and Monetary Union
　　member, 222–223
　Government Procurement Code com-
　　pliance of, 80
　product dumping dispute with
　　Canada, 86
　value-added tax rates in, 197

Jackson, John, 69–70
Japan
　above-threshold contract awards by,
　　146, 147
　Anti-Dumping Practices Code com-
　　plaints about, 75
　baseball bat dispute with U.S., 86–87
　comment period compliance of, 145,
　　146
　corrective rule construction actions of,
　　107, 110
　as economic threat to European Com-
　　munity, 204–205
　Government Procurement Code com-
　　pliance of, 79–80
　Import Licensing Procedures Code
　　compliance of, 73
　restorative rule construction actions
　　of, 123–124, 126–127, 131
　single-tendering procedures and, 146,
　　148
　ski equipment standards dispute with
　　EC, others, 88
Jervis, Robert, 45

Kennedy Round, 51, 55–56
Kenya, 225–226
Keohane, Robert, 6–7, 12–13, 23, 29,
　33–37, 48, 152, 232

Laboratory testing, 124–125, 183–186,
　194–196
Language problems with Customs Valu-
　ation Code, 104–105
Latin America, relative gains problems
　in, 223–225
Latin American Free Trade Association,
　223–224
Leasing provisions in Government Pro-
　curement Code, 109–110
Liberal institutionalism
　basic assumptions of, 4–6
　functional integration theory of, 4–6
　history of, 4–9
　interdependence theory of, 4–6
　neofunctionalist regional integration
　　theory of, 4–6

vs. neoliberal institutionalism, 32
　in postwar period, 7–9
　See also Neoliberal institutionalism
LIC code. *See* Import Licensing Pro-
　cedures Code
Licensing of imports. *See* Import Licens-
　ing Procedures Code
Lipson, Charles, 12–13, 29, 33–37, 152
Luxembourg, 196, 197

Madelin, Alain, 207
Market displacement test in Subsidies
　and Countervailing Measures Code,
　129–130
Material injury, 62–63, 75, 106–109
Mazzeo, Domenico, 226
Meat export dispute (EC vs. Canada),
　98–99
Meat hormones dispute (U.S. vs. EC),
　90–91
Mexico, 224
Middlebrook, Kevin, 225
Milensky, Edward, 223–224
Ministerial Declaration of 1974, Tokyo
　Round initiation by, 57
Mixed interests, 34–35, 151
Morgenthau, Hans, 47

Nationalism in Europe, 8
NATO, relative burden-sharing in, 231
Neofunctionalist regional integration
　theory, 4–6, 27
Neoliberal institutionalism
　anarchy view of, 2, 28, 36, 48, 49, 50
　background conditions for cheating
　　and, 136, 150–165
　basis for (liberal institutionalism), 4–9
　as challenge to realism, 29–36
　cheating problem and, 10, 19, 34–35,
　　48, 135–136, 144–150
　core arguments of, 27–28, 35
　defects of, 2, 49–50, 217–220
　economic cooperation and, 12
　empirical findings of, 216–220
　failure of, 165, 167
　history of, 3–9, 27
　individual state action in, 35
　international institutions and, 31, 33,
　　35–36
　vs. liberal institutionalism, 9, 29–31,
　　32
　NTB code effectiveness and, 136–144
　origin of, 9, 27
　Prisoner's Dilemma game and, 31, 33–
　　35
　rational state egoism and, 34–36

Neoliberal institutionalism (*cont.*)
vs. realism. *See* Realism-neoliberalism
controversy
realist arguments accepted by, 29–30
realist response to, 36–49
state utility and, 35, 41, 49
testing of, 11–20
Neoprotectionism, 3, 208
New Zealand, 120
Nicaragua, 224
Nixon, President Richard M., dollar
convertibility renunciation by
(1971), 52
Nongovernmental bodies, good practice
code for, 125–126
Non-tariff barriers to trade codes
(GATT), 54–56
Non-tariff barriers to trade codes (Kennedy Round), 51, 55–56
Non-tariff barriers to trade codes
(Tokyo Round), 51–68
absolute gains from, 20
ADP. *See* Anti-Dumping Practices
Code
background to, 51–57
cheating problem in. *See* Cheating
problem
committee meeting frequency and,
153, 154, 155
Committee of Signatories of, 59, 84,
103
completion of, 57
countervailing measures. *See* Subsidies
and Countervailing Measures Code
countries represented on committees,
155, 157, 158
Customs Valuation. *See* Customs Valuation Code
description of, 15
dispute settlement in, 83–99
dissatisfaction with, 17–18
effectiveness of (neoliberal view), 136–
144
effectiveness of (realist view), 168–215
effectiveness variations in, 18–19, 99–
102, 131–134, 136–138
empirical findings in, 216–220
European Community relative gains
and, 170–175, 176–177
gains from, 20
GPR. *See* Government Procurement
Code
Import Licensing Procedures. *See* Import Licensing Procedures Code
initial expectations for, 15–16

initiation of, 57
interpretation of, 143–144
key accomplishment of Tokyo Round,
15–16, 58
LIC. *See* Import Licensing Procedures
Code
members of, 13, 157
necessity for, 51–57
performance evaluation of, 64–68. *See
also* Dispute settlement; Rule compliance in NTB codes
Protocol to the General Agreement
(1979) and, 57–58
relative gains and. *See* Relative gains
rule compliance in. *See* Rule compliance in NTB codes
rule construction in. *See* Rule construction for NTB codes
SCM. *See* Subsidies and Countervailing Measures Code
signatories associated with, 155, 156
significance of, 15–16
strategic importance to European
Community, 203–209
Subsidies and Countervailing Measures. *See* Subsidies and Countervailing Measures Code
TBT. *See* Technical Barriers to Trade
Code
in testing of realism vs. neoliberalism,
12–20
theoretical implications of real-
ism/neoliberalism and, 216–220
types of, 15, 57–64
working groups for, 59
See also specific codes
Nordek trade arrangements, 221–222,
231
Nordic countries
above-threshold contract awards by,
147
comment period compliance of, 145,
146
free-trade agreements of, 221–222
rule construction actions of, 114, 122–
124, 127, 131
single-tendering procedures and, 148
in value-added tax dispute, 92
Notification of consultation, 110
Notification of derogation, 126
Notification of subsidies, 127–128, 146,
149–150, 177–178
Notification of technical stan-
dards/regulations, 122–123, 189,
190, 191–192, 238

NTB codes. *See* Non-tariff barriers to trade codes
Nye, Joseph, 6–7

OECD (Organization for Economic Cooperation and Development), 53–54, 198, 199, 200
Operative rule construction, 103, 111–119, 132–133, 142
Organization for Economic Cooperation and Development, 53–54, 198, 199, 200
Oye, Kenneth, 151, 153

Pasta products dispute (U.S. vs. EC), 95–98, 178–179
Performance evaluation of codes. *See specific codes*
Peru, 224–225
Poultry processing dispute (U.S. vs. EC), 88–90
Price-undercutting test in Subsidies and Countervailing Measures Code, 129–130
Pricing systems in Anti-Dumping Practices Code, 106–109, 209–214
Prisoner's Dilemma, 13, 31, 33–35, 41–44
Processing and production methods in TBT Code, 88–90, 123
Product dumping. *See* Anti-Dumping Practices Code
Protectionism, 3, 208
Protocol of Provisional Application to the General Agreement (1947), 55
Protocol to the General Agreement (1979), 57–58
Puyana de Palacios, Alicia, 225

Rational state egoism, 10, 34–36
Reagan Administration, standards formulation policy of, 189, 191–194
Realism
 anarchy view of, 28, 32, 37–39, 49–50
 Andean Pact and, 224–225
 basic assumptions of, 3–4
 as basis for international cooperation, 4, 214–215
 Central American Common Market and, 224
 cheating problem and, 10, 36–37, 47
 classical, 3–4
 Deadlock game and, 43–44
 defensive state positionalism and, 10, 28–29, 36–40, 45

East African Community and, 225–226
Economic and Monetary Union and, 222–223
empirical findings of, 216–220
European Community relative gains and, 170–175, 176–177
European Community subsidies rules position and, 177–182
European Community TBT code position and, 182–209
gain balance and, 47–48
gaps in gains tolerance and, 41, 45–47
history of, 3–4
on international institutions role, 32
Latin American Free Trade Association and, 223–224
vs. liberal institutionalism, 32
neoliberal view of, 2, 27–31, 36, 216–217
Nordic countries free trade arrangements and, 221–222
NTB codes variance in performance and, 19–20, 168–215, 218–220
pessimistic views of, 27, 32
policy implications of, 232–234
in postwar period, 7–9
Prisoner's Dilemma amended and, 41–43
rational state egoism and, 10
relative capabilities and, 39–40, 45
relative-gains problem and, 28–29, 40–49, 209–214
research program for, 227–232
state sensitivity coefficient and, 41–47
state utility characterization of, 41, 49
survival of states and, 39
testing of, 11–20
theoretical implications of, 216–220
vulnerability of states recognized by, 38–39
Realism-neoliberalism controversy
 analysis of, 49–50
 anarchy views in, 32, 49–50
 defensive state positionalism and, 230
 durability of arrangements and, 227–228
 empirical findings in, 216–220
 international cooperation and, 49
 international institutions and, 32, 229
 linkage of issues and, 228–229
 long-term horizons in, 227
 neoliberal challenge in, 9, 29–36
 number of partners and, 228
 policy implications in, 232–234

Realism-neoliberalism (*cont.*)
  Prisoner's Dilemma game and, 31, 33, 41–43
  realist response in, 36–49
  states properties and, 49
  states role in world politics and, 32
  theoretical implications of, 216–229
  utility function and, 49
Regime. *See* International regime
Regulations. *See* Technical Barriers to Trade Code; Technical standards/regulations
Relative capabilities of states, 39–40, 45
Relative gains, 14, 20, 23, 28–29, 40–49
  Anti-Dumping Practices Code and, 172, 173–174, 209–214
  Central American Common Market and, 224–225
  Customs Valuation Code and, 171–172
  East African Community and, 225–226
  Economic Monetary Union and, 222–223
  by European Community, 173–174, 176–177
  Government Procurement Code and, 182–183, 186–188
  Latin American Free Trade Association and, 223–224
  Nordic country free-trade association and, 221–222
  in research program, 230–232
  Subsidies and Countervailing Measures Code and, 175, 176–177
  Technical Barriers to Trade Code and, 182–186
Research program for international cooperation, 227–232
Restorative rule construction, 103, 120–131, 132–133, 142
Richonnier, Michel, 206–207
Ruggie, John, 11, 233
Rule compliance in NTB codes, 69–82, 99–102, 138–141
  Anti-Dumping Practices, 74–76, 100–101, 141
  Customs Valuation, 70–72, 100–101, 137
  definition of, 70
  Government Procurement, 77, 79–81, 100–101, 141
  Import Licensing Procedures, 72–73, 100–101, 137
  Subsidies and Countervailing Measures, 81–83, 100–101, 137–138, 141
  Technical Barriers to Trade, 76–78, 100–101
Rule construction for NTB codes, 103–134, 137–140, 143
  Anti-Dumping Practices, 106–109, 113, 121–122, 132, 134, 138, 142, 143
  corrective, 103–111, 132–133, 142
  Customs Valuation, 104–106, 111–112, 119, 132, 134, 137–138, 142
  definition of, 103
  Government Procurement, 109–110, 114–118, 126–127, 133, 134, 138, 140–141, 142, 143
  Import Licensing Procedures, 112–113, 120–121, 132, 134, 138
  operative, 103, 111–119, 132–133, 142, 235–240
  restorative, 103, 120–131, 132–133
  retroactive, 142
  Subsidies and Countervailing Measures, 110–111, 119, 127–131, 133, 134, 137–138, 140–141, 142
  Technical Barriers to Trade, 113–114, 122–126, 133, 134, 138, 141, 142, 143, 235–240
Rules in international regimes/institutions, 23

SCM code. *See* Subsidies and Countervailing Measures Code
Sensitivity coefficient in utility equation, 41–47
Service contracts in Government Procurement Code, 115–118
Simmons, Beth, 23
Single-tendering procedures, 126, 146, 148
Ski equipment standards dispute (EC, others, vs. Japan), 88
Sloan, John, 224
Software valuation, 105–106
Softwood exports dispute (Canada vs. U.S.), 93–94
Spain, 87, 131, 196, 197
Specialty Steel Summary Invoice, 85, 120
Standards, technical. *See* Technical standards/regulations
States
  cooperation among. *See* International cooperation

States (*cont.*)
  as defensive positionalists. *See* Defensive state positionalism
  as rational egoists. *See* Rational state egoism
  as "rational utility maximizers," 34
State sensitivity coefficient in utility equation, 41–47
State utility/utility functions, 35, 41, 49
Steel imports dispute (EC vs. U.S.), 85
Stein, Arthur A., 29, 33, 44–45
Strauss, Robert, 16
Subsidies and Countervailing Measures Code
  actions initiated under, 175, 176–177
  agriculture-related subsidies and, 178–181
  Article 2:6, 81
  Article 4:2, 119
  Article 7:1, 81
  Article 8, 94, 129–130
  Article 9, 63, 95–97, 128–130
  Article 10, 63, 94–95, 128–130
  Article 12:1, 96
  Article 19:5, 81
  committee meeting frequency for, 154
  countries represented on committees, 155, 157, 158
  description of, 62–63
  disputes involving, 93–99, 101, 140–141
  European Community position on, 150, 153, 158, 160, 163, 171, 177–182
  flour market report and, 128–129
  market displacement test and, 129–130
  neoliberal background conditions effects on, 153, 154
  notification in, 127–128, 146, 149–150, 177–178
  performance evaluation of, 67–68, 137–138, 140–141, 143
  price-undercutting test and, 129–130
  relative gains in, 175, 176–177
  rule compliance in, 81–83, 100, 137–138, 141
  rule construction for, 110–111, 119, 127–131, 133, 134, 137–138, 140–141, 142
  signatories associated with, 155, 156
  subsidy notification in, 127–128
  tests for violations in, 129–130
  transparency in, 81–83, 177–182
  U.S. position of, 208–209

Supplier qualifications, 79, 126
Sweden, 213. *See also* Nordic countries
Switzerland
  above-threshold contract awards by, 146, 147
  Anti-Dumping Practices Code position of, 212–213
  Government Procurement Code position of, 198, 200
  rule construction actions of, 118, 124, 131
  single-tendering procedures and, 148

Tanzania, 225–226
Tax, value-added, 91–92, 186–188, 196–198
TBT code. *See* Technical Barriers to Trade Code
Technical Barriers to Trade Code
  Article 2, 86, 113, 238–239
  Article 5:2, 124
  Article 7, 86, 113, 238–239
  Article 10, 113, 240
  Article 14:2.5, 86–87, 90
  Article 15:7, 76
  bilateral standards-related agreements and, 125
  comment period in, 113–114, 144, 145, 146
  committee meeting frequency for, 154
  compliance with, 76–77, 100
  countries represented on committees, 155, 157, 158
  delivery-time requirements and, 126
  description of, 61
  disputes involving, 86–91, 101, 141
  enquiry points in, 113–114, 240
  European Community and, 150, 153, 155, 158, 163–165, 182–209
  good practice code for nongovernmental bodies and, 125–126
  institutional trends and, 188–202
  neoliberal background conditions effects on, 153, 154
  notification rules of, 122–123
  performance evaluation of, 66, 137–138, 141, 143
  processing and production methods and, 123
  regulations notification under, 189, 190, 191–192
  relative gains in, 182–186
  rule construction for, 113–114, 122–126, 133, 134, 138, 141, 142, 143, 238–240

Technical Barriers to Trade (*cont.*)
  signatories associated with, 155, 156
  standards formulation and, 189, 191–194
  strategic importance of, 203–209
  test results acceptance and, 124–125
  transparency in, 76–77
  U.S. position on, 183–186, 194–196
  See also Testing
Technical standards/regulations
  agreements on, 125
  disputes about, 185–186
  formulation of, 189, 191–194
  notification of, 189, 190, 191–192
  as trade barriers. *See* Technical Barriers to Trade Code
Testing
  acceptance of data for, 183–186, 194–196
  agreements in Technical Barriers to Trade Code, 124–125
Threshold of contracts (GPR Code), 115, 146, 147
Tokyo Declaration of 1973, 58
Tokyo Round negotiations, 3, 51, 57–59
Tokyo Round non-tariff barriers to trade codes. *See* Non-tariff barriers to trade codes
Transaction value in customs valuation, 172
Translation problems with Customs Valuation Code, 104–105
Transparency
  in Anti-Dumping Practices Code, 121
  Committee on Trade in Agriculture work on, 128
  in rule compliance, 70–83
  in state actions, 23
Treverton, Gregory, 231
Tsoukalis, Loukas, 222

Uganda, 225–226
Underwriters Laboratories, 192
United Nations Educational, Scientific, and Cultural Organization (UNESCO), 7
United States
  above-threshold contract awards by, 146, 147
  agriculture-related export subsidies and, 178–181
  American Selling Price agreement and, 55
  Anti-Dumping Practices Code actions initiated by, 174

Anti-Dumping Practices Code complaints about, 75
Anti-Dumping Practices Code position of, 208–214
balance of payments erosion in, 52–53
vs. Canada (grain corn exports dispute), 98–99
comment period compliance of, 144, 145
corrective rule construction actions of, 105–107, 109–111
Customs Valuation Code compliance of, 71
customs valuation practices of, 171–172
dollar convertibility renunciation by (1971), 52
vs. EC (meat hormones dispute), 90–91
vs. EC (pasta products dispute), 95–98, 178–179
vs. EC (value-added tax dispute), 91–92, 186–188, 196–198
vs. EC (wheat flour dispute), 94–97
vs. EC (wine industry dispute), 97–98
as economic threat to European Community, 204–205
Export Enhancement Program of, 97–98, 178–181
vs. France (computer contract dispute), 92–93
Government Procurement Code and, 79–81, 196, 200, 202
vs. Great Britain (poultry processing dispute), 88–90
vs. India (almond licensing dispute), 85
vs. Japan (baseball bat dispute), 86–87
Kennedy Round accord rejection by, 56
material-injury test and, 62–63
NTB codes effectiveness and, 18–20, 136–144
NTB codes initial expectations of, 16
NTB codes significance and, 16
operative rule construction actions of, 112–119
restorative rule construction actions of, 120, 122–130
single-tendering procedures and, 146, 148
softwood exports dispute with Canada, 93–94
standards formulation policy of, 189, 191–194
steel imports dispute with EC, 85

United States (*cont.*)
  Subsidies and Countervailing Measures Code actions initiated by, 175, 176–177
  Subsidies and Countervailing Measures Code compliance of, 81–83
  Subsidies and Countervailing Measures Code position of, 181, 208–209
  Technical Barriers to Trade Code position of, 183–186, 194–196
  technical standards/regulations notification by, 189, 190, 191–192
  Tokyo Round proposed by, 57
  value-added tax and, 196
Utility/utility functions, state, 35, 41, 49

Value-added tax, dispute over (U.S. vs. EC), 91–92, 186–188, 196–198

Value of goods in Customs Valuation Code, 59–60
Venezuela, 224, 225

Waltz, Kenneth, 11, 38–40
War, anarchy and, 38
Wheat flour
  dispute involving (U.S. vs. EC), 94–97
  market uncertainty and, 129–130
Wiklund, Claes, 231
Wilkinson, Christopher, 205
Wine industry dispute (U.S. vs. EC), 97–98
Winham, Gilbert, 64
Wionczek, Miguel, 224
Wood exports dispute (Canada vs. U.S.), 93–94
Work Program of Import Licensing Code, 120–121

Cornell Studies in Political Economy

EDITED BY PETER J. KATZENSTEIN

Collapse of an Industry: Nuclear Power and the Contradictions of U.S. Policy, by John L. Campbell

Power, Purpose, and Collective Choice: Economic Strategy in Socialist States, edited by Ellen Comisso and Laura D'Andrea Tyson

The Political Economy of the New Asian Industrialism, edited by Frederic C. Deyo

Dislodging Multinationals: India's Strategy in Comparative Perspective, by Dennis J. Encarnation

Democracy and Markets: The Politics of Mixed Economies, by John R. Freeman

The Misunderstood Miracle: Industrial Development and Political Change in Japan, by David Friedman

Patchwork Protectionism: Textile Trade Policy in the United States, Japan, and West Germany, by H. Richard Friman

Politics in Hard Times: Comparative Responses to International Economic Crises, by Peter Gourevitch

Closing the Gold Window: Domestic Politics and the End of Bretton Woods, by Joanne Gowa

Cooperation among Nations: Europe, America, and Non-tariff Barriers to Trade, by Joseph M. Grieco

The Philippine State and the Marcos Regime: The Politics of Export, by Gary Hawes

Reasons of State: Oil Politics and the Capacities of American Government, by G. John Ikenberry

The State and American Foreign Economic Policy, edited by G. John Ikenberry, David A. Lake, and Michael Mastanduno

Pipeline Politics: The Complex Political Economy of East-West Energy Trade, by Bruce W. Jentleson

The Politics of International Debt, edited by Miles Kahler

Corporatism and Change: Austria, Switzerland, and the Politics of Industry, by Peter J. Katzenstein

Industry and Politics in West Germany: Toward the Third Republic, edited by Peter J. Katzenstein

Small States in World Markets: Industrial Policy in Europe, by Peter J. Katzenstein

The Sovereign Entrepreneur: Oil Policies in Advanced and Less Developed Capitalist Countries, by Merrie Gilbert Klapp

International Regimes, edited by Stephen D. Krasner

Power, Protection, and Free Trade: International Sources of U.S. Commercial Strategy, 1887–1939, by David A. Lake

State Capitalism: Public Enterprise in Canada, by Jeanne Kirk Laux and Maureen Appel Molot

Opening Financial Markets: Banking Politics on the Pacific Rim, by Louis W. Pauly

The Business of the Japanese State: Energy Markets in Comparative and Historical Perspective, by Richard J. Samuels

In the Dominions of Debt: Historical Perspectives on Dependent Development, by Herman M. Schwartz

CORNELL STUDIES IN POLITICAL ECONOMY

Europe and the New Technologies, edited by Margaret Sharp

Europe's Industries: Public and Private Strategies for Change, edited by Geoffrey Shepherd, François Duchêne, and Christopher Saunders

Fair Shares: Unions, Pay, and Politics in Sweden and West Germany, by Peter Swenson

National Styles of Regulation: Environmental Policy in Great Britain and the United States, by David Vogel

International Cooperation: Building Regimes for Natural Resources and the Environment, by Oran R. Young

Governments, Markets, and Growth: Financial Systems and the Politics of Industrial Change, by John Zysman

American Industry in International Competition: Government Policies and Corporate Strategies, edited by John Zysman and Laura Tyson

Library of Congress Cataloging-in-Publication Data

Grieco, Joseph M.
   Cooperation among nations: Europe, America, and non-tariff barriers to trade /
Joseph M. Grieco.
      p.   cm. — (Cornell studies in political economy)
   Includes bibliographical references.
   ISBN 0-8014-2414-3 (alk. paper)
   ISBN 0-8014-9699-3 (pbk.: alk. paper)
      1.   United States—Foreign economic relations—European Economic Community
countries.   2.   European Economic Community Countries—Foreign economic
relations—United States.   3.   Nontariff trade barriers—United
States.   4.   Nontariff trade barriers—European Economic Community
countries.   5.   General Agreement on Tariffs and Trade (Organization)   6.   Tokyo
Round (1973–1979)   7.   Liberalism.   8.   Realism.   I.   Title.   II.   Series.
HF1456.5.E825G75   1990
382'.5'0973—dc20   89-46166